DOSTOEVSKY
1821–1881

The bare events of Dostoevsky's life—his father murdered by peasants, his own ordeal before a firing squad, then exile in Siberia, his epilepsy, gambling, poverty and debts —go far to account for his strange intensity of vision. This biography, with its illuminating chapters on each of the great novels, traces his wayward development, from his strict and secluded childhood to his debut as 'literary pimple', through his years of anguish, to his maturity as artist and final apotheosis as Russian patriot. It was written some fifty years after Dostoevsky's death, when the material necessary for a full study first became available. As a critic remarked, there is no nonsense about it, which is more than can be said of much writing on Dostoevsky.

EDWARD HALLETT CARR

DOSTOEVSKY

1821–1881

[signature]

UNWIN BOOKS

GEORGE ALLEN & UNWIN LTD . LONDON
BARNES & NOBLE, INC. . NEW YORK

First Published in 1931
Second Impression 1949
First published in this edition 1962

This edition © George Allen and Unwin Ltd., 1962

UNWIN BOOKS

George Allen & Unwin Ltd
Ruskin House, Museum Street
London, W.C.1.

*Published in The United States
in 1963
by Barnes & Noble Inc
105 Fifth Avenue New York 3*

PRINTED IN GREAT BRITAIN
in 9 on 10 *pt. Plantin type*
BY C. TINLING AND CO. LTD
LIVERPOOL, LONDON AND PRESCOT

CONTENTS

CONTENTS

BOOK FOUR

INTRODUCTORY NOTE

Two years after Dostoevsky's death, which occurred in 1881, two of his friends, Strakhov and Orest Miller, collaborated to write a biography which was prefixed to the first collected edition of his novels. This work, which is still valuable, is referred to throughout the present book as the 'official biography'. It contains such facts and such of his letters as his widow cared to see published. She survived until 1919; and during her lifetime no further material of importance was allowed to appear. The only existing biography of Dostoevsky in English (by J. A. T. Lloyd—Stanley Paul, 1912) is little more than the official biography in English dress.

The death of the novelist's widow and the Soviet revolution released a mass of information which has gradually been published during the past decade. First came a biography by Dostoevsky's only surviving daughter (published in Germany in 1921), which, though extremely unreliable in matters of detail, revealed for the first time many aspects of his life which had hitherto been concealed from the public curiosity—the murder of his father, the unhappiness of his first marriage, his chequered liaison with Polina Suslova (who is not, however, mentioned by name), and the family quarrels which followed his second marriage. In 1923 appeared his wife's diary, covering in extreme detail a period of four months during the first year of their marriage (English translation, Gollancz, 1928); in 1925 his wife's memoirs, written long after his death and never completed, but full of information about his later years; in 1926 a complete collection of his letters to his wife, 162 in all, ranging over the last fourteen years of his life (English translation, Constable, 1930); in 1928 the diary of Polina Suslova; and in 1930 the memoirs of his younger brother Andrei. In the meanwhile a large number of Dostoevsky's letters had come to light and had appeared in various periodicals (a few have been translated into English); and a complete edition of all his extant letters is now in course of publication by the State Publishing House in Moscow (Vol. I, 1929; Vol. II, 1930). It seems improbable that any documents of importance relating to Dostoevsky's life still remain unpublished or that any vital new light will be shed on it by further discoveries.

There is no modern biography of Dostoevsky in Russian, though Leonid Grossman (*Put Dostoevskovo* and other books) has written some excellent monographs on certain episodes of Dostoevsky's life in the light of the new documents. The latest biographies in French (by Serge Persky—Payot, Paris, 1924) and in German (by Karl Nötzel—H. Haessel-Verlag, Leipzig, 1925) contain none of the new material published in Russia since the revolution.

The standard English translation of the novels is by Constance Garnett (Heinemann). Other translations have been published of some of the principal novels; but these are inferior both in accuracy and in style. The English titles of the novels adopted in the present book are those used by Mrs Garnett, except in the case of *The Devils* (which she incorrectly calls *The Possessed*). The passage from *Memoirs from the House of the Dead* on page 48 is quoted in Mrs Garnett's translation; the author is responsible for the translation of all other extracts and quotations.

Some of the material used in Chapters VIII and XIII has been published by the author in the *Fortnightly Review* for October 1929 (*Dostoevsky and a Russian Minx*) and in the *Slavonic Review* for June 1929 (*Turgenev and Dostoevsky*) respectively.

BOOK ONE
YEARS OF GROWTH
(1821–1854)

'I am a Russian. Life has taught me to think, but thinking has not taught me to live.'

A character in Herzen's novel, *Who is to Blame?*

Childhood

THE family of Dostoevsky derives its name and origin from the tiny village of Dostoievo somewhere in the Pinsk marshes. It is the dreariest tract of country in all western Russia and, ethnologically speaking, the most variegated, Pole, Lithuanian, White Russian and Jew jostling one another in inextricable confusion. The racial origin of the family remains conjectural. A Polish political exile who knew Dostoevsky in Siberia records that 'his features as well as his name betrayed a Polish descent'. The daughter of the novelist, who published in 1921 the least reliable of all biographies of her father, credits him with a Lithuanian ancestry, and attributes to it both his genius and the defects which critics have detected in his Russian style. These ethnological speculations regarding the hypothetical fraction of non-Russian blood in Dostoevsky's veins need not detain us. In every ordinary sense of the word, he was, as he always believed himself to be, a Russian of the Russians.

Some forgotten ancestor of unknown date migrated from the Pinsk marshes to the Ukraine; Michael Dostoevsky, the novelist's father, came up from the Ukraine to Moscow in the early years of the nineteenth century. He studied medicine at Moscow University, and served as a military doctor in the campaign of 1812. In 1819 he married the daughter of a Moscow merchant, resigned his commission, and was appointed staff doctor at the Marinsky Hospital—an appointment which did not prevent him from engaging in part-time private practice. Fyodor Mikhailovich, the second child of the marriage, was born on October 30, 1821. The date is fixed by an entry in the church register; but it is curious that in later years, by accident or design, the novelist not infrequently deducted a year from his age. His elder brother Michael was born in 1820; after Fyodor came Varvara and Andrei (whose reminiscences constitute our main authority for Dostoevsky's childhood); then, after an interval, Vera, Nicholas and Alexandra completed the family.

The birthplace of Dostoevsky, as of his younger brothers and sisters, was an apartment attached to the hospital. It consisted of a hall, a dining-room, a drawing-room and a kitchen. A wooden partition converted a windowless corner of the hall into a bedroom for the two eldest children; the dining-room served also as a play-room and study; in the drawing-room the family assembled in the evening and, when father was not too busy writing prescriptions, engaged in the favourite pastime of Russian families, reading aloud; and at the end of this room, behind another partition, was the sleeping-place of the parents and the younger children. When the fifth or sixth child was born, another room was acquired. 'In olden times,' remarks Andrei drily, 'quarters were provided for officials on a much more economical scale than nowadays.'

The summer brought some mitigation of the winter confinement; but the régime, though healthier, was scarcely less monotonous. The family evening reading was replaced by a country walk. 'These walks,' reports Andrei, 'were very solemn; and even outside the city the children never dared to play any pranks or run about. Father always talked to us on improving subjects. For example, I remember on many occasions his concise explanations of geometrical principles, of acute and obtuse and right angles, or of curved and broken lines, examples of which occur at every step in the various districts of Moscow.' In summer too there were convalescent patients in the hospital garden where the children played, and Fyodor liked to talk to them, especially the younger ones; but father placed a stern veto on this intercourse. The Dostoevsky children never had playmates.

Those who believe that the outlook of the grown man is largely determined by the unconscious impressions of early childhood may study with interest the life of Dostoevsky. Until the age of ten, except on one or two occasions on which he participated in the annual family pilgrimage to the Sergei-Troitsky monastery some fifty miles from Moscow, he had never left the town. The town-boy remained, despite the varied experiences of later life, pre-eminently the novelist of the town. We miss in Dostoevsky the sweeping landscapes of Turgenev and Tolstoy, the country gentlemen, or of Maxim Gorky, the countryside tramp. His few rural scenes are nothing but hastily painted backcloths which do not unduly distract attention from the action or the actors; they have nothing in common with those intimate scenes of city streets in snow, thaw or sultry heat, or of poky attics and dusty courtyards which are part of the very life and being of his characters. 'In a confined room,' says one of his heroes, 'even thought becomes confined'—a phrase which might serve as a motto to many of his novels. A recent critic has mentioned 'a sense of space' as the prevailing impression left

on the reader by the novels of Tolstoy. The effect of Dostoevsky's novels is to create an almost intolerable sense of confinement. His vision, never focused on the wide expanses of nature, contracted itself more and more to the infinite convolutions of human caprice. There is a certain philosophic detachment common to most great artists which is utterly denied to Dostoevsky, victim, both in his life and in his art, of the narrow and narrowing intensity of the great city.

The lack of playmates in his childhood left equally visible traces on his life and work. It would sound paradoxical to speak of the isolated childhood of one who was brought up with six brothers and sisters in a three-roomed flat. But isolated the family was; it had no social life; all its activities and reactions were domestic, not external. Human intercourse was always conceived by Dostoevsky in later life in terms of the intense, intimate relations of the family hearth. A friend must be a brother or more; no lesser tie was tolerable to him. His singular childhood made him incapable of ordinary social intercourse, of those casual and partial relationships which add to the amenities of life without going far beneath the surface. In such relationships, when they were forced on him, Dostoevsky was jealous, exacting, hypersensitive; he both gave and expected too much; and the inevitable quarrels which followed had the vulgar heart-rending futility of family brawls.

The same curious deficiency is revealed in Dostoevsky's art, though here the deficiency carries with it a countervailing element of strength. No great master of fiction is so poor in 'incidental' characters; thumbnail sketches of external characteristics are not his *métier*; he cannot skim the surface. The number of his characters, or at any rate of those we remember, is very small in relation to the body of his work. But each of these characters is conceived with the intensity of one who has spent a lifetime, and a lifetime of isolation, in the contemplation of their souls. The amazing profundity of his observation more than compensates the narrowness of his field of vision.

It cannot be said that this narrowness and confinement were characteristic of the Russian life of the day. It is curious to reflect that the Moscow in which Dostoevsky grew up as a child was also the Moscow of Pushkin and Griboedov, that beside and around the hospital annexe, in which the doctor's family led its cramped and mean existence, was the spacious and lavish world where the aristocracy and landed gentry lived in careless luxury, the Moscow of Homeric banquets in the fashionable English club. It is a collocation not of two strata of society, but of two epochs of history, of past and present. The contemporaries of Dostoevsky—Turgenev,

Goncharov, Saltykov, even Tolstoy seven years his junior—have their roots unmistakably in the past; they belong to the world of aristocracy and serfdom which has passed beyond our comprehension. Of all the great Russian writers of the nineteenth century before Chekhov, Dostoevsky alone is completely modern. The family of Dostoevsky was, under the curious Russian caste system, of 'noble' rank; but their position was precisely similar to that of bourgeois or middle-class families in western Europe.

In Fyodor's tenth year his parents bought the small farm of Darovoe in the government of Tula, 150 versts from Moscow, and from this year onwards mother and children spent the summer there. Father could only leave the hospital for a week or two in the middle of the summer. The journey was made in a carriage and took two days. To the children it meant deliverance from the confinement of Moscow and, perhaps also, from their father's stern control. Life was spent in the open air in games inspired by *Robinson Crusoe* and *The Last of the Mohicans*. There were horses to ride and there were peasants to talk to; but once again the company of children of their own age was denied to them. There was also time for reading; in one summer, at the age of twelve, Fyodor (if we may believe the testimony of a letter written by him in the last year of his life) read 'the whole of Scott'.

Forty and more years later, when he had invested the Russian peasant with a poetic halo and made him the messiah of his political creed, Dostoevsky liked to look back on these summer sojourns on the parental farm—the only periods in his life which he ever spent in the Russian countryside—and to believe that they had left 'the deepest and most powerful impression on his whole subsequent life'. He disinterred a forgotten incident of his tenth year when he had been seized with childish terror of an imaginary wolf and had been soothed and comforted by a peasant called Marei. The incident is first related in *A Raw Youth*, written in 1875, and occupies two lines; in 1876 it has developed into a complete saga, and the description of it, and of its alleged effects when recollected twenty years afterwards in his Siberian prison, fills one of the best-known chapters on *The Journal of an Author*. In this form it may be literature, but it is not biography. It is hard to discern in the intervening years, any perceptible influence of 'the peasant Marei' or of these summer months in the country. We look in vain in Dostoevsky's novels for descriptions of country life; there are none—his heroes live in cities, and preferably in garrets. We look for peasants—and we find only the bourgeoisie and the down-at-heel proletariat of the towns. We look for animals—and we find the wretched street mongrel Azorka in *The Insulted and Injured*, who seems to be drawn from the poodle in *Faust* rather than from real life, and the spiders and tarantulas which Dostoevsky's vivid imagination may have often conjured up in the dark corner behind the partition where he slept as a child. Such are the characteristic fauna of Dostoevsky's world. In his later years Dostoevsky was prone to denounce the 'wanderer', the man who had no roots in the soil; and he even proposed to write a 'Russian *Candide*', which would doubtless have inculcated the cultivation of one's own garden. But in reality Dostoevsky was himself a wanderer among the cities of the world and had no garden to care for.

It was about the time of the first of these annual visits to the country that the education of the elder children was seriously begun. There had been maternal instruction in the alphabet at an early age. The evening family readings had made them familiar with the Bible and with the principal episodes of Karamzin's history. Then there had been two visiting teachers—a priest and a Frenchman. The latter, whose name was Souchard, became a naturalized Russian, adopted a Russian-sounding name which was supposed to be an anagram of his own, Drashusov, and opened a small private day-school. Thither Michael and Fyodor were sent, probably in 1831. As no Latin was taught there, father himself undertook to initiate the two boys into the vagaries of *mensa* and *amo*; and these lessons, during which the pupils were made to stand bolt upright by the dining-table, seem to have left a vivid impression of paternal impatience and irritability.

In 1834 the brothers were sent to a private boarding-school kept by one Chermak and remained there three years. The curriculum was conceived on the generous lines then current—eight hours of school-work in the day, not counting preparation; but the school seems to have been a good one in most respects. It did not, however, break down the barrier which Dostoevsky's temperament put between him and the mass of his fellow-creatures, and from the few references to his school life in his writings we cannot infer that he looked back on it with any pleasure. 'I was of course unused,' writes the hero of *A Raw Youth*, 'to society of any kind. At school I had been on familiar terms with my comrades, but I had very few comrades. I made a corner for myself and lived in it.' Parental suspiciousness accentuated this anti-social disposition; only once did a school-fellow cross the Dostoevsky threshold. The two brothers never went out alone, and pocket-money was unknown. More and more often as they grew older did their father explain to the boys that he was a poor man, that they would have to make their own way in life, and that they would all be beggars after his death.

In this more than puritan atmosphere of monotony and gloom, the mother fell ill and died early in 1837. She had borne eight children of whom Fyodor was the second, and she died when he was fifteen. He always speaks of her memory with reverence, but she can scarcely have played any great part in his life. The mothers of his heroes are generally models of affectionate ineffectiveness. About the time of her funeral, Moscow was ringing with the news of the duel and death of Pushkin, of whom the boys at this time made their idol. 'My brothers nearly went off their heads,' relates Andrei; 'Fyodor in conversations with his elder brother several times said that, if we had not had our family mourning, he would have asked father's permission to wear mourning for Pushkin.'

Before the death of their mother it had already been decided to enter Michael and Fyodor for the Military Engineering Academy at Petersburg, in which their father was able to obtain free places for them. In May, father and sons set out together, by road, for the railway connecting the two capitals was opened only ten years later. The boys, for the first time in Petersburg, and for the first time alone in the world, were left in the boarding-establishment of one Kostomarov, where they were to undergo the final preparation for the entrance examination of the Academy; their father returned to Moscow and they never saw him again. The examination was duly passed in September, and in January 1838 Fyodor entered the Academy, but alone. Michael was rejected as medically unfit, and was admitted some months later into the Engineering Academy at Reval. The unexpected separation between the brothers produced a correspondence whose meagre remains are our principal source for Dostoevsky's biography during the next few years.

An account by an eyewitness of the sixteen-year-old Dostoevsky during his first year at the Academy portrays for us a youth of awkward demeanour, thick-set, blond and abnormally pale; shunning the dancing-classes and other lighter sides of life in the Academy; sitting in the corner of a dark and airless dormitory reading or writing by the light of a tallow candle; or pacing to and fro in precocious discussion of the problems of existence with one or two kindred spirits. The account was penned after Dostoevsky's death more than forty years later for the official biography. The shades may have been deepened, the pathos a trifle forced; but we need not doubt the essential accuracy of the picture.

Consolations there were. In a joint letter to their father soon after their arrival in Petersburg the boys write: 'We have not yet seen Shidlovsky and therefore have not yet been able to give him your greeting.' It was not long, however, before they made the acquaintance of the person in question. His previous relations with Dostoevsky *père* are something of a puzzle; for he turned out to be a romantic poet of about twenty-five occupying some minor official post which he soon resigned. Common devotion to Pushkin sealed the bond; Shidlovsky became for a space of two years the oracle of the brothers Dostoevsky, seeing Fyodor constantly in Petersburg and corresponding with Michael after the latter's departure for Reval.

The Russian literary world caught the romantic fever late, but severely; at the end of the 'thirties it was still at its height. 'This is the one true sign of the great poet, of the man of eminence; trample him in the mud, cover him with dust, drag, crush and torture him—his soul will remain firm, true to itself, and the angel of inspiration will lead it safe and sound out of the darkness of life into the world of immortality on the wings of all-prevailing glory.' Thus writes Shidlovsky in a letter to Michael Dostoevsky which has by chance been preserved. He goes on to discuss Werther, Chatterton and suicide; 'the river bed,' he writes, 'lured me with the same passion as the bridal bed lures the betrothed'. In accordance with the best romantic principles he suffered from an unrequited love, and thereby acquired enormous prestige in the eyes of his young friends. 'Without this love,' wrote Fyodor to Michael, 'he could not have been the pure exalted unselfish priest of poetry that he was.' It is to this period that we must refer the recollection in one of Dostoevsky's later essays that he loved to imagine himself in turn 'a Marius, a Pericles, a Christian of Nero's day, a knight at a joust and Edward Glendeling [*sic*] in Scott's *Monastery*'.

In this atmosphere and under this guidance, Dostoevsky lived through his romantic period. Scott and Pushkin he had discovered in Moscow; the new idols to whom Shidlovsky introduced him were Shakespeare, Schiller, Hoffmann and Balzac. He began to write two verse dramas, *Boris Godunov* (after Pushkin) and *Maria Stuart* (after Schiller), which have happily disappeared. He had taken his first steps as an author, and consoled himself for the uncongenial curriculum at the Engineering Academy.

In his last years Dostoevsky, in a reminiscent mood, spoke to his friend Soloviev of Shidlovsky as one whose influence in his life deserved to be remembered; and subsequent commentators have expended considerable ingenuity in elucidating the extent and character of this influence. The subsequent career of Shidlovsky is known to us only in vague outline, but it is significant. His

romantic youth was followed by a period of debauch, from which
he emerged in middle life to enter a monastery. He thus exemplified
—and perhaps in part suggested (though here we are reduced to
conjecture)—Dostoevsky's later faith in the efficacy of sin as the
path to true holiness. These later adventures of Shidlovsky were
well known to him, although it does not appear that he ever saw
his former friend after their parting in Petersburg; and the influence
of which he spoke to Soloviev probably relates to these subsequent
experiences rather than to the more commonplace romantic aberrations of Shidlovsky's youth.

It was now the winter of 1838–9, the first he had spent alone in
the world, and a new passion, apparently for one of his fellow-
students, declared itself.

I was in a sort of ecstasy [he wrote afterwards to Michael]. My acquaintance
with Shidlovsky afforded many, many hours of higher life; but that was
not the cause of it. . . . I had with me a comrade, a being whom I loved
so! . . . I learned Schiller by heart, spoke of him, raved of him; and I
think that fate never did anything more apt in my life than when it led
me to the knowledge of that great poet at that epoch of my life; never
could I have learned to know him as well as at that time. Reading Schiller
with *him* I verified in *his* nature the magnificent, fiery Don Carlos, the
Marquis Posa and Mortimer. This friendship brought me so much pain
and pleasure! Now I shall remain eternally silent about it; the name of
Schiller has become part of myself, a magic sound evoking a multitude
of dreams. Bitter dreams, brother; and that is why I have never spoken
to you of Schiller and of the impressions he made on me. It is painful to
me to hear the very name of Schiller.

The identity of the object of this adolescent *Schwärmerei* remains
unknown; and the whole episode is insignificant except as an
example of romantic aberration, and an illustration of that passionate
need for exclusive devotion which clung to Dostoevsky throughout
life. It is symptomatic of this stage in his growth that its object
was a man, not a woman. If he had any relations with women at
this time, they must have been of a purely physical kind. It was
only much later that the emotions began to play a role in his attitude
to the other sex. But by the summer of 1839 this romantic passion
had already become a sentimental memory; Shidlovsky had left
Petersburg, and passed out of Dostoevsky's life for good; and news
came from Moscow of the death of his father.

The Dostoevsky family maintained on the circumstances of their
father's death a silence which was not broken for eighty years. The
event is barely referred to in the official biography of Dostoevsky,
and its circumstances are nowhere mentioned in his extant cor-

respondence; the letters which passed between him and his brother Michael during the fatal year have, with one exception, completely disappeared. Some ten years ago, the novelist's daughter lifted the veil for the first time; but she is not an altogether reliable witness and is, moreover, in this matter, concerned to establish an ingenious but conjectural parallel between Dostoevsky's father and Fyodor Karamazov. The main facts are beyond dispute; but some of the details given by her seem apocryphal.

More affected than he would probably have cared to admit by the death of his wife, Dostoevsky the elder, having left his two eldest children in Petersburg and his three next in Moscow (Varvara being married and the two younger boys at school), resigned his post and practice and retired with his two younger daughters to his little country estate. Living there in isolation, he abandoned himself to private drinking-bouts which were particularly fatal to his jagged nerves and irritable temper. Uncontrolled by any sort of public or family opinion, he became more and more eccentric in his conduct and demeanour; it is said that he used every night to search under his daughters' beds (they were scarcely in their teens) for concealed lovers—an incident which is utilized in one of his son's novels. The sternness on which he had prided himself in his dealings with his children turned to brutality in his dealings with his serfs. One day in the summer of 1839, two years after he had left Michael and Fyodor in Petersburg, he was found murdered in circumstances which left no doubt that the crime was one of vengeance and had been perpetrated by his own peasants. Such events were not uncommon. In her well-known memoirs of the period Madame Panaeva remarks on the frequency at this time of murders of landed proprietors by their serfs, and continues as follows:

In the press of the day information of his kind could not appear. Strict instructions were given to conceal such disorders, and to keep watch on private correspondence so that news of these melancholy occurrences could not be spread about.

This ostrich-like attitude of the authorities may well explain the disappearance of the family correspondence relating to the death of Dostoevsky's father; and unless the lost letters are some day recovered or the records of the judicial enquiry extracted from some forgotten bundle of official archives, it is unlikely that we shall learn more of the end of this strange and unattractive man.

Fyodor was now nearly eighteen; and here if anywhere we must draw the line which separates childhood from manhood.

CHAPTER II

Early Years in Petersburg

THE emotional reactions on Dostoevsky of his father's death, about which much has been written in recent years, are almost purely conjectural. His one surviving letter to Michael which refers to the event does not suggest that they were abnormal or in any way remarkable.

Dear brother [he writes], I have shed many tears over the death of our father, but now our position is still more appalling; I speak not of myself, but of our family.

And he goes on to discuss, in a manner free from any suspicion of a complex, the fate of his orphaned brothers and sisters. This letter provides unsubstantial support for the imposing edifice which critics of the psychoanalyst school have raised over the grave of the novelist's father. The report that the news of this tragic event brought on Dostoevsky's first epileptic seizure is unsupported by any reliable evidence and must be rejected as a myth.[1]

We are on firmer ground in dealing with the material consequences of the tragedy; and here we are brought face to face with a theme which is bound to occupy a tiresomely large space in all biographies of Dostoevsky—his financial improvidence and chronic financial distress. Until they came to Petersburg the Dostoevsky boys had never been allowed to handle money or spend a single kopek on their own account. Their father had talked much of money, especially in his later years, but had kept the purse-strings in his own hands. Left in Petersburg, the boys were dependent on remittances from Moscow for which they had to render a strict account. A letter from Fyodor to his father of the year 1839 contains an urgent and detailed plea for 25 roubles for the bare necessities of life, which do not—he explains—include such luxuries as tea. His plight was evidently pitiful; but, judging from the character which he afterwards exhibited, it may well have been due as much to his own extravagance as to the parental meanness on which his biographers delight to dwell.

We are not informed either of the value of the estate of Dostoev-

[1] See note on p. 30.

sky senior (it must have been fairly substantial) or of the provisions of the will. Karepin, a Moscow merchant, husband of the deceased's eldest daughter, was executor and guardian; but after a few futile efforts to act *in loco parentis* to Michael and Fyodor, now on the verge of manhood, he seems, not unnaturally, to have confined himself to the duty of paying out as rapidly as possible the shares due to them. Between 1841 and 1844, Fyodor was in receipt of considerable sums from this source, and enjoyed moments of affluence which he was not to know again until the closing years of his life. These unearned revenues encouraged the habits of easy and lavish expenditure which consorted so well with his undisciplined temperament.

Very little is known of these years of Dostoevsky's life except a few facts of purely external interest. He went through the usual course of the Academy with sufficient credit to obtain in 1843 his commission and an appointment to the Engineering Department of the Ministry of War. Michael had also obtained his commission in Reval, had married a girl of German extraction, and had by now a child. Meanwhile Andrei had come up from Moscow to prepare for the Academy, and shared a flat with Fyodor for some months. It was of absurd dimensions for the two youths, and the rent swallowed up a quarter of Fyodor's income. A year later he had only furnished two of its rooms and could only afford to heat one. Money continued to come in by instalments from Moscow but was spent or stolen, given or gambled away within a few days of its receipt. Dostoevsky could never refuse a beggar or a friend. He was the uncomplaining victim of his tradesmen. His soldier-servant kept a complacent laundress, with all her family and friends, at his expense. Debts accumulated; for after spending one instalment, one must have something to live on until the next is due. On one occasion we find him living on bread and milk—all that the neighbouring shop would supply on credit; on another borrowing 200 roubles from a money-lender at 50 per cent for four months on the security of his pay at the Engineering Department. Finally in 1844 he offered to compound his remaining share of the paternal estate for a sum of 500 roubles down and a further 500 to be paid in monthly instalments; and the offer was accepted.

In the early days of his stay in Reval Michael had made the acquaintance of a German doctor, Riesenkampf by name. The doctor visited Fyodor in Petersburg at intervals during these years and has left memoirs in which he dwells, with true German horror, on these heart-rending details of financial disorder. The winter of 1843–4 was spent by Riesenkampf in Petersburg, and, at Michael's

earnest request, he went to live with Fyodor, partly in order to
share the expenses of the huge apartment, partly in order to 'influence him with an example of German exactitude'. If we may
judge from Dostoevsky's subsequent career, the latter part of
Riesenkampf's mission was imperfectly successful; nor does he
appear to have been more successful in inspiring admiration for the
German character, which Dostoevsky throughout life continued to
denounce, in and out of season, as unimaginative, narrow and self-
righteous.

Save that he visited the theatre, the ballet and 'expensive con-
certs', the good doctor has little to tell us of Dostoevsky's occupations during this period. Literature was still his ruling passion;
but he had abandoned the Germans for the French. Contemporary
French literature particularly attracted him at this time, and he
seems to have run through the whole gamut from Lamartine and
Victor Hugo to Frédéric Soulié and Paul de Kock. Among Russian
authors he had passed on from Pushkin to Gogol, pages of whom
he knew by heart; Gogol's influence was, as we shall see, decisive
in the formation of his prose style.

His financial difficulties gave him a new view of literature. It
was no longer, as in the days of *Maria Stuart* and *Boris Godunov*,
a vehicle for the expression of philosophic doubts and rhetorical
emotions; it was a specific designed to augment his revenues; for,
like other spendthrifts, Dostoevsky attributed his difficulties to the
inadequacy of his receipts, not to the excess of his outgoings. The
moment was not inopportune. Since 1830 literature had, for the
first time in Russia, become not merely an elegant amusement,
but a commercial proposition. Periodicals sprang up like mushrooms;
people were ready to pay not only for original work, but for translations from the great European literatures. Most of the standard
Russian translations of the classics of western Europe date from the
period between 1830 and 1850. Why should not Dostoevsky float
to fortune on the prevailing current? Like Balzac he fills his letters
with abstruse arithmetical calculations and ingenious schemes
guaranteed to make millionaires of all connected with them. He
translated Balzac's *Eugénie Grandet*, and began a translation of
George Sand; Michael in Reval made verse translations of *The
Robbers* and *Don Carlos*, which were to form part of a complete
Russian edition of Schiller.

Most of the schemes fell through for lack of capital, and none of
them made Dostoevsky's fortune. But literary ambitions made his
service in the Engineering Department seem 'as dull as potatoes';
and when he was threatened with transfer to a post in the provinces

which would have put an end to these extraneous occupations, he handed in his resignation. He had just run through the last instalment of his inheritance, and had nothing more to hope from that quarter. He now abandoned the career which had cost him five years of arduous and uncongenial training, and which, at any rate, offered him a regular pittance for life. The exasperated executor brother-in-law, who being a merchant knew the value of money, wrote from Moscow, 'apropos of nothing' as Dostoevsky remarks, and adjured him 'not to be led astray by Shakespeare, who was of no more use than a soap-bubble'. Undeterred by this excellent advice, the irresponsible young man took the plunge, and joined the goodly company of those who have become great writers under the driving lash of poverty. Having now no other source of income but his pen he sat down to write his first original essay in prose fiction.

Poor Folk, a short novel in epistolary form, was written and rewritten during the winter of 1844–5; and the story of its discovery by the critics is one of the most famous episodes in Russian literary history. In May the manuscript was confided by Dostoevsky to Grigorovich, a literary aspirant like himself whom he had met at the Engineering Academy. Grigorovich took it to his friend Nekrasov, a young writer whose poems had already brought him a certain success and standing in the world of letters. The two sat down to read it together, and went on reading it through the twilight of the May night, and at 4 o'clock in the morning came to wake Dostoevsky and congratulate him on having written a masterpiece. The manuscript continued its ascent through the literary hierarchy. It was brought by Nekrasov to Belinsky with the tidings that 'a new Gogol had appeared'; and the famous critic, after a moment of initial scepticism, endorsed the verdict of Nekrasov and Grigorovich. Three days later Dostoevsky was presented to Belinsky. 'Do you understand,' shouted the latter impetuously, 'what it is that you have written ? . . . It is impossible that you at twenty should understand.' And he proceeded to explain to the enraptured and open-mouthed young author the significance of his work. 'Am I really so great ?' Dostoevsky began to ask himself; and thirty years later he described the scene as 'the most entrancing moment of my life'.

Although Nekrasov's *Almanach*, in which *Poor Folk* was eventually published, did not appear until the following January, the approval of Belinsky brought its author immediate recognition in the narrow but influential circle over which he presided. The morbidly self-conscious young man who had never emerged from the awkward age or succeeded in adjusting his angular personality to the curves of his fellow-men, found himself patronized and petted by the most

famous literary lions of the day, Belinsky and Nekrasov, Turgenev
and Tyutchev, Annenkov and Panaev and half a dozen others now
forgotten. A naïvely optimistic temperament, combined with complete ignorance of social usage, led him to mistake encouragement for
adulation, and friendly gestures for passionate devotion. The literary
world had come to gaze with interest on a young writer of promise;
and he fondly imagined it prostrate at his feet. The following
excerpts from a letter to his brother in November 1845 need no
comment:

Well, brother, I think my glory will never reach such a climax as now.
Everywhere unbounded respect and extreme curiosity about me. ...
Prince Odoevsky begs me to favour him with a visit, and Count S. tears
his hair in despair. Panaev told them that a genius had appeared who will
trample them all in the dust. ... Everybody receives me as a prodigy.
I cannot open my mouth without its being reported that Dostoevsky has
said this or Dostoevsky wants to do that. ... I am full of ideas, but I
cannot tell any of them even to Turgenev, without its being known next
day in every corner of Petersburg that Dostoevsky is writing so-and-so.
Well, brother, if I were to recount to you all my successes, I could not
find enough paper. ...

In short, Dostoevsky made a fool of himself. An English youth
would have kept such thoughts to himself and blushed for them in
secret years afterwards. Dostoevsky was self-conscious enough, and
intelligent enough, to know that he was being a fool. But his uncontrolled Russian nature betrayed him at every turn; and his new
friends were not slow to laugh. Turgenev, Nekrasov and Annenkov
all seem to have had a hand in a rhymed lampoon in which Dostoevsky was apostrophized as the 'Knight of the Sorrowful Countenance', and of which the most pungent couplet was the following:

> Upon the face of literature
> You blossom like an over-ripe pimple.

And the 'literary pimple' became the usual sobriquet for the young
man among his friends. An anecdote gained currency that he had
insisted on *Poor Folk* being printed with a special border to distinguish it from the other contents of the *Almanach*. This particular
canard pursued Dostoevsky throughout his life, and not many
months before his death he thought it worth while to publish a
denial of it in the press.

The rift in Dostoevsky's short-lived intimacy with Belinsky and
his circle was accentuated by an extraneous cause. Belinsky and his
closest friends, Nekrasov and Panaev, were on increasingly bad terms
with Kraevsky, the editor of the *Otechestvennye Zapiski*; and in the

spring of 1846 they severed their connection with the journal to which they had for many years been regular contributors. The aesthetic outlook of a contributor and the financial outlook of an editor seldom coincide; and it would be unfair to condemn Kraevsky, on the word of Belinsky, as 'a grabber, a vampire and a cad'. He could at any rate be generous when he chose, and he adopted the surest method of binding a promising but impecunious young author to his editorial chariot. 'Some days ago,' wrote the naïve Dostoevsky to his brother in November 1845, 'Kraevsky, hearing that I had no money, humbly begged me to accept a loan of 500 roubles.' The process was several times repeated, and Dostoevsky was in the spider's web. Before long, his output was mortgaged to the *Otechestvennye Zapiski* for months, even years, in advance; and as Kraevsky's hack, he became, on business as well as on personal grounds, anathema to the friends of Belinsky. His next stories *The Double*, *Mr Prokharchin* and *The Hostess*, disappointingly and unaccountably inferior to *Poor Folk*, met with an increasingly cold reception from Belinsky, who now wrote for the rival journal, the *Sovremennik*; and by the spring of 1847 the breach was complete.

The name of Belinsky, who died of consumption in the following year, was canonised by the Russian radicals, and for half a century Belinsky was honoured in progressive circles not merely as a great literary critic, but as the founder of Russian political thought. When in later life Dostoevsky became a stalwart pillar of orthodoxy and began to execrate everything that savoured of the radical and revolutionary, he liked to imagine, and to tell his friends, that he had broken with Belinsky on grounds of political and religious belief. It is a striking instance of the unconscious dishonesty which makes highly imaginative people like Dostoevsky the most unreliable of witnesses to the facts of their own life. His subsequent explanation of the breach is untenable, if only for the reason that he passed immediately from the circle of Belinsky to a circle whose views were not less advanced, and more distinctly political in complexion, than those of Belinsky. It is indeed difficult to form any clear estimate of Dostoevsky's opinions at this time; like the opinions of any other unformed and impressionable youth, they were borrowed from his environment of the moment. Since, in the last decade of Nicholas's reign, every independent and intelligent young man whom Dostoevsky was likely to meet was more or less of a radical, he too was a radical; and he embraced the cause with the undiscriminating enthusiasm proper to his age and character. There is no evidence that he had at this date reflected at all profoundly on the problems, ethical, political or religious, which afterwards tormented his mind and fertilized his genius. In his spiritual development he remained, until his departure for Siberia, a callow youth.

The two years which elapsed between Dostoevsky's final breach with Belinsky in the spring of 1847 and his arrest for complicity in a revolutionary conspiracy in April 1849 are barren territory for the biographer. Michael Dostoevsky returned with his family in the summer of 1847 to live in Petersburg, and the fertile correspondence between the two brothers was interrupted. Moreover, there is little doubt that Dostoevsky himself in later life, and his friends after his death, deliberately cast a veil over the revolutionary period of his career. We still catch glimpses of him in the drawing-rooms of aristocratic patrons of literature. There was Count Sollogub, authentic Russian Count and author of popular novels, who liked in the literary world to play the aristocrat and in the aristocratic world the man of letters, and by this wilful perverseness made enemies in both. There was also Count Wielhorski, rotund and rubicund, a creditable amateur musician, who collected at his *soirées* the musical talent, native and foreign, of the capital; and Prince Odoevsky, bustling and faintly ridiculous, but loved by the rank and file of the literary world whom he entertained on Saturday evenings to the disgust of the more fastidious Princess. In this world of elegant dilettanti the vanity of Dostoevsky would be more easily tolerated and more gently dealt with than by his rivals in the commerce of literature. But it is hard to believe that he ever felt at home there; the rare scenes from aristocratic life which occur in his novels are as convincing as similar scenes in Balzac or Dickens.

Another and more important intimacy dates from this period. The successor of Belinsky as principal literary critic of the *Otechestvennye Zapiski* was a young man named Valerian Maikov. He lived with his brother Apollon, an estimable but uninspired poet of the classical school, and with their mother, herself a lady of some literary pretensions. In this house Dostoevsky soon became a frequent and welcome guest; and though Valerian died suddenly in 1847, Apollon remained a close friend of Dostoevsky throughout his later career. The impressions of Dostoevsky's intercourse with the Maikov family are among the pleasantest of his early life; but paradoxically enough, it was through Apollon Maikov, whose own youthful radicalism remained tepid and purely theoretical, that Dostoevsky was led to the great catastrophe.

But in all these relationships we never seem to pierce far beneath the surface; and the barrier of reserve which Dostoevsky maintained at this time even against his best friends has not been lifted for posterity. If we seek to explore his sexual life up to the age of twenty-eight when he was carried off into exile, we find ourselves moving in almost uncharted waters. Both Riesenkampf, the German from Reval, and Yanovsky, his medical attendant and personal friend, have left independent testimony that he had no love-affairs of which they were aware and displayed no interest in women. Their testimony, which relates to different periods of his early life in Petersburg, is confirmed by the evidence, such as it is, of his literary output; save for two studies (in *Netochka Nezvanova* and *A Little Hero*) of sexual precocity in children, sex plays a purely secondary role in the stories of his pre-Siberian period. It would, indeed, be absurd to conclude from this negative evidence that Dostoevsky practised in his early manhood an asceticism entirely foreign to his time, his country and his temperament. We have his own witness to the contrary; for in a letter to his brother, written at the moment when the excitement of his first literary success had dissolved his customary reserve, he speaks of 'Minnas, Claras and Mariannes' who 'cost a pile of money', and adds that Turgenev and Belinsky have 'pulled him to pieces for his irregular life'. But this is scarcely the language of an authentic Don Juan; it is rather the noisy boastfulness of the young man who, too shy to be successful with women in his own sphere of life, seeks furtive pleasures on the streets, and would, in moments of expansion, like it to be thought that he keeps mistresses. There is no more justification for depicting Dostoevsky at this period as a debauchee than as an ascetic.

In the same letter, side by side with this crude boast of the mercenary charms of his 'Minnas, Claras and Mariannes', comes a no less naïve confession of calf-love:

Yesterday I was for the first time at Panaev's and, I think, fell in love with his wife; she is clever and pretty, charming into the bargain and extremely frank.

Six months later (it happened in the winter of 1845–6) he writes:

I was seriously in love with Madame Panaeva; now it seems to be passing off—I don't know.

The lady, afterwards for many years the mistress of Nekrasov, has left voluminous memoirs in which she speaks kindly enough of Dostoevsky; but it is clear that she was totally unaware of the 'serious' passion she had inspired, and that he had never made any attempt to declare it. When physical experiences begin at an early age and are entirely divorced from sentiment, the sentimental reactions which we generally associate with sexual attraction may remain immature and undeveloped up to a relatively advanced age; and this probably explains the unfamiliar combination, which we find in the twenty-five-year-old Dostoevsky, of the careless rake and the sentimental hobbledehoy. It was only later that sex began to dominate Dostoevsky's thought and feeling; and his subsequent romance with Maria Dmitrievna in Siberia at the age of thirty-five exhibits all the recognized symptoms of first love.

In all his dealings at this time with his fellow-men Dostoevsky was pursued by the uneasy, nervous temperament which seethed beneath his awkward and unprepossessing exterior. Its physical causes are conjectural. The medical evidence does not enable us to assert with confidence whether his condition was the forerunner of the epilepsy which, in its overt form, first attacked him in Siberia. It is clear that Dostoevsky did not think so himself; for he more than once declared in later life that the nervous disorders of his early manhood had been cured by prison and exile; and the specific physical disability with which he connected them was not epilepsy, but piles. The memoirs of his doctor-friend Yanovsky mention among his symptoms an irregular pulse and nervous headaches; but Yanovsky evidently thought his patient something of an hypochondriac. From him Dostoevsky borrowed books on nervous diseases and on phrenology. Like Balzac, he endeavoured through the latter science, then in the heyday of its popularity, to detect in himself the physical manifestations of genius; and he liked to be told that his skull resembled that of Socrates.

The moral symptoms of his disorder—fits of extreme elation succeeded by equally extreme depression, outbursts of ludicrous braggadocio followed by moods of insuperable shyness and self-depreciation—were revealed in all his dealings with the outside world. He belonged to the unhappy race of men who perceive the depths of their folly even at the moment of committing it, and whose remorse is almost simultaneous with the action to which it relates. He writes to his brother Michael in 1847 after a visit to Reval:

I recollect how angular and unbearable I was with you in Reval. I was a sick man, brother. I remember you once said to me that my behaviour excluded all idea of mutual equality. Dear friend, that was completely unjust. But I have such an unpleasant, repulsive character. I have always esteemed you more highly than myself. I would give my life for you and yours, but sometimes when my heart is overflowing with love, you can't get from me an affectionate word. My nerves are beyond my control at such moments.

One of the most pathetic and revealing letters of Dostoevsky during this period is written to Madame Maikova to apologize for some incident at a reception of hers:

> I fear you thought me abrupt and (I grant it) rude, and imagined that I acted strangely. I fled by instinct, conscious of the weakness of my nature which will break out violently and exaggeratedly. You will understand: my weak nerves make it hard for me to tolerate and answer questions with a *double entendre*, hard not to be infuriated by the mere fact of the *double entendre*, and most of all infuriated at my own inability to treat them as straightforward well-meant questions. ... Of course, feelings ran high; taunts, deliberate and unintentional, were exchanged; and I instinctively took refuge in flight to prevent these taunts assuming still more unseemly proportions.
>
> But do not judge the weaknesses of a nature like mine.

It is part of the pathos of his temperament that Dostoevsky could not only describe so well the phenomena which he was unable to control, but could analyse their causes with equal clairvoyance. He writes to his brother in the letter already quoted:

> The external ought to balance the internal. Otherwise, in the absence of external impressions the internal acquires too dangerous a supremacy. Nerves and imagination have a very large place in the composition of a man.

Many years later he wrote to another correspondent:

> Do not bottle yourself up in isolation, give yourself up to nature, give yourself up—if only a little—to the external world and external things.

It was the fruit of hard experience. The boy who had had no playmates and who at school had 'made a corner for himself and lived in it', had become incapable of expanding to the normal measure of human intercourse and giving himself to the external world. More and more, like Raskolnikov or the hero of *A Raw Youth*, he shrank back into the morbid self-absorption of his garret existence. It is indeed possible, and perhaps reasonable, to argue that this intense concentration was a necessary element in the growth of his unique genius, on which it left such profound traces. But for the moment its effects seemed purely prejudicial to his talent as well as to his happiness; for by the common consent of contemporaries and of posterity his early work subsequent to *Poor Folk* showed a progressive decline from that brilliant *début,* and revealed a more and more artificial note. These firstfruits of his literary activity must, however, be passed in review before we proceed to the calamity which proved to be the first great turning-point in his life.

NOTE TO CHAPTER II

The psychoanalysis of a genius is an attractive pastime. The fact that in his youth Dostoevsky lost his father by murder, and in his last years wrote a novel about the murder of a father by one of his sons, has proved an irresistible temptation for the high priests of the Oedipus-complex. Many abstruse pages in learned German treatises have been devoted to the elaboration of hypotheses in which Dostoevsky's epileptic seizures and his gambling mania play a prominent part. No less an authority than Dr Freud himself (in the *Realist* of July 1929) regards the death of Dostoevsky's father as the crucial event which moulded the novelist's life, and asserts that his epilepsy dates from this occurrence. On the former point, one can only plead absence of any evidence to support the assumption; on the latter, evidence can be produced to disprove the assertion.

It is natural, but unfortunate, that these scientific investigators are not fully familiar with the literary sources relating to Dostoevsky's epilepsy, which are for the most part still available only in Russian. The voluminous and complicated evidence has been examined in an article in the *Slavonic Review* for December 1930, and only the conclusions need be stated here. The authority for the supposed connection between Dostoevsky's epilepsy and the murder of his father is a passage in the biography by his daughter. 'According to family traditions,' she writes, 'it was on learning of the death of his father that Dostoevsky had his first fit of epilepsy.' But the testimony of this always unreliable source is contradicted by the letters of Dostoevsky himself written soon after his release from prison in Siberia, in which he speaks of his fits as a new phenomenon and is uncertain whether to regard them as epileptic. On February 22, 1854, he wrote to his brother Michael: 'From the disorder of my nerves, I have had an attack of epilepsy; but it does not come on often.' On July 30th of the same year he wrote, also to Michael: 'I have written to you already about my illness. Strange attacks like epilepsy, but not epilepsy. Sometime I will write about it in more detail.' Even three years later he was still in doubt; for he wrote to his friend Wrangel on March 9, 1857: 'The doctor has told me that I have genuine epilepsy.'

The nervous disorders from which he suffered in Petersburg before his exile to Siberia were never regarded either by himself or by his friends as epileptic in character; and there is no proof that they were. In any case they can scarcely be traced back to his father's murder, since they first declared themselves eight or nine years after that event.

CHAPTER III

Firstfruits

THE state of prose literature in Russia in the 'forties of last century has been described by a recent critic as a 'fertile chaos'. The romantic movement had spent itself. Scott had less influence in Russia than elsewhere in Europe (for Russia was a country poor in historical traditions); and Byron's supremacy ceased abruptly when Lermontov died. Despite Pushkin and Lermontov, it may indeed be doubted whether Romanticism ever struck very deep roots in Russian soil; and Panaev gives us the view of a superficial but honest observer when he describes Russian culture in the 'thirties as consisting of 'French conversation, the more or less successful acquisition of the external forms of vulgar European dandyism, and the reading of Paul de Kock's novels'. It was the end of the aristocratic age of Russian literature; in the 'forties literature had already passed into the hands of the professional writer.

The principal influences, native and foreign, which were moulding Russian fiction when Dostoevsky began to write, were three in number—the sentimental novel (mainly French), the fantastic novel (mainly German and English) and, gradually overshadowing and superseding both, the 'naturalistic' novel created by Gogol. It would be a mistake to press this classification too far. For the Russian fiction of the period is essentially eclectic; and Dostoevsky, though acclaimed on his first appearance as a 'new Gogol', borrowed much —as indeed had Gogol himself—from the 'sentimental' and 'fantastic' schools.

The favourite themes of the sentimental novel, which generally ran to three or four volumes, are the loves and misfortunes of noble heroes and pure-minded heroines. The essence of the sentimental novel is to place virtuous people in pathetic situations, and then extract from these situations the last available ounce of pathos. Its origins may be traced back, not without a side-glance at *Werther*, to Rousseau, and through him to Richardson and Sterne. The school had already produced one classic in Russian literature, Karamzin's *Poor Liza*, which had been read in the family circle when Dostoevsky was a boy. The young author of *Poor Folk* can hardly have forgotten Karamzin when he selected the title of his first story; but he had probably not reread *Poor Liza* since childhood, and the sentimental influences more directly traceable in his early work are those of French novelists of the school, who were still in vogue when Dostoevsky came up to Petersburg. The hero of *Poor Folk* is made to quote Ducray-Dumesnil's *Le Petit Carillonneur*, a typical specimen of the *genre*, as one of the only two novels he has ever read; and the servants are named after the hero and heroine of another then fashionable, but now quite forgotten, sentimental novel, *Thérèse et Faldoni*.

Even more popular was the fantastic novel, the tale of the supernatural and, preferably, of the blood-curdling. The English branch of this school of fiction used to be called by English critics the 'Gothic' in honour of Horace Walpole whose *Castle of Otranto* did so much to set the fashion; and its leading exponents Ann Radcliffe, 'Monk' Lewis and Maturin were all still esteemed in Russia in the 'forties. In Germany, the fantastic had always flourished; the names of Hoffmann and Jean-Paul were household words all over Europe in Dostoevsky's youth, and a sane critic like Belinsky could rank Hoffmann with Goethe and Shakespeare. The influence of Hoffmann is clearly enough attested in more than one of Dostoevsky's pre-Siberian tales; and his name recurs again and again in the novelist's letters to his brother.

The 'naturalistic' novel (the name is as convenient and as inadequate as most literary labels) began in part as the product of, in part as a reaction from, the sentimental and fantastic schools. The first requisite of 'naturalistic' fiction was that the scene should be laid not in some distant or imaginary country or in some remote age, but in contemporary Russia; and almost invariably its heroes and heroines were of humble birth. 'The most downtrodden, the lowest of mankind is also a man, and calls himself thy brother'—such was the motto of the school. The story which may be said to have created it was Gogol's *The Cloak* (in some translations called *The Overcoat*), published in 1842. It is the serio-comic story of a poor government clerk who, by dint of incredible self-denial, scrapes together enough money to buy himself a new cloak, of which he is inordinately proud; the first time he dons it, it is stolen from him by robbers, and, despairing of its recovery, the poor man falls into a delirium and dies. It was currently said that all Russian writers of fiction of the 'forties 'came out of Gogol's *Cloak*'; and of its influence on Dostoevsky's début, it is sufficient to remark that the heroes of all his first three stories were poor government clerks. By his contemporaries Gogol was taken for a realist, as the label 'naturalistic' implies; but to posterity much about him seems purely romantic. His exuberant, overloaded, ultra-romantic style proved as infectious as his matter. The question of Dostoevsky's style is of secondary interest to the English reader, but it has attracted great attention in Russia during the last few years, and several essays have been written to demonstrate how closely his early manner was modelled on that of Gogol. The predominant influence of Gogol's style on Dostoevsky continued unabated until his return from Siberia at the end of the 'fifties.

The circumstances of the writing of *Poor Folk* in 1845 and its publication in January 1846 have been described. It is the hybrid offspring of the sentimental and naturalistic schools. The poor official, Makar Devushkin, comes straight from the pages of Gogol; the heroine, forced by poverty and humiliation to marry an old *roué* who offers her material security, derives her pathos from the sentimentalists. The epistolary form—the novel consists of an exchange of letters between hero and heroine—is borrowed directly or indirectly from Richardson and Rousseau, the great forefathers of the sentimental school. But whatever the elements embodied in *Poor Folk*, it is not to be dismissed as a purely derivative work. The misfortunes of the poor official in Gogol are purely comic; the pathos of the ordinary sentimental heroine is merely lachrymose. Dostoevsky has raised both to tragic height, and has made the story of Makar and Varvara one of the great minor tragedies of literature. His genius is, as Belinsky pointed out in his first review of *Poor Folk*, not descriptive or satirical, like that of Gogol, but creative.

He does not obtain his effects [wrote Belinsky] by that knowledge of life and the human heart which comes from experience and observation. He knows them and knows them profoundly, but *a priori* and therefore in a purely aesthetic and creative spirit.

It was a rare stroke of critical intuition which thus detected at the very outset of Dostoevsky's career the fundamental nature of his genius. The figures of Makar and Varvara have not the reality of everyday life, nor are they mere lay-figures of convention; they have the peculiar exalted vitality of beings set in the world, but not of it, which Dostoevsky imparts to all his greatest characters. The only important blemish in *Poor Folk* is that, although scarcely more than a long short story, it gives in certain passages an impression of being unduly drawn out. The vein of true inspiration is there; but it is not yet deep and, in the hands of a young and inexperienced writer, it shows signs of becoming exhausted before the story is at an end.

If *Poor Folk* represents a cross between Gogol and the sentimentalists, Dostoevsky's next production is a cross between Gogol and Hoffmann. *The Double* is a theme from Hoffmann applied to the

C

familiar Gogol character of the poor official, as such themes had, indeed, already been applied by Gogol himself. But here Dostoevsky introduces a new element. The appearance of his hero's double is at first purely fantastic; but we soon perceive that the writer has a deeper purpose in view. The 'double' is the direct issue of what can only be called the hero's inferiority complex; Golyadkin junior, as the double is facetiously dubbed, is the vision of what Golyadkin himself might have been had he asserted his real self, had he not allowed the weight of men and circumstances to hold him down in the miserable rut of the poor official's life. And this vision dogs Golyadkin at every step until it drives him into madness. The double is therefore in a very real sense the product of the hero's dreams. Though the story is told in the main on the fantastic plane, there are moments when Dostoevsky seems to conceive Golyadkin junior not as an objective creature of the magical world, but as a purely subjective hallucination of Golyadkin senior's mind; and the culmination of the story, when Golyadkin is carried off to the madhouse, fits in with the latter conception rather than with the one which dominates the greater part of the narrative. The uncertainty of touch, the tendency to hover between the magical and the pathological, pervades the whole story. It is this incongruity, added to its unnecessary length and tiresome mannerisms, which has made *The Double* an almost complete failure. It was read when it first appeared mainly as the second effort of the promising young author of *Poor Folk*; and nobody would read it on its merits now. In point of style, it is the nearest of all Dostoevsky's writings to Gogol; but the imitation is clumsy and uninspired and is confined largely to verbal tricks and peculiarities.

Many years later, on his return from Siberia, Dostoevsky referred to *The Double* in a letter to his brother as 'the greatest and most important social type which I was the first to discover and proclaim'. The boast is better justified than many which authors have uttered about their own work. In *The Double* Dostoevsky was feebly groping for the first time after a figure which was eventually to become one of his most profound and characteristic creations; the figure of the man crushed by circumstances or driven by his temperament in upon himself; of the introvert who compensates himself for habitual self-control by violent sallies of self-assertion, who, like the hero of *Memoirs from Underground*, has been humiliated himself and wishes to humiliate others; of a being not at unity with himself, a victim, beyond the rest of mankind, of what R. L. Stevenson calls 'the fundamental duality of man'. Such is the thought which makes its first fantastic appearance in the pages of *The Double*; and the story has therefore, for the student of Dostoevsky, a wider importance than that to which its intrinsic merits entitle it.

The productions of the next two years, ten or more in number, none of them exceeding the dimensions of a long short story, may for the most part be passed over in silence. The most ambitious of them, *The Hostess*, has good claims to be regarded as one of the worst stories ever written. The central figure is the possessor of mesmeric powers, the familiar magician-villain of 'Monk' Lewis or Hoffmann; he exhibits a strange combination, not unknown in real life, but here most unconvincingly portrayed, of sincere saintliness and unabashed rascality. Belinsky dubbed it a 'strange incomprehensible piece'; and to the modern reader, far removed from the obsolete conventions of fantastic fiction, it seems merely an astonishing farrago of nonsense. Several of the shorter tales are flagrant potboilers; and one or two of them suggest a passing ambition on the part of the author to enrol himself among the innumerable Russian disciples of Paul de Kock.

The best written of Dostoevsky's pre-Siberian stories after *Poor Folk* are *A Weak Heart* and *White Nights*, both published in 1848. *A Weak Heart* is a study of a young official who, in the ecstasy of requited first love, neglects his work, is disgraced and finally goes off his head. The type of the young man 'unable to endure his own happiness' is perhaps too distinctively Russian to have a strong appeal for the western reader; and the story, though it may be called in many ways characteristic of Dostoevsky, does not stand in any specific relationship to his later work. *White Nights* is described on the title-page as a sentimental novel (though it is only some fifty pages long); and the unreality of the opening scene, where a pure maiden and a shy well-intentioned young man meet by night on the riverside of Petersburg, might be held to justify the adjective. But the story does not conform to the usual conventions of sentimental fiction; it is, in fact, a first study of the triangular situation—two men and one woman—which Dostoevsky afterwards handled in his own peculiarly subtle and unconventional manner in *The Insulted and Injured* and *The Eternal Husband*, and in its converse form— two women and one man—in *The Idiot*. The hero of *White Nights*, assisting the woman with whom he has fallen in love in her endeavours to win another man, is the exact prototype of the hero of *The Insulted and Injured*; and the coincidence should give pause to those critics who regard the later novel as an accurate reflection of the circumstances of the author's first marriage. To *White Nights*, a story not very significant in itself, must be assigned an important place in the development of Dostoevsky's technique.

The following year saw Dostoevsky's first attempt at a full-length novel, *Netochka Nezvanova*. Two instalments only, amounting to some 150 pages, had been published when, in April, Dostoevsky was arrested; and the story was never resumed. If more was written the manuscript has disappeared. The cessation of the story is in any case scarcely a matter for regret; Dostoevsky, to the end of his days, never thoroughly mastered the technique of construction, and in *Netochka Nezvanova* his apprenticeship had hardly begun. The fragment as it stands presents us with four successive tales grouped around the heroine's childhood; the link between them is purely external; and though Dostoevsky might, had the novel been completed, have tidied up some of the loose ends, it is clear that the work as a whole could never have achieved real unity. It is as diffuse and ill-knit as the earlier works of Dickens; but the touch of genius of a Dickens is altogether lacking.

One more story of the pre-Siberian period, remarkable not so much for its merits as for the circumstances in which it was produced, may be mentioned. *A Little Hero* was written by Dostoevsky in the Peter-and-Paul fortress during the summer and autumn of 1849. It is a study of the attraction exercised on a married woman by a boy on the eve of adolescence, still entirely innocent but just awakening to the possibilities of sentimental interest. It is a theme which figures in Rousseau's *Confessions*, and passed thence into many works of the sentimental school. *A Little Hero* is a slight piece of work, neither particularly pleasing nor particularly important; but unlike *Netochka Nezvanova*, it is relatively well-constructed and is written throughout in one style. It is always hard to resist the temptation, often legitimate enough, to connect the individual works of an author with the circumstances in which he wrote; but it should act as a deterrent to reflect that this straightforward untroubled story was written by Dostoevsky in a prison cell in the midst of desperate uncertainty as to his subsequent fate. It was eventually published in 1857.

Had Dostoevsky died on the scaffold in 1849 or afterwards in Siberia, *Poor Folk* would have shared the fate of another novel of the same decade, Grigorovich's *Anton Goremyka*; it would have become a minor half-forgotten classic, read in schools and honourably mentioned in textbooks of Russian literature. His other stories of this period would have passed into complete oblivion; and there is little in them to attract the modern reader. For the student of literature they have a stronger interest; for they foreshadow and explain certain features of Dostoevsky's later novels for which it would be otherwise difficult to account. Of the elements which went to the making of these early stories, the sentimental vein scarcely survived; it can be traced here and there in *The Insulted and Injured*, the first novel written after the return from Siberia, and then disappears. The influence of Gogol did not last much longer, and had been outlived before the great novels came to be written. But the fantastic strain proved more vigorous. The magical and supernatural make an occasional rather incongruous incursion even into Dostoevsky's latest work; and though critics are often tempted to interpret these manifestations in terms of mysticism and symbolism, the student will be more disposed to find in them the legacy of Dostoevsky's youthful passion for the fantastic. Two familiar examples will suffice by way of illustration. The figure of Rogozhin in *The Idiot* reveals a clearly marked fantastic ancestry. His uncanny piercing eyes, which haunt his intended victim, are the eyes of the magician Murin in *The Hostess* and of a dozen well-known heroes of fantastic fiction; and the scene in which he leads Myshkin to the dead body of Nastasya Philippovna is repeated from a scene in *Netochka Nezvanova* where the wicked stepfather (another half-magical figure) displays his wife's body to her little daughter. A still more striking instance is the scene in which the Devil appears to Ivan Karamazov—a scene on which volumes have been written by critics of the metaphysical school. The apparition is described in language which echoes, across the interval of more than thirty years, the passage in *The Double* where Golyadkin junior first dawns on the horizon of the distracted hero; and the opening conversation between Ivan Karamazov and the Devil is no less clearly inspired by a melodramatic favourite of Dostoevsky's callow years, Eugène Sue's *Mémoires du Diable*.

The pursuit of parallels between the earlier and the later Dostoevsky is, generally speaking, an unprofitable task. The survivals of his earlier style, and of the taste of a past generation, are more often a source of weakness than of strength in the great novels of his maturity. For ten years Dostoevsky was cut off from the literary world; and when he once more emerged, the spiritual environment of the Russian man of letters had been so profoundly changed, and the new impressions which he had himself amassed were so powerful and so engrossing, that he found himself in the position of a man beginning a new career rather than of a man resuming an old one. We cannot treat the pre-Siberian stories of Dostoevsky, like the works of most authors, as the first links in an unbroken chain of development. The continuity between the two periods is intermittent and illusory; and it is for this reason that we have felt justified in devoting less attention than is customary to these firstfruits of a great literary career.

CHAPTER IV

Catastrophe

THE history of the affair which brought Dostoevsky at the age of twenty-eight to penal servitude and exile is well known in its main outlines; the occasional uncertainties of detail are due to a super-abundance of unreliable testimony. The participants, most of whose written depositions before the Commission of Enquiry have come down to us, displayed ostentatious frankness in things which they believed to be known to the Commission and ingenious mendacity on points which they hoped to conceal. The official proceedings of the Commission, and of the military court which tried the offenders, show wearisome insistence on trivialities and complete failure to grasp the fundamental nature of the alleged conspiracy; and in one important matter at least, closely affecting Dostoevsky, commission and court were successfully hoodwinked. The subsequent references of Dostoevsky himself to this episode in his career vary in tone and substance, and betray the moralist rather than the historian. Some-times he seems inclined to disclaim any spiritual kinship between himself and the protagonists of the affair; at other times he rather exaggerates the extent of his participation, partly, it would seem, from vanity—the vanity of the arm-chair philosopher who likes to remember that in his youth he too was a man of action—partly from timidity, lest he should be thought, by minimizing his offence, to criticize the government which condemned him. The official bio-graphers, and their successors prior to 1917, are concerned to gloss over as far as possible the revolutionary aspect of Dostoevsky's early career; and Russian writers since 1917 have been no less anxious to magnify it. In the midst of so much tendencious material the objective biographer treads warily the path of sober fact.

The ringleader was an official of the Ministry of Foreign Affairs called Petrashevsky, and his followers were dubbed after him Petrashevtsi, or Petrashevsky's men. He was in the middle twenties; his gloomy countenance and long black hair, his large Spanish cloak, broad-brimmed soft hat and thick stick suggested the Byronic hero or the conspirator of melodrama. His début was ingenious and unusual; assisted by two or three intimates he published early in 1846 the first two volumes of a *Dictionary of Foreign Words In-*

corporated into the Russian Language. The work possessed in a high degree two qualities generally eschewed by makers of dictionaries; it was tendencious and it was readable. It described *Optimism,* for example, as an 'unsuccessful attempt to defend theism against the crushing attacks of practical atheism which is inspired by the facts of life itself', and *Christianity* as aiming at 'the establishment of liberty and the abolition of private property'. It defined *Nationality* harmlessly enough as 'an agglomeration of typical characteristics distinguishing one people from another', but went on to explain that progress consisted in the elimination of these distinguishing characteristics in favour of cosmopolitan development. The idea, if not the execution, was brilliant. The censor, thinking himself absolved from the necessity of reading a dictionary, passed it out of hand; and this inflammatory matter circulated for several months legally and openly. It was detected by the eye of authority, the censor censured and the unsold copies seized. It is now a great bibliographical rarity.

Encouraged by the success of the dictionary, Petrashevsky began to invite his friends and sympathizers to meet every week at his house for improving conversation; or, to use the fashionable idiom of the day, he formed a 'circle'. Every Friday the members of the circle, some half-dozen or dozen men at first, climbed the rickety staircase lighted by one night-light, drank tea, smoked innumerable cigarettes, exchanged forbidden books, and above all, talked, talked till two or three in the morning, talked as only Russians can, talked of the freedom of the press, of the liberation of the serfs, of the abolition of the family and of the establishment of the ideal commonwealth. It was all vague, unpractical, ill-defined. They went there, as Dostoevsky remarked to a friend in a phrase which defies idiomatic translation, 'to satisfy their little passion for playing the liberal'. 'I never found in the society of Petrashevsky,' wrote Dostoevsky afterwards in his deposition, 'any unity, any policy, any common objective.'

Valerian Maikov was an early intimate of Petrashevsky and a contributor to the dictionary. It was probably through him that Apollon Maikov and Dostoevsky made their first appearance in the circle in the winter of 1846–7. Later Dostoevsky brought in his brother Michael, and the following winter the circle was in the heyday of its prosperity with a regular membership of twenty or thirty.

The young Russian intellectuals of 1845 had abandoned German philosophy and German poetry, which had been the rage ten years before, and took their fashions in literature and in politics from

France. The French writers of the Utopian school are now scarcely remembered; but in their day their influence was world-wide. The fundamental tenet of their creed came from Rousseau: 'Everything comes beautiful from the hand of the Creator and is perverted only by the hand of man.' The followers of Saint-Simon proclaimed the 'brotherhood of man' and tried to found a new social religion deriving directly from primitive Christianity. Lamennais, whose *Paroles d'un Croyant* was probably the most popular book published in Paris during the 'thirties, endeavoured to accommodate the social movement within the fold of the church; and, by identifying Christianity with the cause of the oppressed peoples against their rulers, became the father of that not very hardy modern growth, Christian Socialism. Cabet (whose book *Le Vrai Christianisme suivant Jésus-Christ* was found in Dostoevsky's possession at the time of his arrest) was definitely hostile to official Christianity; salvation was to be found not within the gates of the church, but only in an ideal commonwealth based on communist principles which he sketched in his once famous utopian novel *Voyage en Icarie*. George Sand evoked in her early novels that uneasy consciousness of social inequalities which is the germ of all revolutions; and, strange as it may appear, her influence in politics was, at any rate in Russia, greater than her influence in literature. Finally, and most important of all, came Fourier, that half-mad visionary who, on the basis of an obscure analysis of human psychology, declared the ideal unit of society to be a 'phalanx' of 1,600 persons inhabiting an institution called a 'phalanstery', which was to combine the advantages of a military barracks and a garden city. It was one of the most serious indictments against Petrashevsky's circle that they had organized a banquet on Fourier's birthday and pronounced speeches in honour of the French sage.

It is perhaps easier for us than it was for the Russian police to understand the state of mind of these young men, in whom youthful enthusiasm, youthful naïveté and youthful affectation were about equally blended. They were no doubt desperately in earnest in their studies of utopias made in France; they regarded the official religion with aversion and had a touching faith in the political implications of the Christian ethic; they believed fervently in 'mankind', and there was a tendency to identify 'mankind' with what the French called *le tiers état*, the unprivileged masses. But they were not political revolutionaries; their primary and fundamental impulse was merely the desire to escape from the intellectual and moral oppression of life in Petersburg under Nicholas I into an ideal world of their own invention. Still less were they practical reformers;

'these young men', wrote a casual visitor to the circle, 'are learned, it is true, but they know nothing of the real life of the poor'. In many respects, they were typical of Russian ineptitude for political life; and they were certainly not of the stuff of which tyrant-killers are made.

But while they talked in Petersburg, events occurred elsewhere which transformed this company of dreamers, in the heated imagination of the Russian police, into a nest of potential conspirators. In February 1848 a revolution in France overthrew the monarchy of Louis-Philippe and spread rapidly to Central Europe. Nicholas I, seeing thrones totter, looked anxiously around for danger to his own; and, finding nothing more substantial to justify his fears, ordered the Petrashevtsi, permeated as they were with the ideas of these noxious French communists, to be put under 'secret supervision'.

At first there was indeed nothing to discover; but the young dreamers, like Nicholas himself, had had their eyes turned westwards; and the intoxicating example of French and German revolutionaries roused the hotheads, Dostoevsky among them, to a desire for something more active than tea, tobacco and endless discussion. The glamour had gone from the crowded, inconclusive meetings in Petrashevsky's flat; the circle no longer seemed the *ne plus ultra* of daring and enlightenment. The moment had come for enthusiasm to find vent in action; but what action nobody quite knew. About the beginning of 1849, certain members of the group, still unaware of the close watch now kept on their proceedings, resolved to form a more select society. It was to meet on Saturdays in the apartment of Durov, a man of thirty who had recently resigned from a post in the Ministry of Marine; among its members were the two Dostoevskys and Speshnev, a young aristocrat just returned from five years' residence abroad, where he had imbibed not only revolutionary ideas, but more practical energy than distinguished the average member of Petrashevsky's circle.

The first few meetings were devoted to discussions which differed little from those of Petrashevsky's group, and even to literary and musical recreations; but soon Speshnev, one Lvov, and a hotheaded young man named Philippov propounded the idea of setting up a printing-press for the purpose of secretly circulating articles written by members of the circle. The more timid, who had no intention of proceeding from conspirative talk to conspirative action, vetoed the proposal. But the leaders were not deterred and sections of the press were secretly ordered by Philippov, in order to avoid suspicion, from different parts of the city.

So much was subsequently discovered by the Commission of Enquiry. A recently published private letter of Apollon Maikov written many years later makes it clear—for there is no reason to doubt the evidence—that Dostoevsky himself was an active participant in the affair of the printing-press; he was commissioned by Speshnev and Philippov to approach his friend Maikov with a request for assistance which was refused. The commission never discovered either the fact of Dostoevsky's participation or the actual existence of the press, which by a stroke of fortune was removed undetected from the apartment of one of the confederates at the time of their arrest. Had the true facts come to light it is not improbable that Dostoevsky's life would have ended on the public scaffold in 1849.

But if the authorities had little knowledge of what went on in Durov's group, it was otherwise with the larger circle of Petrashevsky. Following their usual tactics, the police had succeeded in introducing into the entourage of Petrashevsky a secret agent, Antonelli by name; the credentials which secured him admission to the group seem to have been a slight personal acquaintance with Petrashevsky and the possession of a red waistcoat; and from March 11th to April 22nd detailed reports of the weekly meetings were furnished by this man to his employers. This was sufficient; on the night of April 22nd-23rd, the leading members, to the number of thirty-four, were arrested, the two Dostoevsky brothers among them. By a strange error Andrei Dostoevsky, who had never had any connection with Petrashevsky, was arrested instead of Michael; and it took nearly a fortnight to rectify this mistake.

Exactly eight months were spent by Dostoevsky in the Peter-and-Paul fortress in conditions approaching to solitary confinement, and for the first part of the time without books or writing-materials. The first four months were occupied by the Commission of Enquiry, which released some of the arrested (including Michael Dostoevsky), arrested other suspects, and finally handed over twenty-three persons to the military court for trial. During this period, Dostoevsky made a written deposition, and was cross-examined by the commission five or six times. It can scarcely be doubted that this ordeal inspired some of the most famous pages in *Crime and Punishment*, the long duel between Raskolnikov and the detective Zosimov, in which the victim is tortured by uncertainty as to the extent of his questioner's knowledge, how much it will pay him to confess, and how much he can hope to conceal. The sole definite charge against Dostoevsky was that he had, at the meeting of the circle on April 15th, read the famous letter, prohibited of course in Russia, in which

Belinsky had lashed Gogol for his conversion to religious and political orthodoxy. The defence put forward by Dostoevsky in his deposition, that he had read the whole correspondence between Gogol and Belinsky as a 'literary curiosity' without indicating on which side his sympathies lay, is singularly unimpressive. But it is unfair to criticize too severely the deposition extorted by months of imprisonment and physical suffering. Its false humility and its insincere efforts to belittle his relations with Petrashevsky make pitiful reading; and the best commentary is perhaps to set beside it a rather too eloquent passage written by Dostoevsky twenty-four years later:

We Petrashevtsi stood upon the scaffold and heard our sentence without the faintest repentance. I cannot, of course, speak for all; but I think that I shall not be mistaken if I say that the vast majority, if not every one, of us would have thought it dishonour to renounce our convictions.

It was easy in 1873 to thunder this retrospective defiance from the pages of *The Journal of an Author*; but in 1849, when he penned the deposition, Dostoevsky knew that he was struggling for his liberty if not for his life.

The military court sat from September 30th to November 16th and recommended the death-sentence for twenty-one out of the twenty-three accused. By the decision of the Auditor-General, which received the Tsar's confirmation on December 19th, the death-sentence was remitted. Petrashevsky was condemned to penal servitude in the mines for life; Speshnev to the same for twelve years, altered in the Tsar's hand to 'ten years'; and Dostoevsky and Durov to penal servitude for eight years, altered in the Tsar's hand to 'four years and then to serve as a common soldier'. Similar sentences were passed on the rest. Speshnev, Durov and Dostoevsky were lucky in the imperial caprice; in several cases the Tsar increased instead of diminishing the penalty.

It is hard to write with patience of proceedings which treated the half-baked lucubrations of a handful of rather simple-minded young enthusiasts as a first-class conspiracy against the government; it is harder still to record the sequel. The recommendation of the death-penalty by the military court had been overruled; but it was decided to make a show of carrying it into effect. It is perhaps fair to attribute this decision to a brutal but honest desire to give these young men a terrifying lesson rather than to a mere whim of imperial vanity, anxious to present a spectacle of imperial clemency. The condemned, uninformed of the reprieve, were conducted in vans to the usual place of public execution; the death-sentence was read;

the priest held up a cross and invited confession; the victims were arranged in order; and the first three were actually tied to the posts and confronted with the firing-party. This was the cue for the well-timed entrance of a messenger bearing the imperial reprieve; the real sentences were now for the first time read, and the prisoners taken back to their cells.

The scene left an ineffaceable impression on Dostoevsky; and had there not been abundant evidence of his abnormally nervous temperament before this time, modern opinion would certainly have been inclined to attribute it to this soul-shattering experience. Again and again he returns to it in his writings:

To execute a man for murder [says Myshkin, his favourite hero] is an incomparably greater punishment than the crime itself. To be executed is incomparably more terrible than to be murdered by a highwayman. The man who is killed by highwaymen, whose throat is cut by night in a forest, for instance, is sure still to hope up to the very last moment that he will escape. . . . But in executions this last hope, which makes death ten times easier, is taken away for a certainty; there is a definite sentence, and in the certainty that you will not escape it resides the whole horrible torture; and than this torture there is none greater on earth. . . . Who can say that human nature is able to endure this without going mad? To what end this inconceivable, unnecessary, useless humiliation? Perhaps there is some man to whom the sentence has been read, whom they have allowed to undergo the torture and then have said: Go, you are reprieved. Such a man perhaps could tell. Of this torture and of this horror Christ has spoken. No, it is not lawful to treat any man thus.

There was no delay in carrying the real sentence into effect. Two days after the pretended execution—it was Christmas Eve—Michael Dostoevsky was admitted to the prison to take farewell of his brother in the presence of warders. About midnight fetters were riveted on the prisoners. The party to be despatched that night consisted of Dostoevsky, Durov and a Pole named Jastrzembski, whose principal offence was that he had 'nodded approval' while Dostoevsky was reading Belinsky's letter. They were placed, each with a guard, on three open sleighs and driven out of Petersburg, past the lighted windows of friends and relatives in the midst of their Christmas celebrations. It was over four years before Dostoevsky walked without fetters, and ten before he again saw the streets of the capital.

They drove all night, and in the morning reached Schlüsselburg on the shores of Lake Ladoga. After eight months of virtual solitary confinement, motion through space and the possibility of conversation at the stopping-places were at first new and delightful sensations. The novelty of the journey and the exhilaration of the bitter night air helped to obliterate the painful impressions of the departure. At Schlüsselburg, the prisoners were transferred to closed sleighs. For seventeen days they travelled almost continuously. At one point the thermometer fell to forty degrees below zero. In crossing the Urals they were stopped for some hours by a snow-drift. The moment invited sentimental reflections and, judged by other than Anglo-Saxon standards, not unmanly tears: behind them Europe and the past; in front, Asia and the unknown future. Dostoevsky, improvident as ever, had failed to take sufficiently warm clothing and was 'frozen to the heart'; his companions both suffered from frost-bite.

At Tobolsk there was a halt of six days. Here the prisoners were visited by the wives of some of the survivors of the Decembrist conspiracy of 1825, who had followed their husbands to Siberia and remained there for twenty-five years. From them Dostoevsky received gifts of money, food and clothing, and a copy of the Bible, the only book which prisoners were officially allowed to possess.

At Tobolsk, Jastrzembski was left behind; and three days' further travelling brought Dostoevsky and Durov to the convict-prison of Omsk.

CHAPTER V

The House of the Dead

THE accounts given by Dostoevsky of the four years spent by him in the prison fall into three categories—the letters which he wrote from Siberia during the two or three years after his release; *Memoirs from the House of the Dead* published, under the transparent guise of a novel, after his return to Petersburg at the beginning of the following decade; and numerous references, direct and indirect, in his subsequent writings. Each of the three categories reveals markedly different characteristics. In the first, memories of suffering and insult are still green and bitter; the letters, sent for the most part by private messengers and not exposed to the risks of censorship, provide a healthy corrective to the rosier hues of the later accounts. In *Memoirs from the House of the Dead*, though they conceal nothing of the horrors and the hardships of a convict's life, the mellowing influence of time has combined with fear of the censor to produce an attitude of unresentful detachment. In later references, beginning with the epilogue to *Crime and Punishment* and ending with *The Journal of an Author* and *The Brothers Karamazov*, Dostoevsky carries to its conclusion the moralising process of which faint traces may be found here and there in the *Memoirs*, and treats his prison years, not without an occasional hint of smugness, as a vital and salutary stage in the salvation of his soul. These later writings are, from the strictly biographical point of view, valueless. But the business of posterity is, after all, not so much with what Dostoevsky underwent during these years of imprisonment as with the view of his sufferings which ultimately expressed itself in his art; and from this standpoint the latest verdict is the most important of all.

It is in the letters to his brother Michael written in the first weeks of his freedom that we must seek the most vivid and objective picture of the conditions in which he passed those four years:

Imagine to yourself an old, tumble-down wooden building which it has long ago been decided to scrap, and which is no longer fit for use. In summer intolerably stuffy, in winter unbearably cold. All the floors rotten. An inch of filth on the floor on which you slip and fall. The little windows frosted up so that the whole day long it is impossible to read. On the panes ice an inch thick. Drips from the ceiling—draughts everywhere.

We packed like herrings in a barrel. The stove is fed with six logs; no heat (the ice scarcely melts in the room) and awful fumes—and so it goes on all the winter. Here in the barrack the convicts wash their clothes, and the whole of the little barrack is splashed with water. No room to turn round. From dusk to dawn it is impossible to go out to satisfy one's needs, the barracks being locked; a large tub is placed in the corridor and the stench is insufferable. All the convicts stink like swine and say that it is impossible not to behave like swine 'since we are living beings'.

And in another letter to Michael he speaks of what was probably even worse than all the physical hardships of the prison:

For five years I have lived under the control of warders in a crowd of human beings, and have never been alone for a single hour. To be alone is a necessity of normal existence, like drinking and eating; otherwise, in this forced communal life you become a hater of mankind. The society of people acts like a poison or an infection, and from this insufferable torment I have suffered more than from anything these four years. There have even been moments when I hated everyone who crossed my path, blameless or guilty, and looked on them as thieves who were stealing away my life with impunity.

In *Memoirs from the House of the Dead* this bitter mood has already been softened or stifled, and the feeling has become altogether impersonal. The book provides a complete record of the life of a Russian convict in a Siberian prison in the middle of the nineteenth century. If you would know the conditions in which these men were confined, and the conditions in which they were driven out to work; their occupations, their quarrels and their rare amusements; the weight and the fashion of the fetters which, waking or sleeping, in health or in sickness, never left them; the manner in which they performed (not more, of course, than two or three times in a year) the complicated operation of dressing and undressing themselves under the fetters; the capricious brutality and no less capricious indulgence of officials and guards; the moral torments of those about to undergo the brutal flogging which formed the only instrument of discipline in the prison, and the physical sufferings of those who had just undergone it—all these things may be found in the unique pages of the *Memoirs*. There are here and there acute psychological observations, but less than one would expect from the future author of *Crime and Punishment*; the strength of the book lies in straightforward narrative and description; and in this respect it may be called the least Dostoevskian of all Dostoevsky's work. One scene, the description of the convicts in the bath-house, was called by Turgenev 'Dantesque'; and the appositeness of the epithet, as much as the vigour of the original, has made this the most famous passage in the book:

When we opened the door into the bathroom itself, I thought we were entering hell. Imagine a room twelve paces long and the same in breadth, in which perhaps as many as a hundred, and certainly as many as eighty, were packed at once, for the whole party were divided only into two relays, and we were close on 200; steam blinding one's eyes; filth and grime; such a crowd that there was not room to put one's foot down. I was frightened and tried to step back, but Petrov at once encouraged me. With extreme difficulty we somehow forced our way to the benches round the wall, stepping over the heads of those who were sitting on the floor, asking them to duck to let us get by. But every place on the benches was taken. Petrov informed me that one had to buy a place and at once entered into negotiations with a convict sitting near the window. For a kopek the latter gave up his place, receiving the money at once from Petrov who had the coin ready in his fist, having providently brought it with him into the bathroom. The convict I had ousted at once ducked under the bench just under my place, where it was dark and filthy, and the dirty slime lay two inches thick. But even the space under the benches was all filled; there, too, the place was alive with human beings. There was not a spot on the floor as big as the palm of your hand where there was not a convict squatting splashing from his bucket. Others stood up among them and holding their buckets in their hands washed themselves standing; the dirty water trickled off them on to the shaven heads of the convicts sitting below them. On the top shelf and on all the steps leading up to it, men were crouched, huddled together washing themselves. But they did not wash themselves much. Men of the peasant class don't wash much with soap and water; they only steam themselves terribly and then douche themselves with cold water—that is their whole idea of a bath. Fifty birches were rising and falling rhythmically on the shelves; they all thrashed themselves into a state of stupefaction. More steam was raised every moment. It was not heat; it was hell. All were shouting and vociferating to the accompaniment of a hundred chains clanking on the floor. . . .[1]

The scene is a lurid but not unfair picture of the system of mass confinement to which the Russian convict was condemned; and it is safe to say that the system with all its abominations was less intolerable, not merely to the average prisoner, but to Dostoevsky himself, than would have been any scientific European prison system, based on order, cleanliness and twenty hours of solitary confinement in every twenty-four. For the Russian system, which brought with it filth and fleas, stench and disorder, brandings, floggings and fetters, brought with it also that intangible sense of a common life, of freedom, within the bars of the cage, to love and to hate, to brawl

[1]Quoted from Mrs Garnett's translation (Heinemann).

and to barter. 'A convict has no property', ran the regulation; but many of them succeeded in smuggling in small amounts of money—Dostoevsky brought 25 roubles pasted in the lining of the Bible—and, as between the prisoners themselves, every object and every service had its price. The inexorable laws of economics did not cease to operate even within the prison; money was so scarce that a rouble was wealth, and practically any article to be found within the walls was purchasable for a few kopeks. Vodka was smuggled in when funds allowed under the eyes of more or less complacent guards; and Christmas Day ended in an orgy of song and drunkenness. Other still more surprising indulgences were not unknown; women sometimes found their way into the prison compound, or could be met—once more if the guards were kind—when the prisoners were marched out to work. The critic of the *Athenaeum*, reviewing the first English translation of *Memoirs from the House of the Dead*, confessed that 'on some occasions the convicts were allowed liberties the idea of which would horrify an English warder'.

It was not, however, the shocking barbarities, or the no less shocking relaxations, of prison discipline at Omsk which rendered *Memoirs from the House of the Dead* distasteful to its first English readers. The defect which mitigated against its success was of a different kind and may be suggested by a somewhat incongruous comparison. The years of Dostoevsky's life at Omsk witnessed the publication of a book which, also under the guise of fiction, had depicted another and more terrible system of horrors. Written in terms of scorching protest, *Uncle Tom's Cabin* swept the world and made its contribution (which has been exaggerated, but was still very real) to the suppression of the abuse to which it related. *Memoirs from the House of the Dead* not merely did not contribute a jot to the amelioration of the conditions in which convicts lived in Siberia, but palpably did not even aim at such a result. In practical reform Dostoevsky neither displays nor feels any perceptible interest.

How much youth is buried within these walls in idleness, what great strength has perished here for naught! For it must be said frankly: these are remarkable men. These are perhaps the most gifted, the strongest of all our people. But this mighty strength has perished for naught, perished unnaturally, illegally, irreparably. And who is to blame?

Yes, who is to blame?

The passage quoted is the nearest approach to a note of indignation which we can find in the *Memoirs*, and it must have seemed pale and inadequate indeed to a generation which was used to reforms propagated by means of fiction.

D

The shrill rhetoric of Mrs Stowe is now apt to set our teeth on edge, and modern criticism would probably accord to her book a place in history rather than in literature. But in other periods the *saeva indignatio* of the injured and humiliated has found expression in other keys; and even a writer so unused to moralizing in any ordinary sense of the word as Oscar Wilde makes his *De Profundis* a cry of bitter protest. The detached resignation and humility of *Memoirs from the House of the Dead* cannot be paralleled in English, and not easily in any other, literature. The threat of the censorship was, of course, constantly in Dostoevsky's mind as he wrote; but it would be a mistake to attribute the tone of the book primarily to any external consideration. It is characteristic of the man. The renunciation of moral judgment is a faculty which Dostoevsky not infrequently practised in his own life, and it is one which the indulgent reader may sometimes be required to exercise in his favour. The injunction not to judge has good authority; and it is followed to artistic perfection in the *Memoirs*. But there is something to us almost inhuman in this matter-of-fact, unemotional narrative of more than human suffering.

There is only one independent source of any importance for these four years of Dostoevsky's life, the reminiscences of Tokarzewski, a Polish fellow-prisoner who is referred to by Dostoevsky under the initial T. The reminiscences, which display bitter hatred of Dostoevsky, were written in the 'eighties and not published until 1907. Their value as unique first-hand evidence is impaired by their tendencious character; for the bitterness which they betray is all too clearly a Polish answer to the Russian novelist's subsequent caricatures of Polish adventurers and persistent hostility to the Polish cause. They serve, however, to throw some light on the obscure question of Dostoevsky's relations with his fellow-convicts.

It is a charge levelled more than once by Dostoevsky at the Polish prisoners that they looked down with hatred and contempt on the other convicts, and never ceased to boast that they were political offenders. Curiously enough, Tokarzewski makes precisely the same accusation against Dostoevsky, who when he first arrived in the prison, eternally repeated parrot-wise the one phrase: 'I am a noble'. There is no inherent difficulty in believing both these mutual accusations to have been substantially true. In *Memoirs from the House of the Dead*, or more bitterly and frankly in his letters to Michael, Dostoevsky speaks of the enmity of the ordinary convict towards the 'noble', and clearly attributes his unpopularity to this cause:

Their hatred of 'nobles' [he wrote to Michael] passes all bounds; they greeted us nobles with every mark of hostility and with malicious joy at our sufferings. They would have eaten us alive if they had got the chance.

On the other hand, another witness who has written, at second-hand it is true, on Dostoevsky's sojourn at Omsk, declares that his comrade Durov, who was also of noble rank, was universally beloved. While Durov greeted all with a smile and friendly words, Dostoevsky thrust his cap over his eyes 'looking like a wolf caught in a trap', never spoke unless he was obliged, appeared to have a morbid fear of all communion with his fellow-men, and was at one time not even on speaking terms with Durov. It is difficult to reject this testimony, at any rate for the earlier months of Dostoevsky's prison-life. In the morose convict we recognize the familiar traits of the morose solitude-seeking student at the Engineering Academy and the morbid hypochondriacal young writer who made himself intolerable to his best friends.

By one of those contradictions peculiarly frequent in the life of this least rational of human beings, it was here in prison, among men 'coarse, enraged and embittered', who 'stank like swine', and whose constant company was the worst of all torments, that this reserved and hypersensitive nature received the first seeds of that idealization of 'the people' which formed so important a part of his later political and religious creed. 'The more I hated individuals', says a character in *The Brothers Karamazov*, 'the more I loved humanity'; and it would seem that Dostoevsky's development followed the same course. The ground was not unprepared. Self-righteous condemnation of other men's sins found no place in Dostoevsky's nature. In his youth he had borrowed from Schiller that familiar lay-figure of the Romantics—the criminal with the heart of gold; he had even written a story called *The Honest Thief*. In prison, he lived for the first time with thieves and murderers and perceived, or thought he perceived, that there was more foundation in real life for this romantic idea than he had ever suspected. He began to conceive for these heroes—for such they were, if only heroes of crime—a romantic admiration which almost suggests Lermontov's admiration for the brigands of the Caucasus. In the relations, at first mistrustful and half furtive, which he began to form with the other inmates of the prison, he met the same variety of qualities, the same baffling contradictions as in the world outside, the same vicious practice and the same potentialities of virtue.

Even in prison among robbers [he wrote to Michael] I have in four years ended by discovering human beings. Will you believe it? There are here profound, strong, beautiful natures; and how joyous it is to find gold beneath that coarse crust! Not one, not two, but many. Some you cannot help respecting, others are downright beautiful.

He echoes the thought in *Memoirs from the House of the Dead*:

Amid the gloomy and hostile faces of the other convicts, I could not fail to notice some kind and cheerful faces. 'There are bad people everywhere, and among the bad there are good ones,' I hastened to reflect by way of consolation. 'Who knows? These people perhaps are not after all so much worse than those, the others, who have remained outside the prison walls?' So I thought, and shook my head at my own idea. But God! if only I had known how absolutely true the idea was!

The process of idealization may be traced even further in another passage of the *Memoirs*:

There is not much that our wise men have to teach the people. On the contrary, I would even say positively that they themselves have much to learn from the people.

In later life, Dostoevsky came to hold a sort of mystical faith in 'the people' and thanked his prison experience for having 'brought him back to the people'. The full development of this faith took place after his liberation (to idealize from a distance is always easier) and, in the main, after the writing of the *Memoirs*. But its beginning must be connected, biographically, with the process of breaking down the barriers of hatred and reserve with which he had surrounded himself in the first months of his captivity, and of establishing points of contact with the convict whom he had at the outset merely detested and despised.

It might be too bold a paradox to maintain that, but for Siberia, Dostoevsky would never have developed his idealization of the Russian people; but the form of the cult bears the clear impress of these prison years. As we have seen, Dostoevsky had not, either in childhood or in later life, any close acquaintance with the Russian countryside; and when in his subsequent works he writes of 'the people', he is in fact thinking of the people as he learned to know them in the prison at Omsk.

Judge the Russian people [he wrote more than twenty years after] not by the degrading sins which it so often commits, but by the great and holy things to which, in the midst of its degradation, it constantly aspires. ... Judge the people not by what it is, but by what it would like to become.

The Russian peasant, as he was known to Turgenev or Tolstoy or

Leskov, remained a sealed book to Dostoevsky; look at the peasants as they appear in his pages, and you will find the marks of the fetters and the shreds of the grey-and-black uniform of the convict.

Dostoevsky never drew up a balance-sheet of the good and evil which came to him from his prison experience, and it is difficult for us to do so now. Even on the physical side the question is full of obscurities. Dostoevsky speaks in the *Memoirs* of increased health and strength resulting from hard physical labour, and in a letter to Michael written shortly after his release he writes:

Pray don't imagine that I am the same melancholy and suspicious fellow I was in Petersburg those last years; all that has completely vanished as if by magic.

And many years later he wrote to Yanovsky:

You loved me and looked after me when I was sick of a mental malady (I recognise that now) before I went to Siberia, where I was cured.

But if the Siberian prison cured these nervous disorders of Petersburg days, it brought in their place the terrible scourge of epilepsy which, from this time onward, pursued Dostoevsky throughout the remainder of his life with varying frequency and intensity. Irresponsible mystics and no less irresponsible psychoanalysts have in recent years amused themselves with ingenious speculations regarding the origins and symptoms of Dostoevsky's malady, and have woven around it fantastic theories bearing little relation to the known facts. It is, as we have seen, impossible to establish any certain connection between the nervous disorders of his early manhood and the specifically epileptic symptoms which declared themselves for the first time in Siberia. The first seizures occurred in the prison. In the absence of medical attention, they were not definitely diagnosed until some time after his release; and there was a short period in which Dostoevsky encouraged himself to believe that his fits were 'like epilepsy, but not really epilepsy'. Nor do we find, at this stage of his career, any attempt to idealize his malady or to attribute to it any mystical significance; it is only about 1865 that we begin to hear of moments of illumination and a sense of spiritual harmony preceding the seizures. The significance of Dostoevsky's epilepsy as we first meet it in Siberia is purely material; and he was fully entitled to assert, as he did in 1859 in his petition to the Tsar, that it was the product of his prison experience.

But when, leaving the relatively firm ground of physical symptoms, we seek to analyse the spiritual legacy of the House of the Dead, we are compelled to abandon ourselves to unsubstantial speculation. Before he reached the end of his life, Dostoevsky had sought and obtained peace of mind in a piece of heroic sophistry which found expression in the climax of his last great novel. Like Dmitri Karamazov, he had been the victim of 'a judicial error'; but like Dmitri, though innocent of the offence for which he was condemned, he had suffered justly for his own sins and those of his fellow-men, and through this suffering had 'risen from the dead'. It was, however, only by a gradual evolution that Dostoevsky reached the quietist position from which he was able to accept and glorify his punishment; and in the ten years of ferment which followed his release from prison very different thoughts must have assailed him as he surveyed his broken life. A man who has undergone such a punishment for such an offence is unlikely to retain any belief in a relation between crime and sin or between human and divine law. In Dostoevsky's case the rebellion went deeper. He met in Siberia men who had been sentenced for offences condemned not merely, like his, by the state, but by the generally accepted sanctions of moral law, for crimes of murder, lust or theft; and these men not only felt no conventional repentance or remorse for their deeds, but displayed, in the ordinary commerce of life, as many qualities of courage, generosity and loving-kindness as their fellows, and enjoyed as large a share of the general esteem. The prison overthrew every standard of morality of which Dostoevsky had ever heard. The conventional categories of virtue and vice no longer seemed to be placed at opposite poles of the moral horizon; indeed it was clear that they were not even mutually exclusive. It was in the House of the Dead that Dostoevsky first learned to perceive the inadequacy not merely of human law, but of the ordinarily accepted code of moral values, and to ponder on the quest for a remoter truth beyond the frontiers of good and evil as ordinarily defined. It was there that he caught his first dim and uncertain glimpses of the ethical problem which was to form the burden of *Crime and Punishment*.

There were also subtler subconscious influences. 'He who strives with monsters,' writes Nietzsche in *Jenseits von Gut und Böse*, 'must beware lest he himself become a monster; and when you look too long into an abyss, the abyss begins to look into your soul.' In the prison at Omsk, Dostoevsky lived for four years with outcasts exempted from the ordinary conventions and sanctions of human society, beings who had returned to an almost subhuman plane of existence; he had gazed into the abyss where the crude element of disembodied human passion boiled and seethed, and the abyss entered into his soul. He was perhaps himself, when he entered the

THE HOUSE OF THE DEAD

prison, an abnormal man; he learned there to adjust himself to an abnormal world; and when he emerged his distorted vision was incapable of adjustment to any other focus. Normal men are as rare in Dostoevsky's novels as they must have been in the prison compound. His world was no longer peopled with men of normal stature; it was a world of criminals and saints, of monsters of vice or of virtue. Dostoevsky was in his thirty-third year when the fetters were struck off his feet in the prison blacksmith's shop and he walked once more in the world of free men; but it was a world transfigured for him for ever by the experience through which he had passed. The years of growth were over; but there were long years of fever and ferment ahead before his genius found artistic expression for the problems of good and evil which had gnawed his soul in the dark shades of the prison-house.

BOOK TWO
YEARS OF FERMENT
(1854–1865)

CHAPTER VI

Exile and First Marriage

WHEN Dostoevsky emerged from prison on February 15, 1854, to serve his further term of punishment as a common soldier, he found himself allocated to the 7th Siberian Infantry Battalion and despatched to Semipalatinsk, where he was to spend the next five and a quarter years of his life. It was a small town of 5,000 inhabitants on the edge of the Kirghiz steppe, not far from the Mongolian frontier. Socially, the transfer to Semipalatinsk had little to offer; for the garrison and officials of the administration, who composed the local society, were not likely to have any dealings with a political prisoner condemned to serve in the ranks. Intellectually, it was a change from darkness to faint twilight; save for the possibility of obtaining them with many delays from friends in Petersburg, books and newspapers were as rare in Semipalatinsk as they had been in the prison. The sense of regained liberty, and the renewed possibility of communication with family and friends, can alone have rendered tolerable to Dostoevsky the first months of his military service. At Semipalatinsk he could at any rate maintain intermittent correspondence with Petersburg by a post which took from three to four weeks each way; but the post was of course subject to a rigorous and suspicious censorship, and anything intimate must wait for the rare chance of a private messenger. His letters from Semipalatinsk to Michael and other members of his family are voluminous, and uniformly dull.

Our most intimate knowledge of Dostoevsky's life at this period is derived from the memoirs and correspondence of a Baron Wrangel, who came to Semipalatinsk as District Prosecutor in November 1854. It was the first stage of a long official career which flowed on uneventfully till 1906, when he retired from his last post as Russian Minister at Dresden. In 1854 he was a young man of average intelligence and more than average good nature, possessed of some means and of sufficient originality to prefer the society of an obscure and discredited man of letters to that of the local military and official world. The two became intimate, and Dostoevsky began to visit his new friend several times a day.

Materially, the gain was all on the side of Dostoevsky, who availed himself not only of the Baron's unending hospitality but also of his generous purse. Wrangel introduced him personally to the Governor, and may be presumed to have contributed by his influence to the mitigation of the material hardships of his position. But what Dostoevsky's expansive nature most needed, and found in this new friend, was a confidant to whom, for the first time in five years, he could pour out his sorrows, his ambitions and his hopes. His principal preoccupation at the moment was a love-affair. Before Wrangel's arrival he had made the acquaintance of a family named Isaev, consisting of husband, wife and a son of seven or eight. The man had held a small post in the customs department ot Semipalatinsk; but by the time of Dostoesvky's arrival his sole occupation appears to have been the consumption of alcohol, which hastened, and rendered tolerable, the slow progress of a painful kidney disease. It is clear that the Isaevs enjoyed no great repute in Semipalatinsk, and Wrangel pointedly declined Dostoevsky's repeated invitations to visit them. But Maria Dmitrievna Isaeva was, to quote the Baron's memoirs, 'a rather pretty blonde of middle height, very thin, passionate and *exaltée*'; and Dostoevsky was completely infatuated. He began to spend 'whole days' at the house; and it is reasonable to conclude, though explicit evidence not unnaturally fails us, that Maria Dmitrievna became his mistress.

It was a commonplace affair. To the lady it was an agreeable, and perhaps not unprecedented, diversion. To Dostoevsky, released from four years' isolation among convicts, it was a *grande passion*. The two points of view coincided well enough until the blow of separation fell. In the spring of 1855 Isaev found employment at Kuznetsk, another frontier post some 600 kilometres distant. Dostoevsky stormed and wept. It was not clear what he expected his mistress to do; but emotion is more than action, and he had at least expected emotions comparable with his own. Maria was philosophically resigned. Kuznetsk was a dismal spot; but it would at any rate be a change, and could scarcely fail to provide attractions equal to those of a devoted but sickly political exile whose rank and pay were those of a common soldier.

The kindhearted Baron lavished his best champagne on the husband in order that the lovers' parting might be undisturbed and unembarrassed. The journey was made in a country cart, the only form of conveyance the Isaevs could afford, and was begun at night. Dostoevsky and the Baron drove with them for a few miles. The Baron took Isaev, now sleeping heavily, into his own carriage, and Dostoevsky joined the lady in the cart. At length they alighted, and the parting took place under a fir-tree, on which Dostoevsky made a commemorative notch. It was a moonlight May night; and as the cart bore away his mistress over the unknown steppe, he stood 'stiff and silent, the tears streaming down his cheeks'. 'A memorable day!' comments the Baron drily, writing fifty years after.

The parted lovers corresponded. Maria's first letters spoke of privation, sickness and loneliness, and wrung her lover's tender heart. Subsequent letters referred to the devotion of a high-minded and sympathetic young school-teacher, who had befriended her husband; and these wrung Dostoevsky's heart still more. Presently the untiring Wrangel arranged a secret meeting between the lovers at a point half-way between Semipalatinsk and Kuznetsk. The journey of more than 200 miles was undertaken; but at the last moment the lady failed to appear, and sent a letter excusing herself on the grounds of her husband's health. Dostoevsky was plunged in despair.

The excuse sounded hollow; but Isaev was really ill, and by the beginning of August had drunk himself to death. The position of the widow with her boy was unenviable. Her husband had probably left debts; he had certainly left her nothing else. Her father was a teacher in Astrakhan and there were younger sisters to provide for. Despite Dostoevsky's subsequent reiterations that she was 'of good family', it is clear that the family was in no position to support her financially; and there was no question of a return to Astrakhan. The generosity of Wrangel, exercised at Dostoevsky's pressing request, helped to relieve her immediate needs; and anything that Dostoevsky had, or could borrow from his friends, reached the same destination. But much in the affair remains obscure. Of the mass of letters, which we know to have passed between Dostoevsky and Maria Dmitrievna in 1855 and 1856, one alone survives, and that, being a letter from Dostoevsky evidently intended for the eyes of Isaev as well as of his wife, tells us little enough. The passages in Dostoevsky's letters to Wrangel referring to her have been thickly scored through in ink (perhaps by the hand of his second wife), and have not all been completely deciphered; from one crucial letter two pages have been removed. The biography of Dostoevsky by his daughter contains many details concerning her; but unconfirmed statements from this unreliable and violently hostile source cannot be accepted. The relations between Dostoevsky and Maria Dmitrievna, both before and after their marriage, are surrounded by a haze of uncertainty which will probably never be dispelled.

In January 1856, Wrangel left Semipalatinsk for other employment, but continued to advise and assist his friend by correspondence. The year was a troubled one for Dostoevsky. His correspondence with Maria Dmitrievna passed through the common vicissitudes of jealousy and uncertainty. In the spring she wrote of a proposal of marriage which she had received, and asked his advice. Dostoevsky was distracted. He begged both his brother and Wrangel to write to Maria Dmitrievna assuring her of the early prospect of an imperial pardon and of his ability to support her once he could return to Petersburg. He obtained leave to go to Barnaul, the next town, and pushed on secretly to Kuznetsk ('I would risk punishment, if only to see her') he stayed two days and returned without mishap. 'In these two days,' he wrote to Wrangel after the return, 'she remembered the past and her heart turned again to me.' There was, however, a serious rival, the high-minded and sympathetic teacher previously mentioned. His name was Vergunov, and he was a native of Tomsk. He was on the spot; he was only twenty-four; and his attraction for the passionate and romantic widow was obvious. But marriage was a matter of interest; and the older man, who would one day return to Petersburg and perhaps to fame, offered more solid prospects for the future. Maria Dmitrievna evidently hesitated. Dostoevsky's unexpected promotion to commissioned rank in October—a mark of returning favour—must have sensibly improved his chances. He redoubled his efforts on her behalf; he begged his friends to use their influence to hasten the payment of a small sum due to Maria from the Exchequer on her husband's death, and to obtain a free place for her boy, Paul, in the Siberian Cadet Corps at Omsk, an educational establishment for future officers. In the spirit of self-effacing generosity which was practised by his heroes in *White Nights* and *The Insulted and Injured*, he declared Vergunov to be 'dearer to him than a brother', and made efforts to secure his advancement. His infatuation rose to insane heights. In a letter to Michael in November he describes Maria as 'an Angel from God who met me on my path'; and to Wrangel about the same time he writes:

Don't shake your head, don't judge me; I know that in much that concerns my relations with her I am not acting reasonably, having practically no hope—but whether I have hope or not, it is all the same to me. I no longer think of anything. Only to see her, only to hear her! I am an unhappy madman. Love in this form is a disease. I feel it. I ran into debt over my journey (I tried a second time, but only got as far as Zmiev, couldn't get further). Now I shall go again; I shall ruin myself, but what do I care! For Christ's sake, don't show this letter to my brother. I am infinitely to blame towards him. The poor man helps me with his last resources, and this is how I waste the money.

It   one more instance of Dostoevsky's capacity for remorseless analysis of his own folly. The consuming passion of a pent-up nature, loosed on the world after years of seclusion, has seldom been more vividly or frankly portrayed by its victim.

The further flying visit to Kuznetsk foreshadowed in this letter took place at the end of November, and brought the still hesitating Maria to the verge of a decision. Two months later, Dostoevsky obtained a more prolonged leave, and the marriage was celebrated at Kuznetsk on February 6, 1857. It was, on the lady's side, a marriage of convenience rather than of passion. It is probable that she would have preferred the young, but friendless and impecunious, schoolmaster; and Dostoevsky's daughter asserts, though we are scarcely entitled to believe it on her sole evidence, that she had been Vergunov's mistress up to the very eve of the wedding. On his way back to Semipalatinsk with his bride and stepson, Dostoevsky had at Barnaul an epileptic fit of extreme violence. Incapacitating him for four days, it dissipated the doubts which he had hitherto encouraged himself to entertain regarding the real nature of his intermittent malady; and it revealed for the first time to Maria Dmitrievna that she was the wife of an epileptic.

Having achieved marriage, Dostoevsky was free to devote himself to the other great hope of his heart, release from his indeterminate exile in the Siberian steppes. A year after his arrival in Semipalatinsk, Nicholas I had died in the midst of the scandal of the Crimean War. Alexander II was received everywhere as the bringer of peace and reform; and the Siberian exiles looked eagerly for some act of clemency on the occasion either of the conclusion of the Peace of Paris or of the Tsar's coronation. Dostoevsky remembered that he had once met the hero of Sebastopol, General Todleben, whose brother was a contemporary of his at the Engineering Academy. The ever-helpful Wrangel was employed to deliver a letter to Todleben, and it was the latter's influence with the Tsar which secured the promotion of Dostoevsky to commissioned rank. But the imperial grace went no further; and a patriotic ode composed, not without intention, by Dostoevsky failed to reach Alexander's eye. It was not until January 1858 that he was at last permitted to send in a formal petition to be allowed to resign his commission and return to Russia.

Another year of suspense followed. In the spring of 1859, Dostoevsky learned, in the first instance from his brother in Petersburg, that an imperial decree of March 18th had accepted his resignation. In the petition he had asked to live in Moscow; but the decree fixed Tver, a town some 150 kilometres north of Moscow on the Moscow-Petersburg railway, as his dwelling-place. Official confirmation of the decree reached Semipalatinsk at the beginning of May; local formalities occupied another two months; and on July 2nd, Dostoevsky and his wife turned their backs for ever on Semipalatinsk. Paul Isaev joined them at Omsk, where his education had begun. By the middle of August they were all in Tver.

The literary output of these years of exile was insignificant. In Semipalatinsk, there was little enough stimulus to intellectual effort; and, as he himself confesses, his relations with Maria Dmitrievna absorbed him to the virtual exclusion of all else. He had come out of prison, as he tells Apollon Maikov in a letter written nearly two years later, with an idea in his head for 'a great final story'. We have hints from time to time in his letters from Semipalatinsk of a 'great novel' which he had on the stocks but we find no evidence that any substantial part of it was written, and the conjecture that it was a first draft of *Crime and Punishment* has nothing to support it. Of the course of Dostoevsky's ideas at this time we learn very little. Among the books which he begs Michael to send him are Kant's *Critique of Pure Reason*; Hegel's *History of Philosophy*; the Greek and Latin historians in French translations; modern French historians; 'the economists'; the early church fathers; the Koran; a textbook of physics; and a German dictionary. A list so catholic and comprehensive gives us little enlightenment; nor have we any idea whether these books were actually received and read by him.

The three works definitely associated with Dostoevsky's Siberian life, *Memoirs from the House of the Dead*, *Uncle's Dream* and *The Village of Stepanchikovo*, are among the simplest and least problematical of all his writings. If his mind was already busy with the problems of good and evil which were to inspire the great series of novels beginning with *Crime and Punishment*, we find no trace here of such preoccupations. The genesis of *Memoirs from the House of the Dead* may be found in jottings begun in Semipalatinsk for the benefit of his friends in Petersburg. But there was at that time no thought of publication, and the *Memoirs* as we know them were probably not conceived until after Dostoevsky's return to Russia. How far the original jottings entered into their composition it is impossible to guess.

It was not until 1857 that the censorship removed in Dostoevsky's favour the ban on the publication of the writings of a political exile; and in August of that year Michael was able to arrange for the publication of *A Little Hero*, the story written in prison in 1849. Kraevsky paid 200 roubles for it in cash, despite Dostoevsky's large undischarged debt to him—an act of generosity which the novelist ungraciously and disingenuously tried to belittle. His marriage to Maria Dmitrievna had now freed his mind from the anxieties of his chequered courtship, and had at the same time increased the stringency of his financial needs. He set to work on two short novels, *Uncle's Dream* and *The Village of Stepanchikovo*, which, after much bargaining conducted by Michael on his behalf, were eventually published in different journals about the time of his return to European Russia. *Uncle's Dream* is the story of a scheming mother's efforts to marry her daughter to an old and imbecile prince, who is persuaded by the mother to make a formal proposal of marriage, and subsequently persuaded by other interested parties that the proposal was merely part of a dream. It is, in short, a farce of no particular merit. *The Village of Stepanchikovo*, a more ambitious production, relates how a pseudo-religious charlatan, Foma Fomich Opiskin, insinuates himself into the household of a retired colonel, a widower with an hysterical mother; rules the whole establishment with a rod of iron; and takes a perverse delight in torturing and humiliating the weak but amiable colonel. The story pursues its anecdotic course until one day, to everybody's surprise (and not least that of the reader), the colonel evicts his tormentor with physical violence. Foma Fomich, nothing daunted, comes back confused and reformed; marries the colonel to a young lady on whom he has previously pressed his own unwelcome attentions; and continues (so we gather, not very clearly, from a hurried epilogue) to exercise on the household as powerful an influence for good as he had previously exercised for evil.

It is not easy to disentangle the influences under which Dostoevsky wrote these two stories. Few biographers have credited Maria Dmitrievna with anything that is good in his life or work; but the first stages, at any rate, of his marriage with her seem to have inspired an unwonted mood of light-heartedness, in which the world and its evils could for once be treated as a joke rather than as a problem. He no longer probes the psychological foundations of visible human relations; he is content to describe external phenomena in a spirit of exaggeration and caricature. The humorous situation appeals to him more than the subtle study of character. Much of the material comes, it is clear, from the narrow provincial scandal-mongering society of Semipalatinsk; but the spirit is so different from that in which he had depicted his Petersburg surroundings in the days before his exile that we must look for some other influence to explain the change. He had, if we may believe Wrangel's memoirs, reread Gogol since his release; and *Uncle's Dream* and *The Village of Stepanchikovo* are, like his early works,

E

saturated with Gogol's vocabulary and mannerisms, which he finally puts behind him only after his return to Petersburg. But this gives no clue to the change in spirit and method. The new influence at work in these Siberian stories seems to be that of Dickens, most of whose novels were translated into Russian within a few years of their original publication. One tradition, which reaches us at second-hand but is not otherwise open to suspicion, declares that the only books which Dostoevsky would read in his captivity were *Pickwick Papers* and *David Copperfield*; and a casual phrase in a letter of 1857 shows that Dickens was familiar to him at this period of his life. It has always been recognized by critics that Nelly in *The Insulted and Injured*, the first novel written by Dostoevsky after his return from Siberia, is taken straight from the pages of *The Old Curiosity Shop*; and it seems as little open to doubt that Foma Fomich is the spiritual progeny of Uriah Heep and Mr. Pecksniff. The straightforward, melodramatic dramatis personae; the substitution of caricature for analysis; the physical castigation of the villain; the sudden conversion leading up to a wildly improbable happy ending—all these elements, profoundly alien both to the earlier and to the later Dostoevsky, are in the true Dickensian tradition. And if *The Village of Stepanchikovo* is a failure, it is because Dostoevsky has the smallest possible capacity for sustained humour, and because he is, in this novel (and to some extent also in *Uncle's Dream*), writing under the influence, and in the manner, of one whose genius was poles asunder from his own.

Of Dostoevsky's four months' sojourn in Tver little need be said. His faithful brother Michael came to visit him shortly after his arrival; but such amenities as Tver had to offer did not make him any less impatient. 'Although I am sitting here in Tver,' he wrote to his brother, 'I am still a wanderer on the face of the earth'; and he assured Wrangel that Tver was 'a thousand times worse than Semipalatinsk'. His letters teem with plans for getting back to his beloved Petersburg. He wrote once more to General Todleben, not without much fear of being thought importunate; and finally, the decision being still delayed, he addressed a petition to the Tsar himself. The petition, in which he begs not only for his own return to the capital, but for the admission of his stepson Paul to a free place in one of the Petersburg educational establishments, has been preserved and is a curious document. Couched in the servile phraseology in which it was customary to approach the great Autocrat of All the Russias, it inevitably makes an unpleasant impression on modern readers; but there is no ground whatever for doubting its sincerity. Dostoevsky shared the general enthusiasm for the person of Alexander II during the first years of his reign, and in letters to his brother refers to 'the Angel Emperor' and 'the revered being who rules over us'.

Your Majesty [concludes the petition] is like the sun which shines on the just and the unjust. You have already made happy millions of your people; make happy a poor orphan, his mother and an unfortunate sick man, from whom the ban has not yet been removed, but who is ready, at this moment, to give his whole life for the EMPEROR who has blessed his people.

Even before the petition was received, a favourable decision had been given. It was communicated to Dostoevsky on November 25th, and about the middle of December he left Tver, his wife and stepson remaining behind until he should have found quarters for them. His brother met him on the station at Petersburg. It was a few days short of the tenth anniversary of that chill Christmas Eve when the sleighs had carried the fettered prisoners out over the snow.

CHAPTER VII

Journalistic Experiment

THE decade of Dostoevsky's absence from Petersburg had witnessed three events of outstanding importance: the loss of the Crimean War, the end of the thirty years' reign of Nicholas I, and the opening of the railway from Petersburg to Berlin. These events had had a profound effect on Russian life; but none of them had much altered the external aspect of the capital as Dostoevsky had known it in the 'forties; and when Michael met him at the station on his arrival from Tver, the intervening ten years may well have seemed no more than an incredible nightmare.

The first months after his return were occupied by the installation of his family, by the preparation of a collected edition of his works, his sole financial resource, and by the renewal of old relationships. Amid much that was new in the political and literary firmament, one thing had not changed; it was as necessary in the 'sixties as it had been in the 'forties for an intelligent man, who wished to be taken seriously in literature, to belong to some group or 'circle' having a more or less definite creed or tendency. The centre of the group to which Dostoevsky gravitated was an old-time acquaintance Milyukov, now editor of a newly founded journal the *Svetoch*; among its members were two other old friends, Apollon Maikov and Yanovsky; and it was here that Dostoevsky first met Strakhov, who was to become his official biographer. During his absence, brother Michael had flourished in the unexpected role of a cigar and cigarette manufacturer; it is his title to fame that he was apparently the first to conceive the original and lucrative idea of distributing 'gifts of trifling value' gratis with his wares. But the aroma of tobacco had not stifled the literary yearnings of his earlier manhood; and the return of his more gifted brother decided him. He resolved to sell the factory and start a new literary journal with himself as editor and Fyodor as principal contributor. An advertisement of the *Vremya* ('Time') appeared in September 1860, and the first number duly saw the light in January 1861. Its principal attraction was the first instalment of a new novel by Fyodor, *The Insulted and Injured*, a diffuse, sentimental and melodramatic story, now interesting only in the foretastes it gives of later and better work; and in April

Memoirs from the House of the Dead, which had begun to appear in the previous autumn in another periodical, were transferred to the *Vremya*. Nor did these contributions exhaust Dostoevsky's fertile brain, never more active than at the moment of his return to the world of letters; for he was from the outset a regular contributor to the *Vremya* of articles on literature and politics. For the space of more than four years he was absorbed in journalistic hack-work to the almost complete exclusion of fiction. But the period is of the utmost significance in his spiritual development. It witnessed the evolution of the passionate young radical into an equally passionate, though scarcely more clear-headed, champion of orthodoxy, and of the clever imitator of Hoffmann and Gogol into the creator of Raskolnikov and Myshkin.

When Dostoevsky was arrested in the spring of 1849, Russian thought, fast in the severest censorship which even Russia has ever known, looked hopefully towards Europe where revolutionary enthusiasm was ablaze. The succeeding years reversed the position. Europe, after the revolutionary disturbances of 1848, had passed rapidly over to reaction. 'Europe is not sleeping, she is dead,' wrote Herzen in 1850; and in this famous phrase the great revolutionary leader summed up the disillusionment so often expressed by Russians, and not merely by Russian radicals, during the next thirty years. But while European political thought remained listless and tepid, Russia began to awake. The humiliations of the Crimean War had damned the defunct régime of Nicholas I; vague ideals of liberty and progress, concrete reforms such as the liberation of the serfs and the abolition of the censorship, were in the air; and Russia seemed, in these early years of Alexander II, to be on the eve of a new epoch of reform and regeneration. Radicals like Herzen, liberals like Turgenev, and Slavophil conservatives like Konstantin Aksakov, celebrate in similar language the contrast between the effete old man, Europe, and the fresh young giant, Russia. The thoughtful Russian of the 'forties had gazed in hope and admiration on Europe; the Russian of 1860 could regard with similar feelings, not perhaps the achievements, but at any rate the aspirations of his own countrymen.

The years of Dostoevsky's absence had seen the growth of a new cult of 'the people', which in Russia at this epoch meant the peasant. The canonization of the peasant had been inaugurated in Moscow by the Slavophils, whose programme was to exalt everything purely Russian at the expense of everything European or Europeanized; and it was fostered by the appearance of some notable tales of peasant life, Turgenev's *Sketches of a Sportsman*, Grigorovich's *Anton*

Goremyka, and others. It reached its culminating point with the decision of Alexander to liberate the serfs, which was taken as early as 1857, though it was not actually promulgated until 1861. The young Tolstoy, in one of his earliest stories, pays his tribute to the cult; *Three Deaths*, written in the winter of 1857–8, contrasts the anguished death of the aristocrat with the simple untroubled passing of the peasant. In short, the peasant was in fashion; and the cult fell in with Dostoevsky's mood when he returned from Siberia. In the 'forties men had sought their ideal in French text-books; they had now only to look around them and find it in 'the Russian people'. In the Petersburg of 1860 it was as easy for a man of warm heart and small political insight to become an enthusiastic patriot as it had been for him in 1845 to become an enthusiastic revolutionary; and Dostoevsky in each case followed the line of least resistance.

The process was assisted by a linguistic confusion. The Russian word *Narod*, like the German *Volk*, covers the two ideas which we prefer to distinguish by the words 'nation' and 'people'. When Dostoevsky, in his journalistic utterances, insisted on basing Russian civilization on 'the national spirit' and on 'national principles', he might equally well have meant—and probably believed that he did mean—'the popular spirit' and 'popular principles'. The word *Narod* and its derivatives, already popularized by the Slavophils, jostle one another not only in the pages of the *Vremya*, but in all Dostoevsky's subsequent political writings; and the unperceived confusion of thought painlessly assisted the transition from the democratic ardour of his youth to the reactionary patriotism of his later years.

The rapid evolution of Dostoevsky's opinions during the years after his return was predominantly affected by the influence of Apollon Grigoriev, a critic of much ability though no great judgment, whose vigour and originality still entitle him to a minor niche in the history of Russian literature. Grigoriev had begun his literary career in the 'forties as a poet; and from 1850 to 1855 he was on the staff of a Moscow journal which, though not officially associated with the Slavophils, practised the cult of the Russian peasant and found the ethical ideal of humanity beneath his unpromising exterior. In Moscow Grigoriev fell in with Ostrovsky, the dramatist of the lower strata of Moscow and provincial society, and conceived for him an unbounded enthusiasm. Ostrovsky was a pleasant, somewhat simple, person, and his dramas are decidedly free from any conscious tendency, Slavophil or other; but he was addicted to that particularly Russian form of sentiment which believes that the minor vices, such as drunkenness and dirt, ordinarily cohabit with the major virtues. Under the transfiguring light of Grigoriev's criticism, Ostrovsky became an exponent of the Russian soul second only to Pushkin; and one of his characters, the hero of *Poverty No Vice*, was celebrated by Grigoriev in doggerel verse, of which one couplet remained for many years famous in Russian literature:

> Wretched, drunken and in tatters,
> But with his pure Russian soul.

The influence of Grigoriev, or of Ostrovsky as interpreted by Grigoriev, is traceable in several of Dostoevsky's characters, finding its completest expression in Marmeladov of *Crime and Punishment*.

When the *Vremya* started publication at the beginning of 1861, Grigoriev, a quarrelsome person who seldom remained long in any employment, offered his services and became a regular contributor. The first advertisements had already explained the programme and policy of the new journal. They expressed a lofty indifference to the 'domestic quarrels' of Slavophils and westerners, and professed to have discovered a new synthesis to reconcile and transcend the views of both. But these professions of originality were emphatic rather than convincing. The divorce between the educated classes and the 'people' produced by the reforms of Peter the Great; the assertion of the distinctive character of Russian civilization and Russian institutions; the need for basing Russian society and Russian culture on the 'people'—all these ideas, with their innumerable implications and ramifications, had been the stock-in-trade of the Moscow Slavophils for fifteen years. Such were the shop-soiled articles of faith displayed in the windows of the *Vremya*. In order to give them some appearance of freshness, it remained to find a new label; and the need was supplied by Grigoriev.

The new label consisted of the simple word *Pochva*, the Soil. The symbol of the doctrine preached by the *Vremya* was the Soil; the men of the *Vremya* called themselves, and came to be called, *Pochvenniki* or Men of the Soil; there was the abstract quality, *Pochvennost*, or attachment to the Soil, which suggested not only devotion to the Russian people, but also a quality of thought which, being rooted in the soil, must be a hardy, wholesome, native growth; and there was the negative *Bezpochvennost*, which characterized your opponents, and which implied not merely that they cared nothing for Russia and for the people, but that their thoughts were mere airy speculations having no effective contact with reality or with the soil. The word was, in short, a brilliant stroke of talent. It was in vain that hostile journals like the *Sovremennik* called the *Pochva* a meaningless phrase. Its strength lay in its superabundance of meanings; and the *Vremya* could scarcely have existed without it. The situation was summed up two years later by the caricaturist of a comic paper who depicted Strakhov as office-boy addressing Michael Dostoevsky the editor: 'Our opinions may be borrowed, but the labels are at any rate our own.'

The sympathies of the new journal were not long left doubtful. The second number (February 1861) contained an article on the theory of art in which Fyodor Dostoevsky vigorously attacked the critics of both the prominent radical periodicals, the *Sovremennik* and the *Otechestvennye Zapiski*. In the same number Grigoriev began a series of articles in which he sang the praises, and expounded the philosophy, of the founders of the Slavophil school, Khomyakov and Kireevsky. Fyodor and Strakhov were enthusiastic converts; but Michael, the business man, less impressionable and more concerned with circulation than with ideas, became anxious. The intelligentsia of Petersburg had not forgotten the traditions of the 'forties, and still faintly despised Moscow. The name Slavophil inevitably suggested the Russian blouses and high-boots affected by the first converts; and Petersburg, even if it had lost faith in Europe as a pattern of democracy, still clung to the traditions of London tailors and Paris *modistes*. Moreover, the *Vremya* had after all inscribed on its programme its proud indifference to Slavophils and westerners alike; and the open profession of Slavophil tenets could, in Michael's cautious opinion, only lead to a falling-off of subscriptions. The first result was a quarrel between Michael and Grigoriev, who with his customary impulsiveness fled to Orenburg in the furthest corner of Russia and spent a year there teaching in a school. He then returned to Petersburg, and wrote occasional articles for the *Vremya* and its successor, the *Epocha*, until his premature death in 1864. He is one whose influence on his contemporaries depended on his vigorous personality, and cannot be adequately measured either by the volume or the quality of his literary remains.

Meanwhile the embarrassment of Fyodor Dostoevsky's position had been most clearly betrayed in an article in the *Vremya* for November 1861, in which he attempted to define his attitude to *The Day*, a new journal just started in Moscow by Konstantin Aksakov and his Slavophil associates. The article is aggressive in tone; but we soon perceive that the bitterness is not that of an enemy, but of a would-be friend whose friendship is spurned and ignored. There is a little mild fun at the expense of Slavophil devotion to the older capital and to medieval traditions; for Dostoevsky, even after he became a full-blown Slavophil, remained at heart a Petersburger, not a Moscovite. There is a little indignation with a writer in *The Day* who is represented (not quite fairly) as speaking of the 'divinely ordained' institution of serfdom; for Dostoevsky, in these early days of his Slavophil conversion, still retained the strong liberal prejudices of his youth. But these are criticisms by the way, proffered as it were in evidence of impartiality. The real offence of *The Day* is a 'rare capacity for not recognizing its friends'. It will not believe that anything good can come out of the *Vremya*; for the Slavophil finds nothing good unless it fits to a millimetre 'the mould of their ideals as cast once for all in Moscow'. An Anglo-Catholic divine gently chiding the Papacy for intolerance and inflexibility might afford a modern parallel to Dostoevsky's attitude. The article pleased nobody. It did not impress the Slavophils; and the liberals and westerners read it as treason to their cause on the part of one who still did lip-service to it. The charge was not unjust; but it is unnecessary to accuse Dostoevsky. He was guilty not of insincerity, but of confusion of thought; he had neither the clear-headedness to know, nor perhaps, even had he known, the courage to admit, how completely and how irrevocably he had transferred his allegiance.

The winter of 1861–2 was a critical one in the history of Russian thought. The liberal enthusiasm, having reached its culminating point in the proclamation of the emancipation of the serfs, began to waver. Some thought that the reforms had gone far enough; others that they had only just begun. There was the usual regrouping of parties; the former left, and Dostoevsky with it, had more or less imperceptibly moved to the right; and new groups of extremists, recruited chiefly from the young generation, formed on the left flank. The 'new men' began to be the subject of serious and disapproving discussion in more orthodox circles; and the inappropriate label 'Nihilists' (apparently invented by Turgenev) was affixed to them. Trouble started in the autumn of 1861 in the University of Petersburg, where the students began to engage in anti-Government —some said, revolutionary—propaganda; the Government replied by closing the student organizations, clapping some of the demonstrators into the fortress of Peter-and-Paul and ultimately sending a handful of them to Siberia. The university was closed; and the students, deprived of any other occupation, devoted themselves to the surreptitious printing and distribution of incendiary pamphlets.

The *Vremya*, with its profession of liberal opinions, had at first sympathized with the students; and Michael Dostoevsky, who had learnt the uses of advertisement in the tobacco trade, roasted a large joint of beef in the offices of the journal and carried it round to the fortress, with vodka and wine, as a present to the imprisoned students. But as the pace grew hotter, the *Vremya* became more lukewarm; the Dostoevskys took fright, and the journal veered round to the Government side. It was only just in time; the *Sovremennik* stuck to its guns, abused the *Vremya* for its desertion, and in the spring of 1862 was suspended by the censorship.

In the midst of these political commotions, at the beginning of June 1862, Dostoevsky left Petersburg on his first journey abroad. He travelled by Berlin, Dresden and Cologne to Paris; he spent eight days in London—his only visit to England—and went to see the exiled revolutionary Herzen, then living at Westbourne Terrace, Paddington; then returning to Paris, he went on via Düsseldorf and the Rhine to Geneva, where he met Strakhov. The two friends proceeded by the Mont-Cenis into Italy, and visited together Turin, Genoa and Florence. From Florence, Dostoevsky returned alone to Russia, where he arrived about the end of August.

It is singularly difficult for us to recapture the impressions which his first European tour made on the novelist; and the few indications we have suggest that, surprisingly enough, they were not very profound. The impressionable young man should have been dazzled by the splendours of European civilization; but he found Paris (so Strakhov tells us) 'a most boring town', and Geneva, more excusably, gloomy and dull. Turin reminded him of Petersburg, which was perhaps a consolation. At Florence, where he stayed a week with Strakhov, he devoured the four volumes of Victor Hugo's *Les Misérables* which had just come out, and had eyes for nothing else. Strakhov dragged him once to the Uffizi Gallery; but he soon tired of it and 'left without having seen the Medici Venus'. Dostoevsky's gifts of observation and description were, in material things, infinitesimally small; and the *Winter Notes of Summer Impressions*, which he contributed a few months later to the *Vremya*, are among the dullest of his writings. Among the few scenes which haunt the reader's memory is the strange nocturnal picture of the Haymarket in London, regularly frequented at this epoch by a motley crowd of prostitutes and their customers, overflowing at every step from the gas-lit pavements into the roadway, while among them went Catholic missionaries, men and women, distributing religious tracts in French and English.

The visit to Herzen, which took place on July 16th, is known to us in greater detail than any other incident of the tour. The two men had met once before, in the autumn of 1846, three months before Herzen left Russia for good. It was the moment when Dostoevsky was beginning to make himself intolerable to Belinsky and his friends; and Herzen's impression of him was 'not particularly favourable'. But in 1862 the past could be forgotten and forgiven. Had not Dostoevsky suffered in Siberia for the great revolutionary cause ? and was he not the author of *Memoirs from the House of the Dead*, which Herzen had made eager haste to read ? The verdict this time was more sympathetic: 'Naïve, not at all clear, but very agreeable; is an enthusiastic believer in the Russian people.'

Some Russian critics, especially since the revolution, have attributed to the great revolutionary leader a marked influence on the development of Dostoevsky's thought; even the official biography remarks that *Winter Notes of Summer Impressions* show traces of Herzen's ideas. It is difficult to believe that the influence was very deep, or that any particular importance attaches to the encounter in London. It is true that Herzen was fond of saying that he hated the Russian government and loved the Russian people; and that the latter sentiment, though less concrete and active than the former, gave him some sympathy with Slavophil tenets. It is true that he had for some time been denouncing the rottenness of Europe in terms on which the most ardent Slavophil could scarcely have improved. But these ideas were commonplaces of the time; and the points of contact with Dostoevsky were purely superficial. In reality, neither Herzen nor Dostoevsky knew much of the Russian people; and whereas Herzen, familiar with western democratic theories, used the downtrodden Russian peasant as an argumentative bludgeon to belabour the Russian autocracy, Dostoevsky, whose manner of thought was Russian and not European, was rapidly approaching the orthodox opinion which regarded an idealized peasant as the base and foundation of the whole autocratic system in church and state. The 'Russian people' evidently bore the brunt of the conversation; and had the conversationalists sought meanings, instead of being content with words, they might perhaps have perceived that the 'Russian people' could be enlisted, quite as easily and quite as legitimately, on one side of the argument as on the other. But the Russian peasant must, on that July day in Westbourne Terrace, have seemed a vague, distant and rather incredible figure; and the conversation ended, as it had begun, in a pleasant summer haze of mutual satisfaction. In his writings many years later, Dostoevsky contested with some asperity Herzen's qualifications to speak in the name of the 'Russian people'. The criticism is just; but the *tu quoque* would have been equally effective, had Herzen still been alive to answer.

When Dostoevsky wrote his *Winter Notes* he refrained, from motives of caution, from mentioning his visit to Herzen. His caution was unnecessary and useless; the Russian political police had their agent in London, perhaps in Herzen's own entourage, to report on suspect persons who came to the house. The visit of Dostoevsky, who, as a former political prisoner, for many years remained a suspect to the authorities, was soon reported to Petersburg. The police list of Herzen's suspect visitors, including the name of Dostoevsky, fell into the hands of a Polish agent of Herzen's, who published it in his paper, the *Kolokol*, as a 'list of persons whom the government has ordered to be arrested on their return from abroad'. This proved to be incorrect. Dostoevsky for one returned unmolested to Petersburg, and the authorities must have taken a lenient view of his visit to Herzen; for he was allowed to go abroad once more next year. But the incident is a curious illustration of the net of espionage and counter-espionage which the Russian government and the Russian *émigrés* of the day had spread over Europe.

The sole direct literary outcome of Dostoevsky's first European tour was the uninteresting series of *Winter Notes* already mentioned; and soon after his return he wrote, also for the *Vremya*, a short story entitled *A Shabby Adventure*. It is a half-farcical, half-satirical account of how the director of a department, from humanitarian views not unmixed with self-righteousness, decides to visit the wedding-feast of one of his subordinate clerks. The result is that he merely terrifies, embarrasses and annoys those whom he has sought to honour, and finally gets himself drunk to the discomfiture of the guests in general and the young married couple in particular. The story is a direct satire on the 'humanitarianism' of the liberals, of which Dostoevsky himself had once been a fervent devotee. It is a slight straw, but it shows from which quarter of the political firmament the wind was blowing. In form, *A Shabby Adventure* was the last of Dostoevsky's stories to reflect the influence of his first master Gogol; and it was the last work of fiction which he was to write for more than a year. The coming months were occupied by a sentimental adventure which is reserved for the following chapter.

Meanwhile the clouds were gathering, and the position of the responsible editor of a journal in Petersburg grew more and more anxious. The Polish insurrection, which broke out in the spring of 1863, caused, apart from its other repercussions, a profound disturbance in Russian political thought. The Slavophil could not without qualms advocate the bloody repression of a brother Slav, even though he were a backslider and a Catholic. The liberal sympathized in theory with Polish aspirations for political liberty, and had greeted with enthusiasm the milder régime inaugurated by Alexander in Poland. But neither Slavophils nor liberals dared to take their stand on the side of the Polish insurgents; and after a moment's wavering, they swallowed their not very solid convictions. The dose was fatal to their independent existence; the Slavophils and the old liberals became from 1863 onwards assimilated to the orthodox conservatives; and the field of opposition was left to radicals and 'nihilists', now more and more openly persecuted by the government, and more and more avowedly revolutionary in aim and character.

The upheaval which had shaken the strongest proved fatal to the timid and faltering *Vremya*. The Dostoevskys chose discretion and were silent on the political aspects of the insurrection; but in the April number they published an unsigned article from the pen of Strakhov entitled *A Fatal Question*. Strakhov mentioned the literary achievements of the Polish aristocracy in the past, suggested that Poland must be fought with the weapons of art and literature, and argued that only when Russian civilization gained the upper hand over Polish culture would the Polish question be finally solved. The article, harmless enough at first sight, passed the censor; but his *imprimatur* did not, under the illogical Russian law, absolve the editor from further responsibility. Certain servile organs of the press, anxious to demonstrate their own orthodoxy, raised a hue and cry; the article, it was said, implied not only disapproval of the policy of the government, but belief in the superiority of Polish over Russian culture. The apologies and explanations prepared by the Dostoevskys for publication were rejected by the censor; the matter was taken up to the Tsar himself; and in June the *Vremya* was suppressed—not suspended, like the *Sovremennik* in the previous year, for a fixed period, but finally and irrevocably suppressed.

The blow which deprived the Dostoevskys of their livelihood was as crushing as it was unexpected. It coincided with a crisis in Fyodor's private life. He hastened his application for the renewal of his foreign passport and in August joined his mistress in Paris.

Financially, the *Vremya* had been a fair success. In the first year it had 2,300 subscribers, in the second year 4,300 and in the third 4,000. A circulation of 2,500 approximately covered expenses, the balance representing profit. Nevertheless, the collapse left the Dostoevskys penniless; and Fyodor borrowed 1,000 roubles from the Fund for Assisting Needy Men of Letters in order to pay for his journey abroad.

CHAPTER VIII

Intimate Life

THE years after the return from Siberia not only developed and matured those ethical and political views which formed the background, and to some extent furnished the inspiration, of his greatest novels; they also provided him with the sexual experience which gave him the key to the hidden recesses of human character. By the time he and his wife established themselves in the capital at the beginning of 1860, passion had given place to reflection, and reflection to disillusionment. So much is clear. But the obscurity which surrounded the earlier years of their union deepens still further after their return to Petersburg; and the assertion of Dostoevsky's daughter that Vergunov followed Maria Dmitrievna thither, and once more became her paramour, is unsupported by any more reliable evidence. It may have been so. The absence of any apparent breach between husband and wife does not dispose of the allegation; for Dostoevsky would have tolerated unfaithfulness in his wife just as he afterwards tolerated it in his mistress. It was a cardinal doctrine in the advanced radical circles in which he moved at this time that the marriage-tie did not justify interference by one partner with the liberties of the other; and even in *The Devils*, written ten years later, Shatov, a character who contains much of Dostoevsky himself, makes it a matter of principle to receive his wife when she comes back to him pregnant by another man.

The question of Maria Dmitrievna's conjugal fidelity must remain open. Before many months had passed, the unfortunate woman was stricken down with consumption, and for the remaining four years of her life became a chronic invalid. Her irritability, of which there are traces even in Siberian days, grew with the disease.

She loved me without limit [Dostoevsky wrote to Wrangel some time after her death], I too loved her immeasurably, but we did not live happily with one another. . . . But although we were decidedly unhappy together, owing to her strange, suspicious and morbidly imaginative character, we could not cease to love one another; the more unhappy we were, the more we became attached to each other.

She continued to live with Dostoevsky in Petersburg until the spring of 1863; and he spent the last winter of her life at her bedside in Moscow. But despite the sentiment with which he managed to surround her memory, the fact remains that during these years she had, except as an object of pity, already ceased to count in his life. The vision of first love had faded and, like the physical indulgences of youth, had left the soul unfed.

The life of Dostoevsky during the years immediately following his return from Siberia is full of dark hints and rumours. In the official biography, Strakhov wrote of the circle in which, at the beginning of 1860, he had first met Dostoevsky:

I noticed with astonishment that no sort of importance was attached to physical excesses and abnormalities of every kind. People who, morally speaking, were extremely sensitive, who were devoted to the highest forms of thought, and themselves, for the most part, refrained from all physical dissoluteness, would nevertheless regard with complete tolerance irregularities of this kind, and would speak of them as idle amusements in which it was perfectly legitimate to indulge in a spare moment. Spiritual sins were judged strictly and precisely; sins of the flesh did not count at all. This strange emancipation of the flesh was infectious, and in some cases led to consequences which it is terrible and painful to recall.

The passage would be irrelevant unless it were meant to imply that Dostoevsky shared the views, even if he did not participate in the practices, to which Strakhov refers; and, as if to add further point to the implication, mention is made on the next page of the 'bifurcation' of Dostoevsky's character, which enabled him to judge with one side of his nature the thoughts and feelings of the other side.

There the matter remained until, soon after Tolstoy's death in 1910, a letter was published which Strakhov had written to him in November 1883. The following are salient extracts:

You have doubtless received by now my Biography of Dostoevsky; please give it your indulgent notice and tell me what you think of it. In this matter, I want to confess myself to you. All the time I was writing, I was engaged in a struggle with my own rising disgust, and was trying to suppress this evil feeling in myself. . . . I cannot regard Dostoevsky as either a good or a happy man (the two really go together). He was malicious, envious and dissolute, and spent his whole life in states of nervous excitement which made him pitiable, and would have made him ridiculous if he had not been so malicious and so clever. . . .

He had a penchant for filthinesses and was proud of them. Viskovatov began to tell me how he boasted that he had fornicated at the baths with a little girl who was brought to him by her governess. Note that for all this, for all his animal sensuality, he had no taste, no feeling for feminine beauty and charm. This can be seen in his novels. The characters most resembling him are the hero of *Memoirs from Underground*, Svidrigailov in *Crime and Punishment*, and Stavrogin in *The Devils*.

The tirade against Dostoevsky's character may pass for an unfair, but still recognizable caricature; but the story alleged to have been told to Viskovatov is more than dubious. It is not made more credible by a later variant, according to which Dostoevsky, by way of penance, confessed his guilt to his bitterest enemy Turgenev. The charge must at least be regarded as not proven.[1] The only thing which the letter definitely proves is bitterness and malice, whatever may have been their motive, on Strakhov's part; and this rather detracts from the credibility of the insinuations already quoted from the official biography. There is sufficient indication in Dostoevsky's subsequent writings of an interest in sensuality, which he shares with the more modern disciples of Freud and Jung; but the extant records are insufficient to enable us to form any judgment on the extent of his indulgence in sensual practices.

The one amatory experience of this period in Dostoevsky's life which we are able to follow in detail is an affair which, divulged to the world for the first time ten years ago, has since attracted more attention than any other episode in his career. In September 1861 there appeared in the *Vremya* a short story by a young university student Apollinaria (or Polina for short) Suslova; and it is permissible to assume that Dostoevsky made her acquaintance on this occasion. It does not appear, however, that their intimate relations began at this time. As we know, Dostoevsky spent the summer of 1862 in Europe; and it is hardly likely that he would have left Petersburg, alone, for upwards of three months, in the heyday of a passionate *affaire de cœur*. It seems that the beginning of the liaison must be placed in the winter of 1862–3, after Dostoevsky's first journey abroad, and during the last months of the existence of the *Vremya*. Some attempt was made to conceal it from Maria Dmitrievna; but it was known to her sister, Varvara Konstant, whose friendly relations with Dostoevsky remained unaffected.

The principal source of our knowledge of the affair is the extremely frank diary of Suslova herself. Beginning in August 1863, it throws back a tantalizing half-light on the earlier stages of the liaison. We can, if we choose, picture to ourselves an innocent girl initiated into the ways of vice by a too experienced man of the world nearly twenty years her senior; or a simple impressionable man tempted from the paths of conjugal virtue by a practised coquette who had fallen in love with his literary reputation. Both pictures have been

[1] See note on pp. 88–9.

drawn; but both depend on the imagination of the artist rather than on recorded evidence. These tempting simplifications contribute little to the understanding of a tangled human relationship. It was— for we have no reason to question her statement—Suslova's first adventure; and conventional sympathies should therefore be on her side. But no reader of her diary can regard Dostoevsky as a cool and calculating rake, or can doubt that Suslova was by nature salacious and by nature a coquette—for she continually depicts herself whetting the appetite of the male even when she had no intention of satisfying it. The beginnings of the liaison still belong to the field of conjecture. But in the sequel, it is Dostoevsky who is impressionable, childish and ridiculous; and she reveals herself an accomplished minx.

It had been the intention of the pair to travel together to France and Italy during the summer of 1863. But Dostoevsky's departure was delayed for several unanticipated reasons. He had to transfer his wife from the unhealthy climate of the capital to Vladimir, a provincial town some distance from Moscow; he had once more to borrow money for the expenses of his tour from the Fund for Needy Men of Letters; and there was difficulty and delay over the renewal of his passport. Suslova started alone for Paris in June; and it was not until the middle of August that Dostoevsky followed her. Even then he did not seem in a hurry; for he stopped for four days on the way at Wiesbaden, and won 5,000 francs at roulette. In the case of another man it would be tempting to draw a deduction as to the relative virulence of his passion for his mistress and his passion for the gaming-table; but in the case of Dostoevsky, it was generally the passion nearest to him which had the upper hand.

On August 27th Dostoevsky reached Paris and sent a note to Suslova's lodgings; and she at once despatched the reply which, she records in her diary, she had prepared more than a week before in anticipation of his arrival. It was couched in the following terms:

You have come too late. A very short while ago I was dreaming of going with you to Italy, and had even begun to learn Italian; but in a few days everything was changed. You used to say that I was not capable of giving away my heart quickly; I have given it within a week, at first call, without resistance, without the conviction and almost without the hope of being loved in return. I was right to be angry with you when you were first attracted by me. Do not think that I blame you; I only mean that you did not know me and I did not know myself. Good-bye, my dear.

I wanted to see you, but to what can a meeting lead? I wanted very much to talk to you about Russia.

Before this missive reached Dostoevsky, he was on his way to her,
F

and the awkward explanation had after all to be given face to face. It was a bitter moment in Dostoevsky's life; and the conversation between them is sufficiently remarkable in itself, and a sufficiently good specimen of the manner and matter of Suslova's diary, to be quoted at length:

'I thought you would not come,' I said, 'since I wrote you that letter.
  'What letter?'
  'Telling you not to come to Paris.'
  'Why not?'
  'Because it was too late.'
  He let fall his head.
  'I must know everything. Let us go somewhere, and tell me, or I shall die!'
  [They went together in a cab to Dostoevsky's lodging.]
  When we got into the room, he fell at my feet and, clasping and pressing my knees, burst out sobbing:
  'I have lost you, I knew it.'
  Calming himself, he began to ask me who it was. . . .
  'Perhaps he is young and handsome, a good talker. But you will never find another heart like mine.'
  For a long time I would not answer.
  'You have given yourself to him completely?'
  'Don't ask! It is not fair of you. . . .'
  I told him that I loved this man very much.
  'You are happy?'
  'No.'
  'You are in love and not happy! How can that be?'
  'He does not love me.'
  'Does not love you!' he shouted holding his head as if in despair; 'but you love him like a slave! Tell me, I must know. You would follow him to the end of the world?'
  'No,' I replied; 'I shall go into the country,' and burst into tears.

The rival was a young Spanish doctor or medical student whom Suslova in her diary calls indifferently 'Salvador', 'Kor' or 'The Planter'. The liaison had been of only a few weeks' duration; but for the first, and perhaps the last, time in her life, Suslova had allowed a man to tire of her before she tired of him; and Dostoevsky's arrival coincided with the moment when he had decided to bring the comedy to an end. Hitting upon a well-worn device, he got a friend to send a letter to his mistress saying that he had typhus. Suslova was in despair; but Dostoevsky, a ready consoler, assured her that 'in this climate and with Parisian doctors' the disease was not dangerous. In the present case it evidently was not; for two days later Polina met Salvador in the Rue de la Sorbonne. The conversation was short and constrained. She went home and had a fit of hysterics, after which, as she frankly records, she felt 'wonderfully well'. At seven o'clock next morning she went to fetch Dostoevsky.

Dostoevsky dealt with the situation with a degree of toleration and outspokenness which disarms criticism:

Fyodor said that it was no use taking notice of the whole affair; I had of course besmirched myself, but that was an incidental. Salvador was a young man who needed a mistress, I had come on the scene, and he had seized the opportunity. Why not? A pretty woman satisfies all tastes.

The upshot of the conversation was the acceptance by Suslova of Dostoevsky's proposal that they should, after all, make their projected trip to Italy together, but as 'brother and sister'. They started in the first days of September. They yielded to a fatal impulse and made a detour to Baden. There the lure of the roulette table, and Dostoevsky's faith in the system he had discovered at Wiesbaden, cost him 3,000 francs, representing practically the whole of the cash in his pocket. From his Wiesbaden winnings he had sent to Varvara Konstant in Petersburg a considerable sum to supply the needs of his wife and stepson. There was now nothing for it but to write to Varvara, begging her to intercept 100 roubles destined for Maria Dmitrievna and send them back to him at Turin, the next intended stopping-place of the irresponsible pair.

Another scene at Baden may be transcribed from Suslova's diary and requires no comment:

At ten o'clock we were drinking tea. I was tired that day and when I had finished I lay on the bed and asked Fyodor to come and sit closer to me. I felt comfortable. I took his hand and for a long time held it in mine. . . .

I said that I had been unjust and cruel to him in Paris, that I had seemed to think only of myself, but that I had really thought of him too, though I had said nothing for fear of hurting his feelings. All at once he got up to go away, but stumbled on my shoes which were lying by the bed, and then hurriedly turned round and sat down.

'Where were you going?' I asked.

'To shut the window.'

'Then shut it if you want to.'

'No, it doesn't matter. You don't know what happened to me just now,' he said with a strange expression.

'What?' I looked at his face, which was quite distraught.

'I wanted to kiss your foot.'

'What for?' I said much embarrassed and almost alarmed, drawing up my feet.

'I wanted to, and made up my mind that I would. . . .'

Thinking to undress and go to sleep, I asked him whether the maid was coming to clear the tea. He said she was not. Then he looked at me in such a way that I felt uncomfortable; I told him so.

'I feel uncomfortable too,' he answered with a strange smile.

I hid my face in the pillow. Then I asked him again whether the maid would come, and again he answered no.

'Then go to your room,' I said, 'I want to sleep. . . .'

He did not bolt his door, and soon came into the room again on the pretext of shutting my window. He came up to me and urged me to get undressed.

'Yes, I will get undressed,' I said making as if I were only waiting for him to go.

He went out, came back again on some excuse, and then finally went out and latched the door.

To-day he mentioned last night and said that he was drunk. He then said that he supposed it was disagreeable for me when he tormented me like that. I answered that it was nothing to me, but avoided any discussion of the subject, so as neither to give him any hopes nor yet make him quite hopeless. He said that I had a very mischievous smile, that I no doubt thought him stupid and that he was conscious of his own stupidity, but that it was unconscious [*sic*].

The record of the tour is divided between these sentimental complications and more vulgar, but no less harassing, financial embarrassments. They left Baden with 120 francs in their pockets and retraced their steps to Geneva. In Geneva Dostoevsky pawned his watch, and the proceeds took them to Turin, where an anxious week of waiting ensued. Suslova pawned a ring; every day they dreaded the presentation of an hotel bill which would disclose their penniless condition; and the town which, only last year, had reminded Dostoevsky of Petersburg, became 'this filthy Turin'. On September 20th the expected succour arrived in the form of the 100 roubles from Varvara Konstant and a larger loan from Michael. Dostoevsky was never hard-hearted, and the revocation of the gift to his wife caused him some pangs of remorse. He could do nothing; for it was unthinkable that he should abandon the journey with his mistress. But he soothed his uneasy conscience by a generous gesture which, for the moment, cost him nothing. He wrote once more to Varvara begging her to lend her sister 75 roubles on his behalf; and next day he and Suslova shook off the dust of Turin from their feet.

They travelled to Genoa and took ship for Rome. It was Dostoevsky's only visit to the Eternal City, but neither he nor his partner has left us their impressions. They had other preoccupations than those of the ordinary tourist. There was another passionate midnight scene, similar to that recorded at Baden, and similarly inconclusive.

Monetary difficulties once more began to assail Dostoevsky's mind. Suslova was an expensive travelling companion; and it was clear that present resources would not suffice to take her back to Paris and him to Petersburg. Family sources of credit had been tapped to the uttermost; but his literary credit remained. On the last day of September he wrote to his friend Strakhov asking him to offer his next novel to Boborykin, the editor of a rather second-rate Petersburg journal; the sole condition was that 300 roubles of the price should be paid in cash forthwith. 'Let Boborykin know,' he adds with quaint boastfulness, 'that, except for *Poor Folk*, I have never yet in all my life written a book without receiving payment in advance.' The theme of the projected story, as sketched in his letter to Strakhov, had evidently been suggested to him by the adventures of the tour; it was eventually written three years later, though not for Boborykin, under the title of *The Gambler*.

From Rome they went on to Naples, where they re-embarked for Genoa. On the steamer they met Herzen and his son Alexander. While Dostoevsky talked politics with the father, Suslova conducted with the young man a mild flirtation which ended only when the Herzens left the ship at Leghorn; and Dostoevsky's jealousy found an outlet in unflattering comments on the younger Herzen. At Turin (it was now mid-October) Dostoevsky found 300 roubles awaiting him from Boborykin. But money, at this period of Dostoevsky's career, was an irresistible temptation, and instead of returning to Petersburg, where he was now overdue, he made straight for Homburg. *En route* Suslova left him. She was back in Paris on October 22nd; and five days later she received a letter from her late companion telling her that he had lost everything and begging her to lend him the money to return home. Lack of generosity is not a Russian fault; Polina's first idea was to pawn her watch and chain; but she eventually borrowed the money to send to him from friends in Paris. This benefaction may have alleviated her pangs of conscience, which she records in a previous entry of her diary, at 'having been unable to recompense him in any way' for all he had done for her.

Dostoevsky and Suslova did not meet again for almost two years, and except perhaps for a few days which they spent together at Wiesbaden in 1865, their intimacy was not renewed. Their liaison, known to us principally through its strange Franco-Italian epilogue, remains a half-deciphered fragment of Dostoevsky's biography. In the period of mutual reproaches which followed, Suslova several times blames him for his intrusion into her life. She began to see Dostoevsky in the role of the traditional seducer, and assumed a tone of moral superiority and injured innocence. 'When I remember what I was two years ago,' she wrote in her diary in December 1864, 'I begin to hate Dostoevsky; it was he who first killed my faith.' His verdict, for which we are once more indebted to her diary, is perhaps more subtle:

You cannot forgive me for the fact that you once gave yourself to me, and you are taking your revenge for that; that is a feminine trait.

Such remained Dostoevsky's diagnosis of the psychology of his mistress; and in subsequent novels, beginning with *The Gambler*, he more than once portrays the woman who gives a moment of exquisite happiness to her lover and then, unable to forgive her own weakness, avenges it on him and on herself. Whether this diagnosis of their relations is historically correct or not, it stands recorded for posterity in the pages of Dostoevsky's novels. The compound of hatred and love, which was the formula of Suslova's ultimate attitude to Dostoevsky, became an important element in his analysis of human psychology.

Three years elapsed before Dostoevsky embodied in fiction his experiences of this summer; but no reader of *The Gambler* will doubt its autobiographical character. Its much humiliated hero is the Dostoevsky of 1863; its heroine (her name, too, is Polina) is an idealized Suslova; the Frenchman De Grieux is a caricature of her Spanish lover, and the insistence in three different passages of the novel on the unfailing fascination for Russian girls of the polished superficial Frenchman reflects the bitterness of her treachery. It is not therefore idle or unjustifiable to invoke the testimony of *The Gambler* in analysing Dostoevsky's passion for Suslova and its influence on his later artistic production.

The keynote of Suslova's character as conceived by Dostoevsky was imperiousness. 'Apollinaria is a great egotist,' he wrote to her sister afterwards; 'her egoism and self-love are colossal. She demands everything from others, and exempts herself from the slightest obligation to others.' 'Man is by nature a despot,' says the hero of *The Gambler* to his Polina, 'and loves to torture; you love it terribly.' A dozen passages from Suslova's diary could be quoted to attest the imperious cruelty of her nature; and the critic Rozanov, whom she afterwards married, compared her to Catherine de Medici.

If Suslova interpreted love in terms of a sadistic passion for domination and cruelty, Dostoevsky on his side conceived it as a passion for suffering, an exultation in undergoing it at her hand, which must, in modern jargon, be called masochistic. But this exultation in his own suffering is compensated by a no less passionate exultation in the suffering of his mistress, even though it is suffering inflicted not by himself but by another. Both Dostoevsky, and his hero in *The Gambler*, feel themselves avenged by the torments which their successful rivals inflict on their mistresses. The passionate phrases of Dostoevsky have already been quoted:

You love him like a slave! Tell me, I must know. Isn't it true, you would follow him to the end of the world?

and beside this we may put the corresponding passage from *The Gambler*:

Miss Polina is his slave. . . . Women are like that; the proudest of them turn out to be the most abject slaves.

It may indeed be doubted whether Dostoevsky's nature remained satisfied with this self-torturing enjoyment of his tyrant's humiliation; and the disagreeable story of the tormenting of a prostitute, which appears six months later in the *Memoirs from Underground*, reads like the literary expression of another form of vicarious vengeance for the sufferings he had undergone at the hands of his late mistress.

The revelation during the past decade of the dramatic details of this previously unknown episode in Dostoevsky's career has led critics to seek in Suslova the original of nearly all the most striking female characters in his later novels. It is difficult to admit this claim. Even Nastasya Philippovna in *The Idiot* and Grushenka in *The Brothers Karamazov*, the likeliest candidates for the honour, have a nobility and a generosity which, except for the limited generosity of the purse, were not in Suslova's nature; and Nastasya Philippovna at any rate had, as we shall see, another model. The influence of Suslova in Dostoevsky's life and art is sufficiently important and well-defined to enable us to dispense with exaggeration. It was she who showed him how intimately hate may be interwoven with love. She had revealed to him the appetite for cruelty and the appetite for suffering, the sadistic and the masochistic, as alternating manifestations of the sexual impulse. He had learnt from her that self-humiliation and self-degradation are the opposite facets of imperiousness and truculence, and that diseased pride will assert itself as readily in the former as in the latter. Others besides Dostoevsky have explored the secret places of the human heart where antitheses are resolved and opposites become one. But none has probed deeper than he; and it was, unless all our evidence misleads us, his experiences with Suslova which first laid bare these dark recesses to his piercing insight.

Note to Chapter VIII

A translation of the letter from Strakhov to Tolstoy quoted in the text was published in the *Criterion* for January 1925; and many references have been made in books on Dostoevsky, both in English and in other languages, to his alleged offence with a young girl. But no serious attempt has yet been made to scrutinize the evidence relating to it.

The allegation recorded in Strakhov's letter reaches us at third hand. Excluding the hypothesis of deliberate falsification, there is a double possibility of honest error; Strakhov may have misunderstood Viskovatov, or (more probably) Viskovatov may have misunderstood Dostoevsky. If we exclude also the hypothesis of honest error, we are still faced with the question of the value of Dostoevsky's confession. A person making such a confession to a casual acquaintance (for Viskovatov was no more) is in a state of mind which can only be called pathological. Did Dostoevsky, in this pathological state, confess a disgraceful action which he had committed? or did he attribute to himself a disgraceful action which in fact he had not committed? It is impossible to answer with confidence; but the latter alternative is prima facie no more improbable than the former. So that if we accept unreservedly the accuracy of Strakhov's statement, we still cannot be sure whether we are dealing with a fact or with a case of pathological self-accusation.

But we should not accept that statement without considering other evidence. Some weight must be given to the indignant denial published by Dostoevsky's widow as soon as she heard of Strakhov's letter. She supports her denial with no serious arguments; but it is palpably sincere. Now Dostoevsky lived the last fourteen years of his life with Anna Grigorievna, falling more and more under her influence and becoming more and more dependent on her. His tendency to 'exhibitionism' and to self-humiliation is notorious; and it is doubtful whether there was much in his past, however unsavoury, which she did not learn sooner or later from his lips. At any rate, it is hard to believe that he confessed to others things which he did not confess to her. The fact that she was totally unaware of this alleged act and this alleged confession constitutes a strong testimony against their authenticity.

But there is other evidence of a more illuminating kind. Early in 1865 Dostoevsky was a frequent visitor at the house of a certain Madame Korvin-Krukovskaya, and a suitor for the hand of her elder daughter Anna, aged twenty. (This episode is described in Chapter X.) He used to relate to Anna and her sister scenes from projected novels; and on one occasion he described how one of his heroes, a respectable, middle-aged landed proprietor, was troubled by the memory that once, twenty years before, 'egged on by drunken companions, he had violated a little girl of ten'. It is perhaps shocking to conventional taste that Dostoevsky should have described such an incident from a projected novel in the presence of two young girls; but it is not merely shocking, but almost incredible, that the incident so described should have been one from his own life.

The fiction theory may be supported by the fact that Dostoevsky did subsequently make use of this *motif*. It first appears in *Crime and Punishment* written in 1866. In one of the nightmares of his last night in the hotel, Svridrigailov dreams of a little girl of five whom he puts to sleep in his bed and whose looks and gestures are already those of seduction and lust. But the character in whom he eventually develops the *motif* is Stavrogin. Not indeed in the published version of *The Devils*; for the chapters in which Stavrogin confesses the offence were rejected by Katkov as unsuitable for the respectable pages of the *Russky Vestnik*, and they remained unpublished until 1922. Stavrogin's victim was 'in her twelfth year'. A curious detail is that the supposed narrator prefaces the story of the confession with the suggestion that it may have been a piece of mere bravado on the part of Stavrogin:

I bring forward no proof, nor do I assert, that the confession is untrue, that is to say, entirely invented and fabricated. In all probability the truth may lie somewhere between.

The theme of these chapters must have been known to many of Dostoevsky's friends and acquaintances. He certainly narrated it himself in other places besides Madame Korvin-Krukovskaya's drawing-room. It is impossible to prove a negative; but there is fair support for the hypothesis that these suppressed chapters of *The Devils*, and narratives founded on them, are the basis, and the sole basis, of the story which Strakhov and others circulated at the expense of Dostoevsky's personal conduct.

CHAPTER IX

Years of Anguish

BEFORE the end of the Russian October, Dostoevsky was back in Petersburg. He joined his wife in Vladimir, and together they moved about the middle of November to Moscow. There all the winter Maria Dmitrievna lay slowly dying, passing through the familiar phases of advanced consumption—depression, irritation and wild pathetic optimism. Except for one or two brief visits to Petersburg, Dostoevsky remained at her side, at first alone, later supported by the dying woman's sister. It was not in his nature to become altogether indifferent to a woman who had once infatuated him. A better man might have been less patient; a more blameless husband might have been less tender to one who had never loved him and whom he had long ceased to love. But the capacity for sinning, and for sinning without remorse, carried with it a capacity for unstinting forgiveness of sins against himself. The wrongs she had done him, the wrongs he had done her, the defects of her character and of his, were forgotten; and there remained on his side nothing but the tenderness of pure pity, pity unspoiled by even the most fleeting sense of condescension or superior virtue.

While his mother lay on her sick-bed in Moscow, young Paul Isaev was pursuing his studies and his pleasures in Petersburg. There was nothing in his parentage to promise stability of character; and an indulgent upbringing had confirmed him in the pleasant habits of an idler and a licensed scapegrace. When at Semipalatinsk the curly-haired boy of ten had 'played the fool and refused to learn', the doting stepfather accepted it as being 'in the order of things'. It was difficult to look with equal complacency on the same behaviour at the age of sixteen. When Maria Dmitrievna was moved to Vladimir and Dostoevsky went abroad, Paul had been left in the Petersburg flat in the charge of a tutor named Rodevich; but this arrangement did not prevent the boy from devoting his time and energies to the acquisition of precocious worldly experience rather than to more orthodox forms of learning. His favourite resort was the Yusupov Garden, the Vauxhall of Petersburg, and it was not long before he had installed a prostitute in the flat. Dostoevsky's letters to his stepson from abroad during the summer and autumn, and from Moscow in the winter, alternate pathetically between expressions of affection, obviously sincere, and confidence, no less obviously misplaced, and bitter heartfelt reproaches—reproaches that he does not take the trouble to write, reproaches, when he does write, that his letters are misspelt and illiterate, reproaches for dissipation and extravagance.

It was even worse when Paul came to Moscow on a New Year visit. His behaviour to his sick mother was so intolerable that he had to be sent back post-haste to Petersburg—probably the very result which he wished to produce.

He is extraordinarily irresponsible [wrote Dostoevsky to his sister-in-law] and the whole trouble is that he does not know how to behave with a very sick woman. Of course, Maria Dmitrievna's illness has made her irritable to the last degree. . . . I am terribly grieved for her, and life for me here is no bed of roses. But I feel I am necessary to her and therefore remain.

There are few moments of Dostoevsky's life which inspire us with more unmixed sympathy than these of his faithful watch by the dying consumptive's bedside.

The spectacle of his wife's agony, the irregular courses of his stepson and, perhaps, the unquiet emotions of the past summer had reacted on Dostoevsky's diseased nervous system. During the first week in Moscow he had two epileptic fits, 'one very severe'. In a letter to his brother in February he records two more fits; he has been ill for a fortnight; his old trouble, piles, has recurred and been followed by inflammation of the bladder; he does not keep his bed, but can 'neither stand nor sit'. Towards the end of the month he risked a journey to Petersburg, but suffered agonies both there and after his return. By the end of March, the main symptoms had passed away leaving an aftermath of weariness, weakness and jagged nerves.

Financial anxieties, except when he was actually on the verge of starvation, never weighed heavily on Dostoevsky; and they probably counted for little among the other troubles of the moment. His position and outlook were indeed rather better than usual. It is true that he had no immediate source of income. But he had returned to Russia with the balance of Boborykin's 300 roubles in his pocket; and at the end of November he received 3,000 roubles as his share of the legacy of rich uncle Kumanin (the husband of his mother's sister) who, having been bedridden with paralysis for eight years, had just opportunely expired. This windfall enabled him to pay back his debt to the Fund for Needy Men of Letters, and to meet the needs of existence for a few months; and as usual when he had money, his pen remained idle. By the spring the money was gone and he was once more reduced to begging small sums from his scarcely less poverty-stricken brother Michael in Petersburg. Finally, in April, Boborykin, who must long since have despaired of getting the promised story, curtly demanded his money back. Dostoevsky tried to digest his humiliation by being rude to his creditor; but he took the only possible course of appealing to Michael, who once more advanced the necessary sum to save his brother's name from disgrace.

The winter for Michael had been one long struggle to repair the family fortunes. The *Vremya* was dead; but the authorities agreed, after a decent interval, to permit its resurrection under a new name. The first name proposed for the revived journal was *Pravda* ('Truth'); but this designation was rejected by the censorship as being dangerous and unduly tendencious. The next title suggested was colourless enough to win official approbation; the new journal was to be called the *Epocha*. But delay followed delay; and instead of the *Epocha* making its bow at the beginning of the year, nothing was published till the last week in March, when a double number for January–February was at last delivered to an attenuated number of patient subscribers.

Fyodor followed the struggles and disasters from Moscow with an agonized interest. After the closure of the *Vremya* in the preceding May, he had not written a line for seven or eight months; and when he at last sat down to write his *Memoirs from Underground* for the second number of the *Epocha*, the words did not flow easily from his pen.

I am a sick man. I am a malicious man. I am an unprepossessing man. I think I have a pain in my spleen. Of course, I really don't understand my pains, and cannot tell exactly what is aching. I am taking no remedies and never have taken remedies, though I respect medicine and doctors. ... No, I refuse remedies out of malice. You probably fail to understand that. Well, I understand. Naturally, I shall not be able to explain to you whom I am getting at with this malice of mine. ... I know better than anyone that I shall harm only myself and nobody else. But all the same, if I refuse remedies, it is out of malice. I have a pain in my spleen; well, let it ache all the worse.

These opening sentences of the *Memoirs* seem pregnant with all the concentrated bitterness of this winter of unalloyed misery: the wife coughing out her life in the next room, the mistress who had played him false in France, the spoilt and heartless stepson wasting his substance in Petersburg, the recurrent attacks of epilepsy, and the painful malady which would let him 'neither sit nor stand'. Even the season of the year played its part· in the mood of the *Memoirs*. Every Russian, and every foreigner who has lived in Russia, is familiar with the enervating effects of those last weeks of the seemingly interminable Russian winter, when frost alternates with thaw and still delays the long-awaited spring.

To-day snow is falling, [concludes the first part of the *Memoirs*] half-wet, yellow, dirty snow. Yesterday it was snowing too, and the day before it was snowing. I think it must be the wet snow which brought this story to my mind. So let it be called *A Story of the Wet Snow*.

The *Memoirs* have in recent years received an almost exaggerated amount of attention from critics and students of Dostoevsky. They fall into two parts: the first is an exposition of the philosophy of malice, the second relates an incident, or rather a series of incidents, from the life of the supposed narrator, the malicious man. The first part may seem inadequate as philosophy, the second is fiction; but in their queer way the *Memoirs* are as original as anything Dostoevsky ever wrote. Many years later the critic Rozanov, Polina Suslova's husband, drew from them the inspiration for some of the most capricious of his writings; and Rozanov declared that, if a statue of him were ever erected, he should be depicted putting out his tongue at the reader. This exactly defines the attitude of the man from 'underground'; his constant delight is to put out his tongue not merely at the reader but at the world at large and even at himself. The *Memoirs from Underground* lack the broad humanity and tolerance which inspire Dostoevsky's greater works; they reflect too much of the pain and distraction in the midst of which they were composed.

The book has, nevertheless, an important place in Dostoevsky's development; it was his first incursion into philosophy, and forms in a certain sense an introduction to the series of his great novels. In the previous year there had appeared a work whose historical significance far exceeds its small literary merit, a novel by the radical publicist Chernyshevsky entitled *What is to be Done?* It is the picture of a Utopian state of society in which perfect happiness is attained by everyone pursuing untrammelled the satisfaction of his own rational desires. In the eyes of Chernyshevsky, a pupil of J. S. Mill, reason and self-interest are the sole sanctions of morality; man commits evil actions only through misapprehension of the true nature of his interests; and intellectual enlightenment is the infallible road to right conduct. The *Memoirs from Underground* are an answer to the philosophy of Chernyshevsky. It had by this time become one of Dostoevsky's strongest convictions that human nature is not, as optimistic utilitarians of Chernyshevsky's kidney believed, fundamentally and essentially good; and that man, in virtue of one side of his nature, may desire and choose evil, knowing it to be evil. This conviction finds its first expression in these *Memoirs*:

Who was it, pray, who first declared and proclaimed that man behaves like a blackguard only because he does not know his true interests; and that if he were enlightened and had his eyes opened to his true, normal interests, he would straightway cease to behave like a blackguard and become good and honourable, inasmuch as, being enlightened and understanding his true advantages, he would see his advantage in goodness? . . . O excellent young man! O pure, innocent babe!

The whole history of mankind, argues Dostoevsky, 'from the flood to the Schleswig-Holstein period' (it was the moment of the forcible occupation of the duchies by joint Austrian and Prussian forces), is a record of human irrationality. Man may love to build, like the ant in his ant-hill; but he also loves to destroy. He loves to indulge his caprice, to sin deliberately against his own interests merely in order to free himself from the tyranny of reason, of 'twice two are four'. Such were the bold paradoxes maintained by Dostoevsky in the year 1864. The age of optimism, of faith in a morality established by science and reason, has now long passed away. The irrational chaos of human nature has become a platitude, and we no longer require a subterranean philosopher to put out his tongue at us in order to compel belief in it. It is one of the most important points on which Dostoevsky anticipated modern psychology.

The *Memoirs from Underground* mark then a stage in the growth of Dostoevsky's thought. Many critics, including most German writers on Dostoevsky and Middleton Murry in English, attach to them a profounder significance. It is suggested that Dostoevsky did in fact pass in this winter of 1863-4 through a spiritual crisis in which he rebelled against accepted morality and vindicated to his own satisfaction the right to sin; and that the *Memoirs* are the record of his own soul-shattering experience. The theory is an illustration of the danger of seeking autobiographical material in professed works of fiction. It will not hold water; and it is hard to believe that the critics who maintain it have read Dostoevsky's private letters of the period, not all of which were available when the theory was first propounded. During his sojourn in Moscow which lasted from November 1863 to the end of April 1864, Dostoevsky wrote twenty-one letters which are extant; of these, twelve are letters to his brother

Michael, from whom he concealed none of his affairs or his thoughts. They are letters of a man wrestling with every form of material difficulty and disaster, and overwhelmed with every kind of mental and physical distress; but they contain no single hint of any spiritual crisis or of any tormenting preoccupation with questions of faith and philosophy. Nor is the evidence exclusively negative. In a letter to Michael of March 26th he refers to the excisions made by the censorship in the first part of the *Memoirs*:

What swine the censors are! The passages where I railed at everything and *made show* of blaspheming [Dostoevsky's own underlining] are allowed; but the passage where I deduced from all this the necessity of belief in Christ is cut out.

These are not the words of a man who has passed through a furnace of doubt and revolt; and they prove that the demonstration of the love of evil as a fundamental element in human nature was followed in the original text (which is lost to us) by an argument of 'the necessity of belief in Christ'. In other words, far from being a cry of revolt, the book was a vindication of religious orthodoxy against the materialistic ethics of Chernyshevsky.

The second and concluding part of the *Memoirs* was published in the April number of the *Epocha*, which did not appear till the first days of June. By this time Maria Dmitrievna's sufferings were over. On April 15th Dostoevsky summoned Paul by telegraph. The boy had not been called earlier to his mother's bedside; for after the previous quarrel Maria Dmitrievna had refused to see him, and his presence would have revealed to her that she was a dying woman. He arrived in time to receive the maternal blessing, and immediately afterwards, on the evening of the 16th, the unhappy woman passed quietly away.

At the end of April or the beginning of May Dostoevsky returned to the capital. The first sequel of the return was a sort of reconciliation with Paul; the tutor Rodevich was made the scapegoat for the sins of his pupil and was dismissed with contumely. It was only after his dismissal that the credulous stepfather learnt for the first time that, during his absence abroad in the previous year, Rodevich had worn his shirts until Paul intervened to protest; had sent his pupil to newspaper offices and to pawnshops to beg the price of a meal; and had introduced prostitutes to the flat, thus tempting Paul to install a mistress for himself. There is no independent evidence of these charges made for the first time more than six months after the alleged events; and we can only consider the character of the witnesses. We know nothing to Paul's credit, and apart from this

incident nothing to the discredit of Rodevich, who afterwards made
an honourable if undistinguished career in the public service; our
sympathies lie with the latter. But Dostoevsky believed Paul; and
the relations between Rodevich and his former employer ended in
acrimonious recriminations and an undignified squabble about
books borrowed and not returned. Paul had once more established
his ascendancy over his indulgent and impressionable stepfather.

Preparations were in progress for another summer excursion
abroad when a blow fell on Dostoevsky more stunning than any
he had yet borne. On July 10th (the date is incorrectly given in the
official biography) Michael Dostoevsky died after an illness of a
few days' duration. He left a widow and four children, of whom the
eldest was twenty-one; a mistress with a child whom he had recognized as his; 300 roubles in cash, which paid for the funeral; debts
to a total of 25,000 roubles, of which 15,000 roubles were represented by bills falling due at various dates in the near future; and
a journal which was run at a loss and the issue of which was two
months in arrears. Such was the inheritance to which Fyodor,
himself shattered by ill-health and misfortune, was the sole effective
heir.

The moral obligation to support his dead brother's families,
legitimate and illegitimate, was recognized by Dostoevsky without
reserve and without hesitation. He had in times past been ready
enough to live on his brother's bounties; and he did not dream now
of contesting the right of his brother's kin to live upon him. He had
no personal debts of any magnitude; and his legal relation to the
Epocha was merely that of a contributor. The dictates of common
sense might have urged him to hand over the journal, and his
brother's other trifling assets, to his brother's creditors, and begin
with a clean sheet the task of meeting his new domestic responsibilities. But the idea of dishonouring the dead man's name by a
posthumous bankruptcy appeared intolerable; and he yielded to the
generous impulse to take upon his shoulders the whole mass of his
brother's responsibilities and obligations. The magnificent gesture
satisfied the moral sense of Dostoevsky and the family; the creditors
were perhaps less profoundly impressed; for actual payments seemed
as far off as ever.

The pressing need of the moment was as always ready money.
Not many months before his death, Michael had borrowed from
aunt Kumanin in Moscow, now a wealthy widow, the 10,000 roubles
which was his prospective share in her estate. Fyodor now obtained
a further 10,000 roubles which represented his own share; and with
this handsome legacy he was able to pay the creditors something on

account and to continue the issue of the encumbered *Epocha*. But scarcely was this difficulty solved when another presented itself. The authorities would not accept as editor of a periodical either Fyodor Dostoevsky, a former political prisoner, or Strakhov, who had earned a bad mark as the author of the article which had brought the *Vremya* to its untimely end. It became necessary to find a presentable man of straw to assume the function of editor. A suitable candidate was found in the person of one Poretzky, formerly an inconspicuous contributor to the *Vremya*; and he was at once approved. For official purposes, therefore, Poretzky became the editor of the *Epocha*; inside the office of the journal, he was a minor member of the staff. Such was one of the ridiculous results of the Russian press law.

For eight months more, amid growing financial difficulties, the *Epocha* struggled on. The May number had appeared a few days before Michael's death, two months late. The June number did not come out until the end of August; and though, by Dostoevsky's superhuman efforts, some ground was made up, the December number was not ready till well on in January of the following year. The business side of the *Epocha*, which had always been in Michael's relatively capable hands, was neglected. We hear of a cashier who had to be dismissed for dishonesty or incompetence. Irregularities in the publication of the journal were aggravated by avoidable irregularities in its despatch to subscribers; and legitimate complaints were ignored. Writers of repute held aloof where prospects of payment for contributions were so uncertain; and Dostoevsky himself, overwhelmed with editorial duties, wrote little or nothing. It is scarcely surprising that the list of subscribers for 1865 reached no more than 1,300, a number inadequate to cover expenses of publication. The fate of the *Epocha* was sealed; it struggled on through the January and February numbers and expired almost unnoticed; there was not a rouble left in the till, and the printers would no longer produce the paper on credit.

Even had the management of the *Epocha* been in more skilful hands, it is doubtful whether its fall could have been long delayed. The political firmament in Russia had seen many changes during the past five years. The *Vremya* had been initiated towards the end of that short-lived era of enthusiasm which had set in with the reign of Alexander II, when the censorship had virtually abdicated and the creation and expression of an intelligent public opinion seemed—for the first, and almost for the last, time in Russia—a worthy and not altogether quixotic cause. But the vision faded. After the political disturbances of 1862 and the Polish insurrection of 1863, reaction

G

once more asserted its power; and, in its dealings with the press and with literature, the new reaction was ten times subtler and more demoralizing than the old. Fifteen and twenty years earlier, the advisers of Nicholas I had acted on the simple and undiscriminating hypothesis that all expression of public opinion was undesirable and potentially harmful; literature was a nuisance, and journalism a positive danger. The conditions were now changed; the advisers of Alexander II recognized that the expression of opinion through the medium of the press had become an essential feature of Russian life; and they saw the possibility, indeed the necessity, of enlisting the press on the side of the government. Public opinion could no longer be dragooned out of existence; it must be instructed. There began a new policy of discrimination; certain select organs were directly or indirectly subsidized to become the mouthpieces of official opinion; the others, if unimportant, were ignored and left to starve, if important, quietly and persistently harassed through the censorship. In a period when nearly every newspaper was struggling for existence (for enormous numbers had sprung up during the early days of Alexander's reign), the financial weapon in the hands of the government was overwhelming; and it far eclipsed in importance and efficiency the direct but clumsy weapon of the censorship.

In such conditions, a journal like the *Epocha* could not long survive. It was too colourless and too conservative to appeal to the radicals; indeed, it engaged in continual polemics with the *Sovremennik*, the leading radical organ. On the other hand, it could not hope to compete with the important conservative journals which enjoyed government support and subsidies; and the records of Dostoevsky and Strakhov precluded all possibility of securing official patronage for the *Epocha*. Its literary merits were insufficient to compensate for its lack of political appeal. Except in the extreme radical camp it had few enemies; but when it ceased to exist it left no friends to regret it and no gap unfilled.

Such was the end of the *Vremya* and the *Epocha*, ephemeral journals whose only title to be remembered is that for nearly five years they absorbed the literary activity of the greatest of Russian novelists. Their failure can hardly be regarded as other than a blessing to posterity. Not many months after the demise of the *Epocha*, Dostoevsky was at work on the first draft of *Crime and Punishment*.

CHAPTER X

Interludes mainly Sentimental

THE first months of 1865, which were the last of the unhappy career of the *Epocha*, were among the most crowded and tempestuous in Dostoevsky's storm-tossed life. The official biographers, and their successors for many years, were content to confine the story of these months to the events described in the last chapter. More recently discovered evidence reveals two interludes of a sentimental character which must be fitted into these already crowded weeks, and which had perhaps a deeper influence on Dostoevsky's artistic development than his journalistic misfortunes or his financial embarrassments. The obscurity which envelops one of these episodes leaves a large field still open for conjecture. But we have no difficulty in sketching in outline the contrasted figures of the two women who played a fleeting but significant part in the novelist's life at the beginning of 1865: Anna Korvin-Krukovskaya and Martha Brown.

In the previous summer, Dostoevsky had received, at the office of the *Epocha*, a letter from an unknown correspondent in a distant province of western Russia. She described herself as a girl of twenty who, unknown to her parents, was sending him the firstfruits of her literary ambitions. He did not think much of the story. It was called *The Dream*, and narrated the untold love of a maiden for a poor young student; he afterwards described it, not unjustly, as 'extremely naïve'. But the *Epocha* in its half-bankrupt condition was hard up for contributions; and *The Dream* appeared in the August number. The following number contained another story from the same hand; its hero was a young monk hesitating between the claims of the monastery and the attractions of the world. It made an impression on Dostoevsky if on nobody else; for ideas borrowed from it occur in *The Brothers Karamazov* written fifteen years later.

The unknown young authoress, Anna Korvin Krukovskaya, was the eldest daughter of a respectable and typical Russian family, which spent ten months of the year in the isolation of a remote and inaccessible country estate, and came up to Petersburg or Moscow for a hectic six weeks in the winter season. Anna was beautiful, romantic and wilful; even at fifteen she did not like 'going for walks, or gathering mushrooms, or rowing on the lake'—the diversions regarded by her parents as suitable for her age and station in life; and even when she was allowed to ride, she insisted on dubbing her honest Russian farm-horse by the ridiculous romantic name of Freda. She dramatized herself as Edith Swan-Neck, wife of King Harold, the heroine of some forgotten English romance (for the girls had an English governess), and shed burning tears over her imaginary sufferings in this character.

Then came a time when she put aside these romantic toys. She began to take herself seriously as a politician; became, naturally, an ardent radical; and was filled with outraged sympathy for the students in Petersburg and Moscow who were being persecuted by the government as nihilists. She even declared she wished to go herself to study at the university; but this proposal received short shrift. 'If you do not understand for yourself,' said her father decisively, 'that it is the duty of every respectable daughter to live at home until she gets married, I am not going to argue with a foolish chit of a girl.' From this time forward, like Aglaya in *The Idiot*, she was definitely regarded by her parents as an 'oddity' and a 'nihilist'; and their affection was mingled with deep anxiety for the future. As Anna is the prototype of Aglaya, so her bovine, but good-hearted father and affectionate, over-anxious mother are the originals from whom Dostoevsky drew the Epanchins, Aglaya's parents. One concession to her 'modern' tastes her father condescended to make. Hitherto, the only periodicals 'solid' enough to secure admittance to this respectable household were the *Revue des Deux Mondes* and the *Athenæum*. Her father now took the altogether surprising step of agreeing to subscribe to a Russian journal. By some odd chance the *Epocha* was selected; and it was the *Epocha* which was destined to receive Anna's first literary efforts.

A new crisis occurred when a letter from Dostoevsky fell into the hands of Anna's father. It was Madame Korvin-Krukovskaya's 'name-day', and the house was full of guests—a circumstance which had prevented Anna from taking the usual precautions to secure her correspondence before the family post reached the old gentleman's hands. He had a weak heart, and in moments of excitement used to go black in the face; on this occasion he nearly died of 'shame and despair'. Shutting himself in his study, he refused to see the guests and, as soon as they had gone, Anna was sent for. The fatal letter contained a draft from Dostoevsky in payment for *The Dream*. 'From a girl,' said her father, 'who is capable, unknown to her parents, of entering into correspondence with an unknown man and of taking money from him, one may expect anything. Now you sell your stories, but the time will come when you will sell yourself.'

The tension lasted for weeks; but, like General Epanchin, Anna's father had a simple heart beneath a rugged exterior, and when Anna was at length permitted to read *The Dream* aloud in the family circle, he dissolved in tears.

The mother took her two daughters to Petersburg in the New Year of 1865. Before their departure the head of the house, half reconciled but still grumbling, had given his consent to a meeting with Dostoevsky, repeating, however, the anxious warning that their prospective acquaintance was 'a journalist, a man not of our world, and has been in prison'. On arrival in Petersburg, Anna wrote to Dostoevsky, and he called the following day. The visit took place in the chilling presence, not only of Anna's mother, but of 'two old German aunts'; and it was a complete frost. Dostoevsky at forty-three was as shy and clumsy in society as he had been twenty years before, and after a short conversation, constrained and largely monosyllabic on his side, took an awkward leave. 'Anna ran to her room,' records her sister, 'threw herself on the bed and burst into tears.' Her disappointment at the unprepossessing appearance and manners of her idol was, however, short-lived. Dostoevsky called again; this time he found the two girls alone, conversation flowed freely, and a firm friendship was established. Dostoevsky became a constant visitor, and it was soon evident that the middle-aged man had fallen in love with the sprightly girl. Anna, like Aglaya, was capricious and inclined to tease; and her suitor, unlike Myshkin, was jealous. There was a terrible scene at an evening reception when Dostoevsky, obsessed with the idea that Madame Krukovskaya was bent on marrying her daughter to a handsome young officer of German blood, broke into an incongruous and impassioned tirade against mothers who, in defiance of biblical injunctions, wished to dispose of their daughters to the highest bidder. This was evidently the origin of the famous scene in *The Idiot* where Myshkin, in the middle of a soirée at the Epanchins, delivers a similarly incongruous harangue on the inquities of the Catholic Church. The scene in *The Idiot* ends with the breaking of a priceless Chinese vase and an epileptic fit. Real life is less avowedly dramatic; Dostoevsky retired into a corner and sulked for the rest of the evening.

The incident seems to have been the turning-point in this curious courtship. Dostoevsky afterwards told his second wife, rather disingenuously, that Anna had been engaged to him, but that he had released her. It is clear from the more circumstantial memoirs of Anna's sister that there was a proposal, but no engagement. Anna, whose romantic disposition did not preclude a strong dose of common sense, told him that 'she loved and very much respected him, but not in such a way as to marry him'. They parted friends, continued to correspond and met again in later years, when both were happily married. Anna Korvin-Krukovskaya is perhaps the most gracious and charming figure which crosses the path of Dostoevsky's life. We owe to her not only the most attractive heroine in the range of Dostoevsky's creation, but a penetrating diagnosis of his character and of their short-lived friendship:

His wife [Anna told her sister] must devote herself completely to him, give up her whole life to him, think of nothing but him. And I cannot, I want to live myself. Besides, he is so nerve-ridden and exacting. He continually seems to be taking hold of me and drawing me into himself. In his presence I can never be myself.

It is a brilliant analysis by anticipation of the self-effacing role which Dostoevsky's second wife, a very different woman from the other Anna, was to play with such conspicuous success.

There is nothing particularly remarkable about Dostoevsky's fleeting passion for Anna Korvin-Krukovskaya. It is not unprecedented for a man in the forties, who has not hitherto found happiness in his dealings with women, to woo a pretty high-spirited girl less than half his age. It is not—or in the nineteenth century it was not—unusual for a girl of twenty to fall in love with her literary idol and to discover subsequently that literary fame, or even literary genius, is unsubstantial food for romantic passion. More remarkable and more characteristic, though much in it remains obscure and conjectural, was the other sentimental relation in which Dostoevsky became involved at the same time. The antecedents of Martha Brown are entirely unknown to us. She can hardly have been of other than humble origin; but she had a sufficient education to be able to write a good literary Russian. When we first make her acquaintance (the information comes from her own subsequent letters to Dostoevsky) she is wandering over Europe with one protector after another. In Austria and Prussia her companion is a Hungarian; then she falls in with some 'adventurous Englishman', with whom she travels through Switzerland, Italy, Spain and the south of France, 'now on foot, now on horseback, with never a moment's rest'. This lasted seven months; then she attached herself to a Frenchman who took her through France to Belgium and Holland. 'I have always believed,' she wrote afterwards, 'that life was made for impressions'; and her thirst for impressions must surely have been assuaged by this fantastic pilgrimage, in which she fell lower and lower in the scale of esteem and security. The flight from France to Belgium and from Belgium to Holland was due to the uninvited interest of the police in the movements of Martha's companion. What became of him we do not know; but she embarked alone at Rotterdam for England, where she arrived penniless and ignorant of the language.

It is a pity that we know so little of her stay in England. It lasted four years and was at any rate not monotonous. She slept on the Embankment, was in prison for two days for attempted suicide, and nearly got into more serious trouble for association with a band of forgers. Then she fell into the philanthropic hands of some Methodist missionaries who, by way of making an honest woman of her, married her to a sailor from Baltimore. She acquired from him the name of Brown and probably not much else. Presently she was compelled, for some reason which she does not divulge, to flee from England, and about the end of 1862 she was back in Petersburg. Her wanderings were at an end; and 'comfort' rather than 'impressions' became the ambition of her later life.

It does not seem, however, to have fallen to her lot. After some further adventures, she became the mistress of a drunken journalist named Gorsky, whose financial position was far from brilliant. He was an occasional contributor to Dostoevsky's journal, and through him Martha Brown found employment, towards the end of 1864, in the office of the *Epocha* as a translator of English. A friendship with Dostoevsky had begun to ripen when she fell ill and was removed to a hospital. There Dostoevsky visited her, gave her money and entered into a correspondence of which her letters to him alone survive. The central element of her feeling for him was gratitude. His emotion may perhaps be described as an infatuated pity; and Dostoevsky's pity easily rose, like his other emotions, to passionate heights. There is no doubt that he would have offered her marriage, as Myshkin did to Nastasya in *The Idiot*; but Russian law made divorce practically impossible except by the express consent of both parties; and she had long lost sight of her legal partner. Instead, Dostoevsky proposed that she should leave Gorsky and come to live with him. The letter in which she replies deserves quotation both for its human and for its literary interest:

In any case whether I succeed in satisfying you physically, and whether or not there is established between us that spiritual harmony on which the continuance of our friendship will depend, believe me that I shall always remain grateful to you for having found me worthy, even momentarily, or for a short time, of your friendship and affection. I swear to you that I have scarcely ever made up my mind to be so frank as I have ventured to be with you. Forgive me for my egotistical enthusiasm; but during these two brutal years since my return to Russia, so much sorrow, disgust and despair have seethed up in my soul that I am glad and happy to have met a man possessed of so much equanimity, toleration, common sense and fairness. It is at the present moment absolutely indifferent to me whether your feelings towards me continue for a long or a short period. But I swear that I prize, incomparably more highly than any material gain, the fact that you have not shunned the fallen side of my nature, that you have placed me higher than I deserve in my own estimation.

Readers of *The Idiot* will at once remember Myshkin's attitude to Nastasya ('I take you as a pure woman, not as Rogozhin's mistress'), and her answering cry:

Nobody ever spoke to me like that before. They bought and sold me, but no decent man ever wooed me.

Martha's letter seems not altogether unworthy to have inspired a great scene in one of the masterpieces of literature.

It is at this tantalizing point that Martha Brown passes from our ken. Her last letter, from which we have quoted, was written in the latter part of January 1865. Its terms, and the subsequent interruption of the correspondence, make it reasonable to infer that she went to live with Dostoevsky; and if so, she must have been living with him at the time of his abortive wooing of Anna Korvin-Krukovskaya which can be definitely placed in February and March of the same year. When nearly three years later he began to write *The Idiot*, Dostoevsky harked back to these events of the first months of 1865 and depicted his hero divided, as he had then been, between passionate admiration for a pure young girl and no less passionate pity for a fallen woman, and loving each with a love which had nothing in common with his love for the other. It would be as extravagant to suggest that Aglaya and Nastasya are mere portraits of Anna Korvin-Krukovskaya and Martha Brown, as to believe that Myshkin is a portrait of the novelist himself. Aglaya seems to reflect something of Dostoevsky's second wife, and Nastasya perhaps something of Suslova. But there is no possibility of doubt that the unique triangle round which the plot of *The Idiot* is woven faithfully reproduces these twin interludes in the strange and complicated history of Dostoevsky's heart.

The narrative of the sentimental entanglements of this stormy year is not yet complete. It would seem that the 'spiritual harmony' of which Martha spoke in her letter was never established, or was quickly broken; for the liaison was not in any event of long duration. The collapse of the *Epocha* came in April; and at the beginning of May Dostoevsky was already laying plans for another European tour. The desire to escape from the scene of his financial and sentimental embarrassments might in itself be sufficient to explain his

Wanderlust. But there were other reasons. There was the question of health, for Dostoevsky always believed, rightly or wrongly, that the European climate mitigated the frequency and severity of his epileptic seizures; there was the secret hope, perhaps unavowed even to himself, that the gaming-table would after all right his fortunes, now that any other remedy seemed hopeless; and, probably the strongest incentive of all, there was the irrational and irresistible impulse to renew the stormy but exciting relationship with the companion of his last European journey. He had not seen Polina Suslova since their parting in October 1863; but we know that letters had been exchanged between them. In the early part of 1865, and therefore presumably in the heyday of his divided affection for Anna Korvin-Krukovskaya and Martha Brown, he had written to Polina a letter, whose contents are unknown to us, but which had bitterly offended her. She did not reply herself, but asked her sister, who lived in Zurich, to write to Dostoevsky on her behalf. Nadezhda Suslova's letter has also disappeared; but we infer from Dostoevsky's answer that she reproached him with 'cynicism' and 'coarseness', and enquired 'whether other people's sufferings and tears were meat and drink to him'. The defence which he wrote to Polina has not survived, but he wrote her sister a bitter letter which has been quoted in a previous chapter.

I love her still, love her deeply, but I now wish that I did not love her. She is not worth such love.

It is unnecessary to proceed further with the analysis of Dostoevsky's state of mind in regard to his former mistress. The very existence of this correspondence is sufficient proof that her attraction for him, however bitter its fruits, had survived his more recent sentimental entanglements. But the material difficulties of a journey abroad were now infinitely greater than two years before; for apart from the cost of the journey itself it was necessary to satisfy in some measure the needs of his dead brother's family and the hungry creditors of the *Epocha*. A third application to the Fund for Needy Men of Letters was not met with the same alacrity as its predecessors; and the 600 roubles eventually given were at once extracted from him by the creditors under a threat to consign him to a debtors' prison. His name in the literary world no longer stood as high as in the years immediately following his return from Siberia. Since *Memoirs from the House of the Dead* and *The Insulted and Injured* he had written nothing but journalistic hack-work, which had not enhanced, or even maintained his reputation. The political tone of the *Epocha* had stamped him as a reactionary—or, still worse, as a false friend—

in the eyes of the radical journals which had published his earlier works. His unreliability had become notorious; and no reputable editor showed any inclination to advance him money on the intangible security of unwritten novels.

In these circumstances, it became necessary to try another expedient. The publisher Stellovsky was ready to pay 3,000 roubles, partly in cash, partly in short-term bills, for the right to issue a collected edition of Dostoevsky's writings, which was to include one new novel of specified length, to be written and delivered by November 1, 1866. Dostoevsky jumped at these terms. But Stellovsky knew his man, and demanded the insertion in the contract of penal provisions; not only did he become entitled to heavy financial compensation in the event of the new novel not being delivered in time, but if it were more than a month late, he was to receive the right to issue in book form, without further payment, all Dostoevsky's writings past or future.

The impecunious author was in no position to bargain; and the contract was signed in this form on July 2nd. If we may believe his own subsequent statement, Dostoevsky retained for his personal use only 175 roubles out of the total of 3,000 roubles; and with this modest sum he left for Wiesbaden. The contract with Stellovsky was destined in the following year to play a decisive role in his life; and there is grim humour in the reflection that, but for the anxiety to rejoin Suslova which impelled him to sign this menacing document, the circumstances would never have arisen which led to his meeting with his future second wife.

We may guess with some approach to certainty the reason which dictated the choice of Wiesbaden as his destination. It had been the scene of his first, and sole successful, appearance at the gaming-table, when he was on his way to Polina in Paris in August 1863. His subsequent visits to Baden and Homburg, had both spelt bankruptcy; and the gambler's superstition led him back to Wiesbaden. He arrived there about August 10th, and was soon joined by Suslova. They were together only a few days, and an inopportune lacuna in her diary deprives us of any intimate knowledge of their relations. By August 15th, roulette had swallowed up the total resources of both, and Dostoevsky wrote despairing letters to Herzen at Geneva and to Turgenev at Baden begging for loans. The letter to Turgenev is a blend of insincere flattery and affected dignity:

I am ashamed and disgusted to bother you with my affairs. But, except you, I have really nobody to whom to turn; besides, you are more intelligent than the others, and to apply to you is therefore easier for me morally. Of course, it is possible I shall not be able to pay you back for three weeks.

Herzen returned an evasive answer and sent nothing. Turgenev sent fifty thalers (Dostoevsky had asked for 100)—a debt which rankled, and remained unpaid, for ten years; and it was this bene- faction which enabled Suslova to escape. On August 20th or 21st she left for Paris; and her still infatuated lover tormented himself with anxiety whether, on changing trains at Cologne, she would have enough money left to buy a third-class ticket to her destination.

For more than a month longer Dostoevsky sat alone at Wiesbaden in a state of acute misery and privation. It was the lowest depth of humiliation to which he ever sank. It reached a point when the hotel would give him no more food on credit and even refused him a candle at night. In a letter to Polina he depicts himself sitting and reading all day long in order not to excite appetite by movement. He compares himself with the hero of Gogol's *Revizor*, who found himself in a similar plight until the comic mayor mistook him for an official inspector. He begged Polina for money; but she was already absorbed, as we know from her diary, in the complications of another liaison; and there is no trace of any reply from her. He wrote to Milyukov in Petersburg begging him to raise money for him; and he wrote to Katkov, the editor of the Moscow *Russky Vestnik*, offering him the novel which was eventually to become *Crime and Punishment*, and asking for an advance of 300 roubles. It seemed a forlorn hope; for he had once before offered a story to this journal and had failed to keep his promise; and the *Russky Vestnik* had now become the richest and most powerful journal in Russia. Dostoevsky scarcely hoped for success in this quarter.

Finally, he bethought himself of his old Siberian friend, Baron Wrangel, now secretary to the Russian Legation in Copenhagen, and appealed to him. They had not met since Semipalatinsk, but there had since been intermittent correspondence of an affectionate character. The faithful Baron once more proved his worth as a friend. He sent not only 100 thalers, but a pressing invitation to come to Copenhagen. Meanwhile Dostoevsky's debts had accumulated; and even the 100 thalers did not enable him to leave Wiesbaden with a clean slate. A Russian priest resident there guaranteed his hotel bill and advanced him a further sum in cash; and it was months before these debts were discharged. The 300 roubles from Katkov were, somewhat to Dostoevsky's surprise, forthcoming; but they reached Wiesbaden too late and were eventually forwarded to him in Petersburg. In the first days of October he turned his back on the humiliations of Wiesbaden and travelled to Copenhagen. By this time Suslova had left Paris for good, and was also making her way back to Russia.

Dostoevsky spent a week with Wrangel in Copenhagen, and returned directly to Petersburg by sea. Wrangel, needless to say, paid his fare; but on arrival in port there was a bill for extras, including five shillings for beer (we infer that it was an English ship); and Dostoevsky, whose pockets were empty, had no alternative but to beg that this also should be presented for payment in Copenhagen. A month elapsed before he found time to write to his late host describing the circumstances of his safe return, and regretting his present inability to repay what he owed.

This is the last appearance in Dostoevsky's biography of the generous and constant friend of the middle years of his life; and it may not be out of place to add a few further details. Wrangel continued to live mainly abroad, and Dostoevsky after his second marriage ceased to correspond with him. There was a brief meeting in Petersburg in 1873, when Dostoevsky called to discharge his financial obligations of eight years before. But the society of those who had seen and helped him in his moments of penury and humiliation had become, with advancing years, more and more painful to the now prosperous and respectable man of letters. The Baron found his old friend cold and formal; and there was no renewal of their former intimacy. After Dostoevsky's death, his literary executors asked Wrangel, through a common friend, for the letters received by him from the great novelist during the period of their friendship. The letters were sent, and most of them published, in a mutilated form and without the consent of their owner, in the official biography. The originals were not returned to him, nor did he receive any thanks. Such are the facts recorded by Wrangel, without undue bitterness, in the reminiscences of Dostoevsky which he wrote after his retirement from the diplomatic service in 1906.

We are approaching the close of an act in the tragi-comedy of Dostoevsky's life, and we have still to witness the last appearance of another of the dramatis personae, Polina Suslova herself. She had returned to Petersburg about the same time as Dostoevsky, and her diary records a meeting between them at the beginning of November. Dostoevsky offered her, probably not for the first time, his hand and heart. 'If you marry,' he added with the untimely insight which so often enabled him to perceive the depths of his own folly, 'on the third day you will begin to hate your husband and abandon him.' Her refusal was a foregone conclusion. 'You cannot forgive me,' he retorted in words which have already been quoted, 'for the fact that you once gave yourself to me, and you are taking revenge for that.' They skirmished for a few moments round that idea. 'What does it matter to me?' she said at last; 'I neither admit it, nor refuse to admit it; but you, with your superfine imagination, were bound to think that.'

Dramatically, this repartee is Polina's exit. In fact, there were a few more encounters during the winter; but in March of the following year she left Petersburg for the country, and it is probable that they never met again. They continued to correspond at intervals, even in the first year of Dostoevsky's second marriage, causing Anna Grigorievna not unnatural pangs of jealousy. Thereafter the letters, or our sources of information regarding them, cease.[1]

[1] In 1880 Suslova married a student many years younger than herself named Rozanov, who became a noted critic of Dostoevsky's writings.

BOOK THREE
YEARS OF CREATION
(1866-1871)

CHAPTER XI

Annus Mirabilis

'THE year 1866,' writes Dostoevsky's official biographer, 'had a great significance in his life. In January the novel *Crime and Punishment* began to appear in the *Russky Vestnik* and in the autumn, on October 4th, he met Anna Grigorievna Snitkina, his future wife.' *Crime and Punishment* placed him beyond dispute among the greatest Russian writers and stabilized his position in the world of literature; his second marriage stabilized his domestic life and, eventually, his financial situation. At the age of forty-five, fortune removed him— for it must be attributed to chance rather than to calculation or any act of will—from the troubled passions and the literary experiments of his earlier manhood, and made of him, by a turn of the wheel, a faithful husband and an established novelist. The period which ran from November 1865, the effective end of his romance with Suslova, to February 1867, when he married Anna Grigorievna, may justly be called the turning-point in his career.

The spiritual conception of a masterpiece is a process which defies analysis. We can trace only the external stages of the growth of *Crime and Punishment*; but we can trace these with unusual precision. In June, not long after the final suppression of the *Epocha*, Dostoevsky had bethought himself of his old publisher Kraevsky and had written to offer him a novel entitled *The Tipplers*, dealing with 'drunkenness in all its ramifications, particularly pictures of families, the bringing up of children in such surroundings, etc.' Kraevsky declined the offer; and there is no evidence that a line of *The Tipplers* was ever written. But we may assume that we have in this project the first germ of the chapters in *Crime and Punishment* relating to the Marmeladov family. Kraevsky's refusal was followed by the contract with Stellovsky; and having money in his pocket for the journey abroad, Dostoevsky ceased as usual to think of the future. Then followed the disastrous days at Wiesbaden with Suslova; and it was—as he told a correspondent in later life—at the moment when he had lost his all at roulette that the idea of *Crime and Punishment* flashed into his mind. He was haunting daily the Wiesbaden pawn-shops in the hope of extracting, in return for clothing and trinkets, a few thalers to save him from starvation. One of these flinty-hearted usurers must have sat as the first model of Raskolnikov's victim; and it was in his own heart, at this moment of direst stress, that Dostoevsky detected the potentialities of a Raskolnikov. Early in September, in his letter to Katkov offering him the novel for the *Russky Vestnik*, he gives a fairly full outline of his plot, 'the psychological *compte rendue* of a crime'. Alone in Wiesbaden, in the throes of humiliation and hunger, he began to write the famous first chapters of *Crime and Punishment*; and from the moment of his return to Petersburg and Katkov's acceptance of the novel, the work proceeded apace.

Dostoevsky was conscious of the magnitude of the occasion, and approached his task with unusual care and deliberation. He had at this period a marked preference for narrative in the first person; his last three important works, *Memoirs from the House of the Dead*, *The Insulted and Injured*, and *Memoirs from Underground*, had all followed this model. He made three attempts to tell the story of *Crime and Punishment* in the person of the hero, in the form first of a diary, then of a confession made to the court, and lastly of reminiscences, supposed to have been penned on his release from prison eight years after the murder. Then all these drafts were set aside (manuscript fragments of them survive), and he plunged into the straightforward third-person narrative in which the finished novel is cast. He worked incessantly through the winter. The first instalment was published in the issue of the *Russky Vestnik* for January 1866. About half the novel appeared in the January, February and April numbers; the balance was spread in a more leisurely fashion over the remainder of the year.

The material conditions in which the writing of *Crime and Punishment* continued in Petersburg were not much better than those in which it had begun in Wiesbaden. The total sum received for it from Katkov amounted to more than 4,000 roubles, most of which was taken by instalments in advance. But this relatively handsome remuneration made little impression on the hopeless mass of the author's indebtedness. Eager creditors awaited the instalments with outstretched hands, and a nice balance of interests was established. They threatened Dostoevsky with the debtors' prison. He replied with the counter-threat that, once in prison, he would be able to write no more and their last hope of recovering any part of their claims would disappear; for assets, other than his genius, he had none. So long as he paid them enough to make it worth their while, they could be counted on to leave him at liberty; but should the payments become too small or too infrequent, they might at any moment prefer vengeance to profit. Nor were the creditors the only claimants; for throughout the period under review he continued to support to the limit of his capacity not only Paul Isaev (who lived with him), but the two families, legitimate and illegitimate, of Michael, and his worthless younger brother Nicholas, a helpless but amiable drunkard who may have served in part as a model for Marmeladov. The sombre background of *Crime and Punishment* is but a dim reflection of the black gloom of despair in which its tortured pages were written.

In the summer, Dostoevsky fled from Petersburg to escape the attentions of his creditors and work uninterruptedly at his novel. Funds did not permit of another foreign excursion, and he went to Moscow. But the heat and the loneliness (his Moscow friends being all in the country) soon drove him from the town; and he moved out to Lublino, in the woods a few miles from the city, where his sister Vera and her family had a summer cottage. Here he passed more than two months. It was many years since Dostoevsky had found himself in the midst of a peaceful family circle; and those short summer weeks of repose and simple pleasures made a vivid impression on the passionate and overstrung writer. Tradition records that Vera's family and their friends served Dostoevsky as models for some of the incidental characters in *The Eternal Husband* written two years later, and a passage in that novel seems to describe his own emotional reaction to the pleasant and unwonted domestic scene:

Here in this family he was simple, naïve, good-humoured, nursed the children, never put on airs, was conscious of and confessed his failings. He often vowed to the Pogoreltsevs that, when he had lived a little longer in the world, he would settle down with them for good and live with them without any further separation. He often turned over this idea in his mind quite seriously.

It was an oasis of calm in his tormented life; and the idyllic mood of this summer proved a decisive factor in turning his erratic brain once more to dreams of domestic felicity.

It was now two years since Maria Dmitrievna's death; and the collapse of his romance with Anna Korvin-Krukovskaya, and the final refusal of Suslova, had not destroyed his hopes of finding happiness in a second marriage. Among the summer visitors at Lublino was Elena Pavlovna Ivanova, Vera's sister-in-law. Her husband, the brother of Vera's husband, was a chronic invalid whose death was confidently anticipated; and Vera suggested to her brother that he should marry Elena as soon as she became a widow. One day—so Dostoevsky afterwards told his wife—he asked Elena whether she would marry him if she were free; she returned an indefinite answer—she could indeed scarcely have done more. Dostoevsky left Lublino at the end of the summer, and married six months later; and Elena Pavlovna's husband lingered on for another three years.

The writing of *Crime and Punishment* continued through these summer days; but Dostoevsky had not yet begun to think seriously of the other novel which, under the contract of the previous year with Stellovsky, must be delivered before November 1st. By July the plan had taken shape in his mind of 'a quite satisfactory novelette which will even contain vestiges of characters'; such is the author's anticipatory, and not unjust, description of *The Gambler*. It was the story which he had originally thought of, and offered to Boborykin, during his journey with Suslova three years before. But the lifelong habit of procrastination was too strong; and he returned to Petersburg in September without a line written. The position was now desperate. If the novel were not completed by November 1st, there was a heavy financial penalty; if it were not delivered by December 1st, Stellovsky obtained the right to issue in book form all Dostoevsky's novels, present and future, without remuneration; and there seemed every chance that Stellovsky would be in a position to exact his pound of flesh. Three friends—Maikov, Milyukov and Dolgomostiev—suggested that they should work in sections on the plan prepared by Dostoevsky, and that the latter should sign his name to the composite work; but the expedient was rejected as impracticable or dishonourable. Then Milyukov proposed that the latest resources of contemporary science should be invoked, and the novel dictated to a stenographer; and, having obtained Dostoevsky's despairing and half-hearted consent, he applied to one Olkhin, who held classes in the new-fangled device of stenography, to furnish what was required.

The sequel is one of the most famous stories in Russian literary history, and may be read at length in the *Memoirs* of the lady who became Dostoevsky's second wife. From this point in his life, these *Memoirs* (together with the same lady's *Diary*, of which a short fragment alone remains) supplant the official biography as the basis of our narrative; and it is therefore the moment to make some acquaintance with their style and character. The story of the meeting with Dostoevsky begins as follows:

On October 3rd, 1866, about seven o'clock in the evening, I arrived as usual at the Sixth Boys' Gymnasium, where the teacher of stenography, P. M. Olkhin, gave his course. The lesson had not yet begun; they were awaiting the late-comers. I sat down in my usual place, and had only just begun to open my notebooks when Olkhin came up, and, sitting beside me on the bench, said:

'Anna Grigorievna, would you not like to take some stenographic work? I have been asked to find a stenographer and I thought that perhaps you would be prepared to take the work.'

'I should very much like to,' I replied; 'I have long dreamed of being able to work. My only doubt is whether I know stenography well enough to undertake a responsible post.'

Olkhin reassured me. He thought the proposed work would not require a greater speed than I was capable of. . . .

If it is a function of art to express character, it seems impossible to refuse the name of art to these *Memoirs*. The passage quoted is one of many which display with equal vividness the personality of the writer. It is not a bad style; for it is unpretentious and seldom strikes a false note. It is not a good style; for it lacks any sense of proportion or discrimination, any power to reject the trivial or throw the essential into relief. The opening passage is admirably expressive of the meticulous love of detail which caused the writer to record in her *Diary* the price of every trifling commodity in every town of Europe in which she stayed; of the clear-headed though modest estimate which she always formed of her own capacities; and of the cool self-possession with which she was always capable of defining her desires.

On the following day, October 4th, Anna Grigorievna Snitkina appeared by appointment in Dostoevsky's apartment and, having undergone the inquisitive scrutiny of Paul Isaev, dishevelled and half dressed, was confronted by the great man himself. The impression of the first two interviews was unfavourable, almost painful. Though friendly and polite, Dostoevsky was embarrassingly nervous; several times asked her name and immediately forgot it; smoked cigarette after cigarette; walked up and down the room as if distracted; seemed at times unaware of her presence; and was quite unable to dictate at his ease. She could, however, look back on her own behaviour with conscious pride:

I had long determined that, in case I should take stenographic work in private houses, I should from the first moment put my relations with persons with whom I was only slightly acquainted on a business footing, avoiding any familiarity, so that no one might have the idea of speaking to me in a free or forward way. I did not, I think, smile once in speaking with Fyodor Mikhailovich, and my seriousness pleased him much. He confessed afterwards that he was pleasantly struck by my knowledge of correct behaviour.

The man of forty-five was nervous and ill-balanced, the girl of twenty calm and self-possessed; but both were impressionable. It was not long before Dostoevsky felt the characteristic Russian need of pouring out his soul to his companion. Day after day, in the intervals of dictation, he told her stories of his life and misfortunes; of his eight months' imprisonment in the Peter-and-Paul fortress; of the sham execution on the Semenevsky Square; of his ten years' exile in Siberia; of his first marriage to a consumptive wife; of his poverty and his debts; of how he had pawned his Chinese vase and his silver spoons and forks; of how he had wooed and lost Anna Korvin-Krukovskaya. The listener became more and more sympathetic and attentive. In reply to a question, she recommended matrimony and assured him it was not too late for him to marry. He inquired why she had not married; and she explained that neither of her two admirers (who were, so far as we know, purely imaginary) had, for all their excellent qualities, yet touched her heart.

The story proceeds with monotony and precision to its pre-destined goal. The habit of dictation, the soothing influence of his methodical young collaborator, and the growing certainty that *The Gambler* would be finished in time, worked a miraculous change in the nerves and demeanour of the novelist. It was many years afterwards, at the beginning of the second decade of the present century, that the heroine of the story wrote up her *Memoirs* from old short-hand notes; and the sentimental flavour of her narrative smacks of the naïve literary artifices of popular fiction. But the main facts are straightforward and undisputed: on October 30th, which was Dostoevsky's forty-fifth birthday, the literary task was accomplished, and the last line of *The Gambler* dictated, a novel of some 40,000 words having been written in twenty-six days; on November 3rd, Dostoevsky paid his first visit to Anna Grigorievna and her mother (who was of Swedish origin, and a widow); and on the 8th, with becoming trepidation, he proposed marriage and was accepted.

The remainder of the year was occupied with the transports of courtship and the dictation of the last two parts of *Crime and Punishment* for the November and December numbers of the *Russky Vestnik*. At Christmas Dostoevsky went to Moscow. The main motive of the journey was, as usual, financial. He told Katkov of his approaching marriage and, well aware how much *Crime and Punishment* had enhanced his value as a contributor, demanded 2,000 roubles as an advance against his next novel. The request was granted; he returned to Petersburg with 700 roubles in his pocket, and the balance followed by instalments. But there were creditors to be satisfied, and the family needs to be supplied; and lest the whole sum should slip through Dostoevsky's unretentive fingers, 500 roubles were handed to Anna for safe custody to defray expenses of the marriage. Thanks to this wise precaution, the wedding took place in the presence of a few friends on February 15th, 1867.

If it be true that every marriage has its critical period, the crisis in the affairs of the new Dostoevsky *ménage* arrived at an unusually early stage, and for the most commonplace of reasons. The marriage of a young girl to a middle-aged widower is ordinarily regarded with disfavour by the relatives of both. Madame Snitkina, indeed, appears to have accepted with extraordinary equanimity a son-in-law who had neither youth nor health, nor fortune to recommend him. The Snitkins were, we gather, socially insignificant; and both mother and daughter were equally impressed by the literary fame and affable demeanour of the bridegroom; it seemed impossible that one so great could be so gentle, so helpless. The relatives of Dostoevsky, on the other hand, had every ground for displeasure. Besides the arguments which could be openly urged against so unsuitable a match, there were more weighty considerations of self-interest. Dostoevsky had too often been a parasite himself not to recognize the rights of parasites; and so long as he could work with his pen, and no extraneous power intervened, Paul, Emilia Fyodorovna (the widow of Michael Dostoevsky) and Nicholas could all rely on receiving their pittance from his encumbered earnings. It was, of course, regrettable that he should from time to time squander his substance on a Suslova or a Martha Brown; but such women were passing phases, and did not claim to manage or dispose of his entire resources. A wife was a different matter; at best, she could hardly be other than a formidable natural rival of her husband's other dependents. Still, Anna Grigorievna was young and untried; and every known engine of diplomacy must be brought into action in order to prevent the management of Dostoevsky's affairs from passing into her hands.

The newly wedded pair had taken a new apartment which they were to share with Paul. The old flat, not five minutes distant, was handed over to Emilia Fyodorovna and her family, Dostoevsky still paying the rent. The skirmishing began within a week of the wedding. The tactics were, without resorting to open hostilities, to discredit Anna in the eyes of her husband, and to prevent her from gaining his confidence; and in view of his well-known instability and impatience, the policy seemed to offer every prospect of success. Paul, if we may believe the wife's *Memoirs*, resorted to such pranks as hiding all the matches and attributing the deficiency to her inefficient housekeeping. Emilia Fyodorovna was less crude and less dishonest—for she was at heart not a bad woman and was greedy for her children rather than for herself; but she was for that reason all the more dangerous. She was critically patronizing; continually offered her help and her advice; and with feline cunning encouraged her older children to frequent the flat at every possible moment on the ground that the younger generation were more suitable and attractive company for the young bride than her husband could possibly provide. The forces of disunion were thus effectively set in motion. Dostoevsky listened to the complaints of Paul and the criticisms of Emilia Fyodorovna with the helpless benevolence of one anxious to believe everybody, and yet think evil of none. He begged his sister-in-law and his stepson to be patient with his inexperienced wife; and he begged his wife to be patient with his stepson and his sister-in-law. He was as incapable of defending her as he had always been of defending himself; and he wounded her young pride by his apparent unwillingness to take her part. With naïve modesty he accepted the view that his nephews and nieces were more interesting companions for his wife than he himself could be. He seconded Emilia Fyodorovna's efforts by encouraging their constant presence; and once more he wounded his wife's heart by appearing not to desire that exclusive attention which her romantic nature longed to bestow on him. She had never heard the maxim of the admirable and experienced Madame Roland that 'marriage is an association of two individuals in which the woman charges herself with the happiness of both'; and she did not yet realize that she must guide and control the emotional reactions, as well as the financial affairs, of her childlike husband. It was a position which she had not foreseen; and she took refuge in bewildered tears.

It was not long before other disagreeable realities of her married life forced themselves on her notice. They were supping one evening at her sister's, when Dostoevsky, worn out by the excitement of the last few weeks, had two successive epileptic fits, the second so severe that 'for two hours after regaining consciousness he cried out with pain'. In Moscow, where her husband's sisters, once the ice was broken, received her more cordially than his relatives in Petersburg, she had an experience of a different kind. A young man whom she met at Vera's had been obviously attracted by her, and they had chatted and laughed together; and on their way back to the hotel Dostoevsky had one of those violent attacks of jealousy which represented the uncontrolled animal side of his nature.

His shrieks and the awful expression on his face terrified me [records Anna in the *Memoirs*]. I began to think that Fyodor was going to have an epileptic fit or that he would kill me. I could not bear it and burst into tears.

The tears were the necessary solvent; Dostoevsky's rage melted in an agony of remorse; and the reconciliation was effected in a moment. The concluding reflection in the *Memoirs* is one more tribute to the matter-of-fact outlook and unemotional common sense which always had the last word in the debates of Anna's heart:

The impression of the night scene was printed for ever on my heart. It made me reflect on our future relations. I understood what profound suffering jealousy caused Fyodor, and promised myself to spare him such cruel impressions.

She had in after years many opportunities of putting this precept into practice. Explosions of jealousy on the flimsiest of pretexts continued throughout their married life; and she records in her *Memoirs* a scene where, not many months before his death, he burst into a storm of rage and reproaches over some polite attentions which she had paid to the old friend and comrade of his youth Grigorovich, a man like himself in the late fifties. But jealousy is a vice which flatters more often than it repels; and the hasty remorse which always followed on Fyodor's side made these helpless childlike outbursts a cementing rather than an estranging influence in their domestic relations.

The practical fruits of the ten days' visit to Moscow were a further 1,000 roubles from Katkov; and it seems to have been in Moscow that Anna conceived the plan of rescuing her husband from his domestic environment by a journey abroad. Her cautious and secretive nature would have led her to conceal the plan until it was thoroughly matured; but on the very day of their return to Petersburg, Fyodor blurted it out at a family council. He proposed to give Emilia Fyodorovna 200 roubles, Paul 100 and Nicholas 100, leaving 100 for immediate household expenses and 500 for the projected trip. The battle was joined; Emilia Fyodorovna roundly declared that she could not be left with less than 500 roubles for the needs of the family; Paul demanded 200; and a forgotten creditor, having got wind of this momentary affluence, presented an overdue bill of exchange for 500 roubles. Dostoevsky could refuse nothing and suggest nothing; in such cases it only remained to hold up one's hands and attribute one's disappointments to fate.

But the clear-headed and strong-willed girl had made up her mind that nothing less was at stake than the ruin or salvation of the hazardous marriage on which she had embarked. Her modest dowry had been spent on a piano and modest items of furniture and jewellery. With the consent of her mother she decided to pawn everything she possessed and take her husband abroad on the proceeds. It was Palm Sunday when they returned from Moscow; on Monday Fyodor had capitulated before the demands of the family; on Tuesday Anna announced her plans to him, overcame his hesitations, and led him unresisting to discharge the necessary passport formalities; on the following day, a valuer came to appraise Anna's effects and to arrange for their removal; and on that evening the astonished relatives learned for the first time that the departure of the pair for Europe was imminent. They had little time to discover objections; their claims for two days earlier had been met in full; and they had at least the consolation of reflecting that the expenses of the enterprise were being met from a purse whose strings would not in any event have opened for them. At 2 p.m. on Good Friday, Fyodor and Anna took their places in the Berlin train, refugees not —as the older biographies tell us—from the fury of his creditors, but from the more insidious importunities of his relatives They did not return to Petersburg for four years and three months. Anna's victory was sudden, complete and final.

CHAPTER XII

First Months Abroad

THE Dostoevskys left Petersburg on April 14th. They halted by the way at Vilna and at Berlin ('where I stayed only one day, where the stupid Germans got on my nerves to the point of exasperation, and where I had a Russian bath', as Dostoevsky afterwards wrote to his friend Apollon Maikov), and established themselves in furnished lodgings at Dresden. Here they remained for some two and a half months. Then after a stay of seven weeks in Baden they arrived towards the end of August in Geneva, which was to be their resting-place for the winter. The period from their departure from Petersburg to their arrival in Geneva is covered by Anna Grigorievna's *Diary*, which must, in point of detail, be one of the completest ever written; for the events of four months occupy nearly four hundred closely printed pages. The *Diary* was kept in shorthand and first transcribed by its writer many years later. It is therefore not quite an original document; for we cannot be sure that it was reproduced exactly as it was written. It is possible that expressions of irritation may have been toned down or removed. But on the whole it displays remarkable frankness and there are no passages where we can detect alteration with certainty. Perhaps we may assume that the untiring hand which, thirty years afterwards, could copy out, page after page, the catalogue of daily hours of waking, rising and sleeping, of casual encounters with total strangers, of the prices paid for rolls in Vilna, for a particular kind of chocolate *éclair* in Dresden, or for mending a pair of boots in Baden, would scarcely have dared to vary the sacrosanct record of those first months of married life.

The *Diary* is full of the pettiest detail, and contains much that is merely dull and stupid. It affords us, nevertheless, invaluable assistance in tracing the early stages of this unpromising, but altogether successful marriage. The character of Dostoevsky was essentially loving and lovable; weak, impetuous as any child, driven hither and thither by every passing breeze, he was yet neither vain and self-indulgent like Turgenev, nor arrogant and self-sufficing like Tolstoy. His helplessness attracted; and there was no hard inner core of selfishness to repel on closer acquaintance. He often acted, but never felt, selfishly; and it cannot be too often emphasized that, in Russian eyes, action is of small importance in comparison with feeling. More than twenty years her senior, he had a vein of boyish impulsiveness which both shocked and attracted Anna's staid matter-of-fact nature. A scene in the Dresden Gallery will illustrate this little-known lighter side of Dostoevsky's character.

Fyodor can never see properly the Sistine Madonna, because he is short-sighted and has no glasses. To-day he had the idea of standing on a chair in front of the Madonna in order to study it more closely. . . . My attempts to dissuade him had no effect. An attendant of the gallery came up to him and said that it was forbidden. No sooner had the attendant gone out of the room than Fyodor said he did not care if they turned him out, but he would certainly get on the chair again to look at the Madonna, and if I didn't like it, I had better go into the next room. . . . I did so, not wishing to irritate him; and in a few minutes he joined me, saying that he had seen the Madonna.

But even when we have made the most generous allowance for Dostoevsky's virtues, we must still attribute to Anna rather than to him the brilliant success of their marriage. His role in the building of their domestic happiness was passive. His qualities made the task a possible one; but it was she who performed it. There could be no equality in so incongruous a marriage; but the effect of equality was achieved by a balance of extremes. Her attitude was divided between girlish worship of her husband's genius (not the less fervent for her utter incapacity to appreciate or understand it) and maternal solicitude for the always helpless and often wayward child. His attitude was compounded half of wondering gratitude to the 'angel-preserver sent to him from God', the first woman who had made his welfare the unique preoccupation of her existence, and half of affectionate paternal amusement at the childish pleasures, and even more comical seriousness, of this slip of a girl of twenty, who had developed 'a decided taste for antiquities' and would fill pages of her shorthand notebooks with descriptions of 'some stupid German Rathaus'. And to crown the whole, both found in marriage the complete physical satisfaction which radiates from the modest pages of her Diary and of his letters to her, and which should be taken into account by those critics who seek to depict Dostoevsky as sexually abnormal.

The clue to Anna Grigorievna's character, which thus strangely combined the qualities of youth and maturity, lies in her natural possessiveness; she was utterly possessive—possessive at once with the naïve romantic exigence of youth and with the hard concentration of middle age. We have seen how systematically she afterwards destroyed every record which might have thrown light on her husband's first marriage; and her daughter, following the same tradition, relentlessly vilifies, in her biography of her father, not only the two other women who had played known roles in his life, but practically every member of his family. During the first period of their sojourn abroad, Anna had much to suffer; but the only moments when she allows herself to despair, or seriously doubts her capacity to retain his affection, are when she reflects on the day of their future return to the bosom of his family:

One thing alone always terrifies me—that once we arrive in Petersburg all this will end. ... It is painful for me to think that when we get to Petersburg, the everlasting quarrels with Paul will begin again, that he will insult me and Fyodor will notice nothing and won't defend me.

Or again:

Now he is alone with me, but there we shall be surrounded by a host of people all hostile to me. Now Fyodor doesn't get angry, is seldom irritated; but then Paul will be there every day to drive him mad. Those endless quarrels with him will begin again. I am more sick than I can say of all those squabbles, and however much I may dream of seeing mother again, I simply get cold shudders down my back to think of our returning to Petersburg and of all this being changed.

The first two months of her marriage had made an indelible impression; and her almost fierce determination to dominate and monopolize her husband was the corollary of those cruel and unforgotten attempts on the part of his relatives to take him from her.

The theory of Anna's possessiveness may seem at first sight to be belied by her passivity in the face of Dostoevsky's renewed correspondence with Suslova. She knew of this episode in her husband's past; had she learnt of it from no other source, his relatives would probably not have failed to enlighten her. She seems to have known enough to guess at once the origin of certain letters which he received at Dresden and did not show to her. She succeeded in reading two of them by stealth and boiled with private rage; but she said nothing. She rightly judged that Fyodor's own embarrassed conscience would prove more effective than reproaches on her part. She elaborately explained, when the occasion offered, that she had no desire to intercept his correspondence. The shot told.

He came up to me [she writes] with his face trembling and began to say that he understood my words, that it was a hint, that he retained the right to correspond with anyone he pleased, and that he had relationships with which I dared not interfere.

Then Anna tried a counterstroke. She made a mystery of one of her letters, declared it to be from 'a certain lady' and, basing herself on his principles, refused further information; in short, by judicious hints, she made her husband believe that Suslova had written to *her*. It seems clear that the supposed letter was a myth, though her *Diary* is not quite explicit on the point; but later we find that she has actually taken steps to discover Suslova's address. Whether she ever wrote to Suslova, or Suslova to her, is a question which must still continue to excite our curiosity; but there is no doubt that Dostoevsky believed, at any rate at the time, that letters had passed between them, and that this incident inspired the famous correspondence between Aglaya and Nastasya Philippovna in *The Idiot*. Of the correspondence between Dostoevsky and Suslova we hear no more after the summer of 1867. The wife's devotion and patience had won the day.

The most serious menace to their married happiness came, not from the dying embers of Dostoevsky's infatuation for his ex-mistress, but from the still active volcano of his passion for roulette. The period of his passion for the gaming-table had hitherto coincided with the period of his most complete abandonment to sexual infatuation. It had borne the same character of unrestrained violence, and the fury of one passion had seemed to minister to the flames of the other. On his way to join Suslova in Paris in 1863 he had stopped for four days at Wiesbaden 'and, of course, played at roulette'. Beginner's luck had brought him in a few hours 10,000 francs, of which half were lost again before he could tear himself away. The infatuation was already complete; and like other infatuated men he soon discovered a rational basis for his passion.

Some hundreds of people gamble here [he wrote to his sister-in-law, Varvara Konstant] and, on my word, I have not seen more than two who knew how to play. The rest lose their last farthing because they do not know how to play. There was one Frenchman playing there, and an English lord; they knew how to play and did not lose—on the contrary, they nearly broke the bank. Please don't think that I am swaggering, out of delight that I did not lose, when I say that I know the secret of how to win and avoid loss. I really do know the secret. It is extremely stupid and simple, and is to restrain oneself at every moment, whatever phases the game goes through, and not get excited. That is the whole thing; and if you stick to that, it is simply impossible to lose, and you are bound to win. That isn't the difficulty. The difficulty is when a man knows the secret, will he be in a state to take advantage of it? With a forehead five spans high and the most iron character, you will still break down. Even the philosopher Strakhov would have broken down!

Thus early did Dostoevsky acquire the fatal conviction that the strait path to riches—infallible if only a man could keep his head and follow it—lay across the pleasant green pastures of the roulette table; and having once acquired the conviction, he retained it firmly for the rest of his life, undeterred by the most discouraging experiences of failure. He persuaded himself that all was well so long as he followed his 'system', and that his losses were due only to the moments of weakness in which he allowed himself to be carried away.

I will stick to my opinion [writes the hero of *A Raw Youth*] that at games of chance, if only a man could maintain perfect composure, and therewith the full possession of his understanding and powers of calculation, he *must* overcome the stupidity of blind chance and win his game.

And long after his death his dutiful widow solemnly recorded in her *Memoirs*:

All Fyodor's arguments about the possibility of winning at roulette by his system of play were perfectly accurate, and might have been crowned with complete success; but only on the condition that it was worked by some cold-blooded Englishman or German and not by a man like my husband, nervous, easily carried away, and prone in everything to rush to extremes.

The notion that he was pitting himself, in a trial of skill and endurance, against the blind forces of chance formed one of the irresistible attractions of Dostoevsky's gambling mania.

From the success of his first essay at the Wiesbaden roulette table, he went on to the humiliation of Paris where he found that his mistress had rejected him for a new lover. Leaving Paris with her on the 'brother-and-sister' excursion to Italy, he paused at Baden and sought consolation for defeat in his other new-found passion. The impulse cost him 3,000 francs; and with empty pockets the pair moved on to Switzerland and Italy. The tour completed, he made straight, as we have seen, for Homburg, and gambled away there the slender resources which should have paid his journey back to Petersburg. So ended the first round of his struggle with the demon of chance. Then came an interval of nearly two years spent in Russia—a period of enforced separation both from Suslova and from the gaming-table. In August 1865 he was back again with her at Wiesbaden, playing more furiously than ever, and seeking once more in the reckless self-abandonment of roulette relief from the stalemate of this inconclusive liaison.

The explanation which Dostoevsky gave to himself and to others of this wild infatuation was the desire to redeem his financial fortunes. The hero of *The Gambler* dwells on the fundamental antipathy of the true Russian for 'the German method of amassing riches by honest toil', and suggests that, since the Russian needs riches as much as anyone, he has no other resource than the roulette table in order to gain them; and the same character, whose utterances are autobiographical in almost every detail, expresses his contempt for those who play for mere amusement without caring, or professing to care, whether they win or lose. But this rational explanation does not contain, at any rate in the case of so purely irrational a being as Dostoevsky, more than a fraction of the truth. It would scarcely be more misleading to explain the phenomenon of falling in love as a rational desire for the blessings of domestic life. The principal, though often subconscious, impulse which drove Dostoevsky to the gaming rooms was not a reasoned calculation of financial profit, but a craving for strong emotions and abnormal excitements, perhaps even the longing, which he often attributes to his characters, to plumb the depths of moral degradation.

My nerves are distraught [he wrote afterwards to his wife in the midst of one of these gambling bouts], and I am tired out, though I am sitting all the while in one spot; but all the same I am in fine fettle. I am in a wrought up and excited state; and my nature demands this from time to time.

It was a sort of intoxication. Anna rarely had the opportunity of seeing him while he was actually engaged in play; but she describes him, on one such occasion, as 'simply terrible to look at, all red and with red eyes, like a drunkard'. He found in his infatuation for roulette the same reckless, exciting experiment, the same turbulent emotions, the same moments of exquisite triumph and no less exquisite humiliation, which had formed the staple of his passion for his mistress.

The Wiesbaden visit of 1865, which ended in weeks of literal starvation and in the conception of *Crime and Punishment*, was Dostoevsky's last excursion abroad up to the time of his second marriage. It might reasonably have been anticipated that the gambling fever, hitherto associated with the excitements and disappointments of the liaison with Suslova, would be dissipated by the more orderly and disciplined course of marital happiness. Such anticipations, if they entered into Anna's mind, were not fulfilled. A fortnight of peaceful inactivity at Dresden exhausted Dostoevsky's taste for domestic tranquillity. He was engaged for the moment on no literary work except an article on Belinsky, which he found both difficult and tedious. Symptoms of the old restlessness declared themselves; and after two or three days of uncontrolled irritability he left his young wife alone in their Dresden lodgings and took train for Homburg. Her *Diary* and his letters give us a complete picture of the episode. Anna's attitude to the new infatuation was the same as her attitude to Suslova. She did not permit herself to criticize; she ignored where she could, and where she could not ignore she tolerated. She sat helpless and almost hopeless in Dresden, half longing for and half dreading the arrival of the letter which inevitably, sooner or later, would announce that he had gambled away all the money that he had taken away with him and all that he could obtain by pawning his watch and the less necessary items of his clothing. It was about a week after her husband's departure. The expected letter arrived; and after many troubles (which she records at inordinate length) in purchasing a banker's order payable at Homburg, she sent the money. Nor did this bring back her wandering husband; for on the following day she received from him another letter.

I had the presentiment [she writes] that I should get more unpleasant news. I went very slowly to the post office, got the letter, read it through and saw that Fyodor very much wanted to stay and try his luck again. I wrote back to him at once that he should stay if he wanted to. . . . What can I do? I suppose it is fated to be. But how much better if he could get this fatal idea of winning out of his head.

We are left to admire or to deplore this amazing tolerance, and to speculate how much of it must be attributed to youth and shyness, and how much to mature and far-sighted calculation. To slacken the line in these early days was perhaps the only means of eventually landing the fish in her basket.

The money was lost; and only the despatch of another banker's order enabled Dostoevsky to return from Homburg to Dresden. Instead of the reproaches which he deserved and had anticipated, he found only pity and 'exhortations not to despair'. There were days of complete hopelessness and abject self-reproach. Then taking heart again, he began to persuade himself that it was only his haste and his anxieties for his absent wife which had spoiled his game in Homburg, and deprived him of the composure and clear-headed-ness which would infallibly have brought him success. If only he could take Anna with him and play undistracted by other cares, he would certainly redeem his fortunes. Anna shared the illusion, or pretended to share it. For it was necessary at all costs to revive his drooping spirits; and his financial position was so desperate that only success at the green table seemed to hold out any prospect of a cure. It was the drug which deadened his senses to the acute misery of his situation and kept his mind still alive and active; to renounce

I

roulette was to renounce the one remaining hope without which existence became morally impossible.

When therefore they at length left Dresden for Switzerland at the end of June, they decided to spend a fortnight *en route* at Baden and once more try their luck on the tables. The fortnight prolonged itself to seven weeks. 'It was a sort of nightmare,' wrote Anna afterwards in her *Memoirs*, 'which held my husband in its grip and would not release him from its iron chains.' It is a story of almost continual losses; for Dostoevsky would seldom leave the table so long as he had any money left in his pocket. His occasional winnings went to redeem clothing and jewellery which had found their way to the pawnshops a few days before, and which were destined, a few days later, to suffer once more the same indignity. At these rare moments of success, he would come home to Anna laden with flowers and fruit and with those little gifts which he always delighted to bring her in times of affluence, and which endeared him to her simple heart. But it was, still more, the moments of failure and mutual despair which sealed the union of hearts and made him, in all matters save that of this overwhelming passion, her willing and obedient slave; she threw her whole being into his successive states of emotion—his hopes and excitements, his elation and his despair. She faithfully records in her *Diary* the trying symptoms of early pregnancy; but she does not complain that he thought always of his own troubles, never of hers. The monotonous but fascinating details of this queer relationship must be studied by the curious in the pages of the *Diary* itself. But the following quotation may serve to illustrate the side of Dostoevsky's nature from which he had drawn the character of Marmeladov:

At 11 o'clock Fyodor came in. He was terribly distracted. He said that he had terribly wanted to come to me these last three hours, but did not know what to do. He said that he had won, in addition to what he had, as much as 400 francs, that he wanted to win more, that he was anxious and had tormented himself about me, but that he could not tear himself from the game. I began to console him, and assured him that all this was nothing, a mere trifle, and that nothing had happened to me in his absence, if only he could be calm and not torment himself. He begged me not to deprive him of the possibility of reproaching himself for his insane weakness, begged my pardon for heaven knows what, said that he was unworthy of me, that he was a knave and I an angel, and so forth— impossible things. I could scarcely quiet him.

Another passage gives a painfully typical view of this phase of their relationship:

More than half an hour passed before he returned, having of course lost everything, and said he wanted to talk to me. He took me on his knee and began to beseech me to give him another five louis. He said he knew that that would leave us only seven louis and that we should have nothing to live on; he knew everything, but what was to be done? In no other way could he calm himself; he said that if I did not give him the money he would go off his head. He was in a fearful state of excitement. ... Of course, I could not stand out against his arguments and gave him the five louis. He said that, though I now acted in this way, some day when I was older I should not allow him to carry on as he was doing; I should say that I had been stupid, and that if my husband played the fool, I ought not to allow it, and that it was a wife's duty to stop him. He said that the way I was now acting was far better, that I was subduing him by my goodness and uncomplainingness, and that he loved me more and more.

By a miracle the five louis, after many fluctuations, were still intact, when Anna eventually dragged her husband from the tables.

We were so rejoiced [concludes the entry for the day] that we laughed merrily all the way home, and Fyodor kissed my hands and said that there was not a happier man than he in the world.

This irresponsible self-satisfaction was short-lived enough. Before the end of July Dostoevsky had perforce practically ceased to gamble. Funds were exhausted, almost to the last shilling; and he and Anna lived only by pawning such articles of value as they still possessed. It was Anna's mother who at last came to the rescue and sent money to enable them, towards the middle of August, to escape from the misery of Baden. But even at the last moment, a considerable part of the sum found its way to the roulette table. When they finally departed, they had little more than the bare fare in their pockets; and many of Anna's most treasured possessions remained, irretrievably lost, in the Baden pawnshops.

The vows of gamblers are proverbially as light as those of lovers. A dozen times during their stay at Baden Dostoevsky had promised his wife not to return to the tables; and a dozen times his promises had melted in the flames of his infatuation. There was no reasonable hope that the same vows made on leaving Baden would prove more durable; and if in fact he never sank afterwards to quite the same depths of ignominy, the credit must be given to Anna's foresight rather than to his own restraint. She never again made the mistake of accompanying him to the scene of these orgies. If he went, he went alone; and, as with the passage of time, prolonged absence from Anna's side grew more and more intolerable to him, his visits to the gambling resorts became fewer and of shorter duration. Three times during the next winter he left Geneva to visit the little Swiss watering-place of Saxon-les-Bains, where roulette was played; and

during their residence in Dresden in 1870–71 he made excursions to
both Homburg and Wiesbaden. All these visits followed the now
monotonous routine of transitory gains, final and irrevocable loss,
pawnshops, letters of abject self-reproach, and the sending of money
by Anna to defray the cost of his return. But these were short
episodes, scarcely comparable with the long agony of Baden; and if
there was no cure, growing dependence on his wife had at last
mitigated the virulence of the disease.

The last occasion on which Dostoevsky appeared at the roulette
table was at Wiesbaden in the spring of 1871. They returned to
Russia in the summer of that year; and although Fyodor travelled in
Germany several times during the last decade of his life, he did not
again succumb to the old fever. Advancing age had perhaps dulled
the fury of his passions. His domestic life had assumed the character
of a satisfying and tranquillizing routine; and in these days of
relative prosperity, there was no longer the feeling that success at
roulette, however problematical, was the sole alternative to despair.
The temptations were much less keen; and at the same time the
opportunities were removed to an almost inaccessible distance. In
1872 a decree of the federal German authorities closed all public
gaming-houses on German territory; and the enterprising managers
of these institutions, expelled from Germany and refused admittance
to France, found themselves obliged to accept the proffered hospitality of the Prince of Monaco. The paternal decree of the German
authorities created the fame and fortune of Monte Carlo; and it
probably played the chief part in freeing Dostoevsky's later years
from this persistent and degrading obsession.

During the stay at Baden there occurred an incident unimportant
in itself, but destined to become notorious in Russian literary history
—the quarrel between Dostoevsky and Turgenev. The character
and circumstances of the two men provided a perfect contrast. The
one was by origin and every instinct a bourgeois; the other a no less
thorough-going aristocrat. The one had for twenty years known
every kind of privation and poverty; for the other, financial embarrassment meant at most the temporary abandonment of a few
superfluous luxuries. The one was reckless, exacting, and spared
neither himself nor his friends; the other was lazy, easy-going and
indulgent even to his enemies. From their first meeting in Belinsky's
circle in 1845, Dostoevsky had regarded Turgenev with jealous,
rather reluctant, admiration; and Turgenev's attitude to his rival
had been one of kindly, but distinctly superior, patronage.

In the circle of Belinsky, it was easy for the aristocrat Turgenev
to regard with half-contemptuous amusement the antics of the

Moscow doctor's son, who wrote like an angel and behaved like a boor. But there was no declared inequality between them; they were both budding authors with their way to make. When Dostoevsky returned from Siberia, the situation had changed. Turgenev was now a recognized figure in Russian literature, and could command the best prices for his work. When Dostoevsky met him again in the early 'sixties, the *Vremya* was just starting its career; and there is extant a considerable correspondence between them relating to a story called *Phantoms*, which was promised by Turgenev for the *Vremya*, and eventually appeared in the *Epocha* a few months before the final débâcle. The correspondence is full of expressions of mutual esteem and seems sincere on both sides; and many literary bouquets are exchanged. Turgenev admires *Memoirs from the House of the Dead*; Dostoevsky replies with a eulogy of *Fathers and Sons*, and compares *Phantoms* to music. But we must not forget (indeed, we are not allowed to forget) that Dostoevsky is an impecunious editor soliciting contributions from a popular author to bolster up the circulation of a none-too-flourishing journal. 'If we could have appeared in January with a story of yours,' he writes in one of these letters, 'we should have had not 4,500, but 5,500 subscribers.' Dispassionate criticism is the last thing to expect from Dostoevsky. He could not afford at this time not to flatter Turgenev; and as the correspondence proceeds, the deferential tone of the anxious editor contrasts more and more sharply with the easy nonchalance of the *grand seigneur*. A curt reminder from Turgenev of an outstanding balance of the payment due to him for *Phantoms* closes this section of the correspondence.

The fall of the *Epocha* was followed by the fatal visit to Wiesbaden in August 1865, during which Dostoevsky, as we have seen, borrowed from Turgenev the sum of 50 thalers. 'They have been a great help to me, though they have not helped me radically,' wrote Dostoevsky in a rather cool letter of thanks. And he forgot all about the debt until, two years later, travelling this time not with his mistress but with his young wife, he saw Turgenev again in the gaming-rooms at Baden. Relations between borrower and lender are notoriously delicate; and they are particularly delicate when the parties to the transaction are Russians. The debt may, as between gentlemen, remain undischarged for an indefinite period. But delicacy requires of the lender that he shall not remind the borrower of the debt; and it demands of the borrower that he shall not even seem to suspect the lender of being capable of reminding him of it. 'As Fyodor owes Turgenev 50 roubles,' writes Anna in her *Diary*, 'it is absolutely necessary he should call on him; otherwise Tur-

genev will think that Fyodor does not want to come out of fear that
Turgenev will ask for his money back.'

In this complicated state of mind, smarting under the double
humiliation of his gaming losses and of the old debt which he could
not pay, Dostoevsky went to see Turgenev in the early days of July.
If we study the psychology of Dostoevsky's heroes, we shall not be
surprised that his humiliation vented itself, at the first opportunity,
in an outburst of assumed truculence. Nor was Turgenev's state of
mind exactly serene. His latest novel *Smoke*, in which he had pil-
loried the indecision and inconclusiveness of the Russian character,
had excited universal disapproval and, in Slavophil circles, bitter
reprobation. Always sensitive to public opinion and greedy of
popularity, Turgenev was stung to the quick by the general outcry;
and Dostoevsky must have seemed to him typical of those who were
leading the campaign against him. The detailed records of this
famous interview both come from Dostoevsky's side, one from the
entry which Anna made in her *Diary* the same evening, the other from
a letter written to Maikov two months later. If we may believe these
accounts, Turgenev himself led the conversation to the subject of
his latest novel, declared that he regarded himself as a German rather
than a Russian and proclaimed himself 'an out-and-out atheist'.
These details are probably in part fictitious; but it is not difficult to
reconstruct the spirit of the conversation. The two antagonists
stand clearly before us: Turgenev, the old-fashioned liberal and
westerner, sure of himself and of his place in the world, in all else
an agnostic, ready to jettison his country and his religion if they
failed to come up to his standards; Dostoevsky, the convert to
conservatism and orthodoxy, sure of nothing, least of all of himself,
but clinging passionately to the new-found faith in Russia and the
Russian God which alone seemed to offer a firm foothold in the
quicksands of this perplexing world. It is immaterial who began the
discussion; but given the two men, it could scarcely end without a
clash. We suspect that Dostoevsky was truculent and ill-bred; we
are sure that Turgenev was frigid and polite. 'He insulted me too
much by his opinions,' wrote Dostoevsky afterwards. In Russia,
more readily than elsewhere, the holding of political or theological
opinions may become a personal insult.

The quarrel had no immediate consequences; and it was only when
Dostoevsky caricatured Turgenev in *The Devils* in the character
of Karmazinov that the victim was stung into an angry and contemptuous retort.

I am told Dostoevsky has taken me off [he wrote to a friend]. Well, let
him amuse himself. He came to me five years ago in Baden, not to pay

back the money he had borrowed from me, but to abuse me roundly for *Smoke*, which according to him ought to be burnt by the public executioner. I listened in silence to all this tirade, and what do I now discover? That I have expressed all sorts of criminal opinions. ... It would be simply libel, if Dostoevsky were not mad—of which I have not the slightest doubt. Probably he dreamt it all.

To Turgenev, who had lived long in western Europe, it may well have seemed an odd proceeding to vilify, in a highly successful novel, a man to whom one had never repaid money borrowed in a moment of bitter distress; but this point of view did not occur to Dostoevsky. The 50 thalers were ultimately repaid in 1875; and in the last year of Dostoevsky's life there was a dramatic but hollow reconciliation when the two men met in Moscow at the unveiling of the Pushkin statue. But Turgenev lived to pen one of the bitterest epitaphs ever written by one author on another. Comparing his old enemy to the Marquis de Sade, he continues:

And to think that for this our de Sade all the Russian Bishops have celebrated masses, and preachers read sermons on the universal love of this universal man. ... Verily, we live in strange times.

CHAPTER XIII

Residence Abroad Continued

'THE departure from Baden,' writes Anna in her *Memoirs*, 'ended the stormy period of our life abroad.' It also brings to an end the extant portion of the *Diary* which has proved so copious a source of information for the events narrated in the last chapter; and we are once more relegated to the *Memoirs*, written nearly fifty years later and possessing none of the freshness and detail of the *Diary*. The travellers took train from Baden to Basel; they stayed there long enough to visit the Museum and to be impressed by Holbein's Descent from the Cross, which is described at length in one of the early scenes of *The Idiot*; and went on to Geneva, where they had decided to take up their winter quarters.

It was the end of August 1867 when the Dostoevskys reached Geneva; and they were destined to remain abroad for almost another four years. The first of these years was spent in Switzerland at Geneva and then at Vevey; the second in Italy at Milan and Florence; and the two further years at Dresden. The Swiss period was devoted entirely to *The Idiot*, which was only finished at Florence in January 1869. The remainder of the Italian period was spent in idleness. *The Eternal Husband* was written at Dresden in the autumn of 1869, and the succeeding eighteen months produced *The Devils*. Such was the output of these years of exile, less prolific than that of some other years in Dostoevsky's life, but yielding to none in greatness. It was the period of his artistic maturity.

The isolation and monotony of these years, following on the ferment of the years after his return from Siberia, were necessary to bring his genius to its full mellowness. They were even more necessary for the establishment of his domestic tranquillity. It was not easy for two such diverse characters, in Anna's sentimental phrase, to 'grow together'. The first tempestuous months of married life had not indeed shattered her firmly planted belief in the romantic vision of love and happiness. But Dostoevsky's faith was a feebler growth, and had ripened slowly amid these early storms. His lack of self-confidence and even of legitimate self-esteem, his consciousness of his own defects, had been accentuated by the bitterness of his experiences with Maria Dmitrievna, with Suslova and with Anna

Korvin-Krukovskaya, and made it particularly difficult for him to believe in his present good fortune. He could not indeed doubt the sincerity of his wife's present devotion; but he tormented himself with fears for its duration. His fears found expression in a letter written to Maikov soon after their arrival at Geneva:

I was afraid that Anna Grigorievna would get bored alone with me. So far we have really been entirely alone. I had no confidence in myself; my character is diseased, and I foresaw that she would undergo many torments with me. It is true that Anna Grigorievna has turned out to be stronger and deeper than I had known or counted on, and on many occasions has been simply my Angel-Preserver; but there is also much of the child and the twenty-year-old, which is charming and naturally inevitable, but to which I have scarcely strength and capacity to respond. All this was in my mind when we started; and though, I repeat, Anna Grigorievna has turned out stronger and better than I thought, yet I am still not free from anxiety.

After the first months abroad these doubts and fears fade imperceptibly away from the pages of Dostoevsky's correspondence. The years of exile and isolation consummated the miracle—for such it seemed to him and such it may sometimes seem to his biographer—of his married happiness. There are days of pain and weeks of distress; but we see no reason to dispute the description of these years in the official biography as the 'happiest of his life'.

Not many weeks after their arrival, Geneva was the scene of an international congress of the League of Peace and Freedom. The Dostoevskys went to the second meeting and listened to some of the orators. It was a strange medley. The sole requisite qualification of a delegate seems to have been opposition to the existing régime in the country to which he belonged; and there gathered together, under the expansive banner of Peace and Freedom, representatives of every shade of opinion ranging from Bakunin the Russian nihilist, who stood boldly for internationalism, anarchy and atheism, to Garibaldi the Italian nationalist, who struck a sympathetic chord in Dostoevsky's heart (he is the only delegate mentioned by name in Dostoevsky's letters) by speaking of the brotherhood of nations, the necessity of religion, and the wickedness of the Papacy as a political institution. Garibaldi found himself in an atmosphere hostile to the propagation of these ideas, and left the congress on the second day; and from this point the more orthodox advocates of revolution found themselves in the ascendant.

It is inexpressible [wrote Dostoevsky to his niece] how these gentlemen, whom I have now for the first time seen, not in books, but in the flesh, these revolutionaries and socialists, talked nonsense from the tribune to an audience of 5,000 people. No description will give an idea of it. The absurdity, the feebleness, the mutual contradictions pass all imagining. And it is this rabble which excites the unhappy working man. Sad! They began by saying that in order to obtain peace on earth it was necessary to exterminate the Christian religion. Abolish big states and make small ones, down with capital so that everything may be made common by order, etc. . . . . First and foremost, fire and sword; and when everything has been annihilated then they think we shall have peace.

The occasion was one of some importance in Dostoevsky's literary career; for it clearly inspired the episode of the young nihilists in *The Idiot*, and sowed in his fertile brain the first seeds of *The Devils*.

His judgment of the revolutionaries *en masse* was trenchant and uncompromising; but one of them, Ogarev by name, an associate of Herzen and a minor poet, was the sole acquaintance he and his wife had in Geneva. Ogarev visited them frequently and, in the apologetic words of Anna's *Memoirs*, 'sometimes lent us ten francs which we returned to him as soon as we had any money'. Even a revolutionary had his uses. But in the winter Ogarev moved south into Italy; and they found themselves once more quite alone in the 'stupid Protestant town'. Once Dostoevsky met Herzen in the street, but the conversation was brief and formal, and no exchange of visits ensued. Herzen was associated with two now unwelcome memories of Dostoevsky's past. He had met him last on the Italian steamer when travelling with Suslova in 1863; and two years later, in the moment of his bitterest need and degradation at Wiesbaden, he had appealed to Herzen for money, and Herzen had turned a deaf ear. It may safely be conjectured that these recollections, rather than any differences of political conviction, explain the lonely exile's coldness to a former friend.

In February occurred an eagerly expected event, the birth of Dostoevsky's first child. Madame Snitkina had intended to come from Petersburg but had been prevented by illness. When Anna's birth pains began, her husband was sleeping off the effects of a severe epileptic fit and lay in a deep coma from which she dared not rouse him. There was nobody else in the house but a half-idiot servant, and she suffered all night alone. In the morning Dostoevsky awaked, and ran in a state bordering on distraction for the midwife, who declared with professional sang-froid that she had been fetched hours too soon. She was right; and after an endless day, throughout which the expectant mother was calm and collected, the midwife cynically unconcerned, and Dostoevsky alone almost insane with agonized anxiety, the child was born in the early hours of the following morning. During the last stage of her labour, Anna again and again sent the midwife into the next room to comfort her husband, who was on his knees praying in a condition which gave every reason to fear another epileptic seizure.

The child was called Sonya, after Dostoevsky's favourite niece and the heroine of *Crime and Punishment*. His relations with Paul had already revealed Dostoevsky in the character of a tender, even doting father. In the passion of parenthood he knew no more restraint than in his other emotions. At the age of two days, Sonya was 'a wonderful, healthy, intelligent little girl, ridiculously like me'; and for weeks he could think of little else but his happiness. The new emotion interrupted the progress of *The Idiot*; and the *Russky Vestnik* had to announce that the March instalment was postponed until the April number 'owing to the illness of the author'.

The infant lived for less than three months, took cold and died. The grief of the parents was as passionate as had been their bliss. Dostoevsky railed at his fate, at the Geneva climate, at the carelessness of the nurse, at the self-assurance of the doctor who had at first pronounced the illness unimportant. The scene of their past joys and present sorrow became intolerable to both. On a day early in June they paid the last of their daily visits to the little cemetery, laid a last wreath on the little white cross, and took the steamer for Vevey at the other end of the lake. Here they passed the saddest summer of their married life. Even the Russian library and the Russian newspapers, which had been Dostoevsky's sole diversion at Geneva, were absent here; and with Anna's mother, who came from Petersburg to visit them, they led a hermit-like existence, speaking and thinking only of the lost child.

Never have I been so unhappy [wrote Dostoevsky to Apollon Maikov] as in these last days. I will not try to describe anything; but as time goes on, the bitterer grows the recollection, the vivider the image of our dead Sonya. There are moments which cannot be borne. She already knew me; and when, on the day of her death, I went out to read the papers, not realizing that in two hours she would die, she followed me with her little eyes and gazed on me with a look which I can see now ever more and more clearly. I shall never forget and never cease grieving. Even if I have another child, I do not understand how I shall love it, where I shall find the love. It is Sonya that I need; I cannot understand that she is dead and that I shall never see her more.

These and other episodes of the Dostoevskys' life abroad must be painted in against a drab background of financial embarrassment deepening sometimes to shades of acute want. When he left Petersburg in April 1867, Dostoevsky had already received from the *Russky Vestnik* 3,000 roubles on account of the novel of which he had not yet written one line. It was not until September that the composition of *The Idiot* began; and the first instalment was sent to Katkov at the New Year, just in time for the January number. In the meanwhile, except for occasional gifts from Anna's mother, and a loan of 200 roubles from Apollon Maikov, his staunchest friend at this period of his life, Dostoevsky had no resources other than further advances from Katkov; and before the first chapter was delivered, the author had already received the formidable sum of 4,500 roubles, leaving only a paltry balance of some 750 roubles to be paid while the novel was actually being written. In these circumstances Dostoevsky was never out of debt. His letters from abroad are crammed with monotonous details of financial difficulties, requests for loans, speculations how soon he dare ask for a further payment from Katkov, and projects for raising more funds by the issue of his novels in book form. The three visits during this winter to the roulette tables at Saxon-les-Bains exhausted their meagre stock of ready money; and they left items of property in the pawn-shops of every town in which they stayed. Just after the birth of Sonya they had 40 francs in hand and 400 francs of debt; ten days later Dostoevsky had pawned his last overcoat—it was with him a common symptom of the approach of spring—and had 30 francs in his pocket. In an unusual burst of humour he dubbed himself and his wife 'Mr and Mrs Micawber'; for every move which they made from place to place depended on some windfall which enabled them to pay their bills, redeem their most necessary belongings, and defray the costs of locomotion.

It is an amazing fact, and one which must be given due weight in any estimate of Dostoevsky's character and conduct, that throughout the period of his residence abroad, or at any rate up to the end of 1869, he was regularly sending money to his dependants in Petersburg. His late brother's mistress and illegitimate child soon disappear from their modest place on the pay-roll; but from practically every payment received by him a sum is set aside, however desperate his own plight, for Paul and Emilia Fyodorovna. It was a strange relationship. He had no illusion of affection on their side; for they never wrote to him except to state their needs and demand, often peremptorily, the wherewithal to satisfy them. He knew by the experience of the first weeks of his marriage that they hated his wife; and Emilia Fyodorovna was apparently ill-bred and ill-advised enough to refuse even to mention Anna's name in her letters to Dostoevsky. He knew that the birth of the children, which caused him such untold joy, was to them a theme of lamentation; and perhaps the most pathetic passage in the whole of his extant correspondence is one in which he begs Maikov not to tell them of the death of Sonya:

By the way, a particular request. Do not tell any of my relations, if you meet them, that Sonya is dead. At any rate I very much want them not to know for a time, including of course Paul. It seems to me that none of them will be sorry about my child, and perhaps will even feel quite the opposite; and the very thought of this embitters me. What harm did the poor little mite do them? Let them hate me, let them make fun of my love—it's all one to me now.

Other men have been bled by undeserving relatives who have thrown dust in their eyes; but there can have been few whose charity, like Dostoevsky's, remained unaffected, even in moments of direst penury, by the most penetrating vision of the unworthiness of its recipients. He could not forget that Paul had been left to him by Maria Dmitrievna on her death-bed and 'had grown up for ten years in his house', or that Emilia was the widow of the man who had once been everything to him; and although Paul was in the twenties and two of Emilia's sons were of age, he continued to shower on them with the generous irresponsibility of his nature (not far removed perhaps from the recklessness which led him to the roulette table) money which might have redeemed from pawn his own overcoats or the jewellery of his wife.

These proceedings were regarded by Anna with something less than her usual tolerance, and had provoked during the stay in Baden the bitterest passage in the whole extant portion of her *Diary*.

Yes, it is already clear that he will not trouble himself about his own family. Fyodor will be far more anxious that Emilia Fyodorovna, that stupid German woman, shall not want, that Fyodor Dostoevsky [Michael's eldest son] shall not have to work too hard, that Paul shall be refused nothing. In the meanwhile, it is a matter of perfect indifference to him that we lack this or that—he does not even notice it. Of course, as I am his wife and therefore belong to him, it follows that he considers me bound to put up with all these petty inconveniences and privations. Perhaps I should not complain if I really knew that he had nothing; but when we are in want in order that Emilia Fyodorovna and company may not want, when my cloak is pawned in order that Emilia Fyodorovna's cloak may be redeemed, then, take it how you will, a very unpleasant feeling arises in me, and it pains me fearfully to find in a man whom I esteem and love such carelessness, such incapacity to understand, such lack of consideration. He says that he is bound to help his brother's family because his brother helped him; but is not Fyodor not bound to help me also, have I not given him my whole life, have I not given him my soul with the fullest desire and willingness to suffer for his happiness? But that he evidently does not prize; that is taken as a matter of course. He does not consider himself bound to trouble that his wife should live in peace and should not at every moment be worried that tomorrow there will be nothing to eat.

But she concludes this very entry with self-reproach for her own bitterness; and Fyodor's weak generosity did not, any more than his more disastrous and less amiable addiction to roulette, impair her fundamental devotion to him. For Anna, despite the meticulous and cheese-paring nature of her own financial transactions, was not at heart greedy for money; and so long as she had Fyodor at her side, dependent on her and on her alone in all the more important relations of her life, she regarded with comparative equanimity these benefactions at a distance to people whom she detested and despised.

In September 1868 the exiles moved on from Switzerland into Italy, travelling by coach over the Simplon pass. They stopped at Milan, not from choice, but because their money carried them no further; and there they stayed, for the same good financial reason, for two months. At the earliest opportunity, which occurred towards the end of November, they resumed their journey to Florence, where those indispensable luxuries, a Russian library and Russian newspapers, were, for the first time since Geneva, once more at Dostoevsky's disposal. When he had last been in Florence with Strakhov in 1862, his companion had been unable to drag him from the pages of *Les Misérables*. But now he visited with Anna the Pitti and the Uffizi galleries; stood in obedient raptures before the Madonna della Sedia, and pronounced the Medici Venus a work of genius; and here at last he finished *The Idiot* in the early days of 1869. A few days later Anna discovered that she was pregnant for a second time.

When the accounts for *The Idiot* (for which, as for *Crime and Punishment*, he was paid 150 roubles a folio) were made up, there was a debit balance against the author of nearly 2,000 roubles, which would have to be set against his next novel. But as the said novel would not be required by the *Russky Vestnik* until the beginning of the next year, and as he had long become incapable of writing anything until the last possible moment, there was leisure to repose from his late labours and look about him. At Florence he received letters from his friend and old collaborator Strakhov, announcing the foundation of a new journal, the *Zarya*, and asking him to become one of its contributors. He was flattered by the invitation, and had some sentimental feelings for the new venture, which reminded him of his own journalistic past. Although he still expected the *Russky Vestnik* to continue to make him payments in advance on account of his next year's novel, he saw no objection to having two strings to his bow; and risking the probable offence to his principal paymaster, he offered to write a short novel for the *Zarya* by the autumn on condition that he received 1,000 roubles in cash forthwith. He exaggerated either the resources of the new journal or its eagerness to secure his collaboration; for his proposal was refused. But Dostoevsky wanted money and was not proud; he lowered his immediate requirements to 300 roubles, and the bargain was struck.

Meanwhile spring was turning to summer, and he had not yet begun to write either the story for the *Zarya* which was due in September, or the long novel promised to the *Russky Vestnik* for January. The heat of Florence was becoming unbearable; and it was imperative before Anna's confinement to move to a country whose language he could speak; for in Italy she had served as interpreter. But there were no funds, and there was the usual accumulation of debts and pawn-tickets; and through May, June and July they sat on in Florence in a state of growing exasperation and despair, their nerves more and more on edge as the thermometer soared to heights unknown in their native north, Anna now heavy with child, and he unable to put pen to paper. Then, after a stream of appeals *ad misericordiam*, it was once more Katkov who came to the rescue with a further advance of 700 roubles; and in the first days of August they at last escaped from the furnace of the Italian summer.

They paused to admire Venice, crossed to Trieste, and took train to Prague, where they planned to fix their headquarters for the winter. It had the main qualification of being a German-speaking town; but being the centre of a Slavonic population, it appealed to Dostoevsky's now strongly developed Slavophil sentiments, and seemed calculated to impart that flavour of Slavonic life which he missed so bitterly in his wanderings in the Teutonic and the Latin world. His judgment of the sister race of Bohemian Slavs might have been of interest; but the plan failed to materialize. Ordinary tourists seldom passed this way, and the city did not cater for them. No furnished rooms were obtainable; and after three days' vain search, the travellers were obliged to continue their journey to their old resting-place in Dresden. They arrived there about the middle of August. They had made the first stage of their homeward journey; but it was nearly two years before they moved again.

In September a daughter, Lyubov, was born, and the story for the *Zarya* seriously begun. It was completed in three months and was called *The Eternal Husband*. It is in subject and texture one of Dostoevsky's lightest works; he was keeping his heavy batteries in reserve for the big novel for the *Russky Vestnik* next year. A Russian

Madame Bovary has died, leaving letters which disclose for the first time to her purblind husband the fact that she had had a series of lovers; *The Eternal Husband* is the story of the subsequent relations between him and one of the lovers, the father of his supposed child. The spiritual link between two men who love the same woman is a theme which Dostoevsky had treated, on a tragic plane, in *The Insulted and Injured* and in *The Idiot*. It is here treated in a vein of pungent comedy which suggests Flaubert or Maupassant rather than Dostoevsky. Incidents are borrowed from *The Idiot* and reproduced in the new setting. The lover peers through the curtains to watch the husband gazing up at his windows, just as Rogozhin in *The Idiot* watches Myshkin; the rivals in the culminating scene once more sleep side by side on divans, and there is the same attempted murder, this time with a razor. It all reads like an extremely clever pastiche; but it is not Dostoevsky himself, but some witty and malicious parodist flippantly turning to base uses the familiar clichés of Dostoevskian art. The story might provide the subject for a unique study in literary psychology; for there is in the concluding 'analysis' a passage in which we seem to detect (and we can scarcely be mistaken) a mocking farewell to his relations with Maria Dmitrievna, to the time when he had held Vergunov 'dearer than a brother':

So they ended after all in Bruderschaft. Ha, Ha! Embraced and shed tears. Oh, you Schilleresque poets!

The blood of the attempted murder (it was only a scratch) made the rivals 'quits'; and perhaps in writing this story Dostoevsky felt himself in some queer way 'quits' with the memory of his first wife. It was written with a speed and gusto quite unusual to him; and it is this which makes it easier to read than almost anything else he ever wrote. The sense of strain on both writer and reader, which can be felt in every line of the greater novels, is here altogether absent.

The appearance of *The Eternal Husband* in the January and February numbers of the *Zarya* for 1870 made Dostoevsky's relations with the *Russky Vestnik* delicate and difficult. For if he had never formally promised Katkov the monopoly of his output, he had promised him a novel at the beginning of the year; and while he was not yet able to deliver a single line of it, he was publishing another story in a rival journal. It was a flagrant breach of faith. But it is impossible to apply ordinary standards of commercial morality to a being as irresponsible as Dostoevsky always showed himself in his business transactions; and it seems incongruous to brand as sharp practice an action so palpably hostile to his own interests. He had risked—and as usual he was perfectly well aware of it—a breach with the man who had virtually kept him for the past three years and who had treated him, as he frankly admitted, with consideration and generosity, for the sake of a sentimental attachment to a new and untried journal which seemed in some vague way to be carrying on the traditions of the *Vremya* and the *Epocha*. He perceived the falseness of his position; but the perception did not deter him from immediate repetition of the same step, though in the reverse direction. For as soon as his relations with the *Russky Vestnik* were patched up again and he had begun to work seriously at *The Devils*, we find him once more, in the spring of 1870, taking advance payments from the *Zarya* for another story to be delivered at the end of the year. The story was never written, and three years later the money advanced to him had not yet been repaid.

The period from January 1870 to July 1871, the last eighteen months of the Dostoevsky's sojourn abroad, produced the greater part of his third masterpiece, *The Devils*. The story of the unusual vicissitudes of the composition of this novel belongs to a later chapter. Other history this period has none. The Franco-Prussian War makes an occasional incursion into the pages of Dostoevsky's correspondence, but did not disturb the monotonous tenor of their life in Dresden. In the family circle the child grew and flourished; Anna was ailing and pined more and more for Russia; and Dostoevsky, under the habitual stimulus of debts and an empty pocket, went on wrestling with the great novel, and becoming more and more acutely conscious of lack of contact with his native land.

The aimless life of self-imposed exile had in fact become intolerable. Already during the first stay at Dresden the 'immeasurable stupidity' of the Germans had enraged the excitable and impressionable traveller. The Swiss seemed to him to possess 'a few good traits which placed them incomparably higher than the Germans'. But we are hard put to it to identify these redeeming characteristics; for in the same letter he assures Maikov that the prevailing habits of 'this vulgar republic' are 'drunkenness, theft and petty trickery which has become a rule in commercial transactions'. He writes from Geneva to dissuade his sister from giving her children a French governess who will merely impart to them 'her vulgar, distorted, ridiculous and uncivilized rules of behaviour, and her perverted ideas of society and religion'. The furious and unreasoning patriotism which so often overtakes the wanderer, especially the unwilling wanderer, in foreign parts makes itself more and more insistently heard in Dostoevsky's letters. Everything that was not Russian began to fill him with angry contempt.

K

But worse than the irritation of incessant contact with the uncongenial foreigner was the gnawing homesickness for Russia. 'Here I am growing dull and narrow,' he wrote from Milan, 'and am losing touch with Russia. I lack the Russian air and Russian people.' Life abroad, he declared elsewhere, is worse than banishment to Siberia; and he seriously canvasses the rival disadvantages of his present exile and the life in the debtors' prison of Petersburg, the threatened alternative. Finally, the letters from Dresden contain incessant references to Anna's failing health and her longing for Russia. In the autumn of 1870 she had again become pregnant; and in the following spring, encouraged by the success of *The Devils*, they decided to risk everything and return to Petersburg for the birth of the child. The usual financial complications attended their departure; it was only at the last moment that funds sufficient to cover their debts and their expenses were received from Katkov. They left Dresden on July 5th and travelled direct to Petersburg, a continuous journey of three nights and two days. Exactly a week after their arrival, Anna gave birth to a son.

When Dostoevsky had last returned to Petersburg from Europe in October 1865, his fortunes were at their lowest ebb; he had written nothing which gave him a clear title to immortality, and had frittered away his early reputation in futile journalistic enterprises. Now in July 1871, he was the author of *Crime and Punishment*, *The Idiot* and *The Devils*, and was beyond dispute one of the great figures in Russian literature. The return to Petersburg is the beginning of the last period of Dostoevsky's career; and before proceeding to it we must turn aside to examine the three masterpieces which give to the years we have just traversed their claim to be regarded as preeminently the great creative years of his life.

CHAPTER XIV

The Ethical Problem—Crime and Punishment

THE publication of *Crime and Punishment* made Dostoevsky one of the world's great novelists. It is the first of the series of five novels, *Crime and Punishment*, *The Idiot*, *The Devils*, *A Raw Youth* and *The Brothers Karamazov*, on which his fame ultimately rests. In all these works (with the exception, perhaps, of *A Raw Youth*, which stands on a somewhat lower plane of inspiration than the rest), Dostoevsky dramatizes the problems of life and philosophy. It will not be supposed that any one of them (not even *Crime and Punishment*, which is the most compact and closely reasoned of them all) is confined to a single theme, or works out that theme with complete precision; for Dostoevsky is an artist, not a systematic thinker; and he is writing fiction, not philosophy. But the central theme is always there, inspiring and informing the whole; and without it the novel would dissolve into diffuse and unrelated parts. The great novels of Dostoevsky are, in the phrase of a recent Russian critic, 'philosophy in action'.

The *roman à thèse*, now so unpopular that the phrase has become a hackneyed term of abuse in literary criticism, was in the middle of last century a respected and recognized form of literature. The once famous German novel *Problematische Naturen*, in which the principal characters personified different points of view in contemporary thought, was published five years before *Crime and Punishment*. Practically every great Russian novel of the classical period was more or less definitely a *roman à thèse*. Even if we ignore novels like those of Herzen and Chernyshevsky, written on a specific propagandist thesis, the moral purpose is almost as clearly marked in Turgenev or Tolstoy as in Dostoevsky. It was not until the last two decades of the century that a divorce was pronounced between art and morality. It would not have occurred to Dostoevsky to deny that his novels were written with a purpose. One of the unrealized ambitions of his later years was to write a 'Russian *Candide*'; and if ever a story deserved to be branded as a *roman à thèse*, it is Voltaire's masterpiece.

The Russian character was fertile soil for the philosophical novel. The 'certain shade of unconcern' which, in the words of Walter

Pater, 'may be thought to mark complete culture in the handling of abstract questions', is too exclusively Anglo-Saxon to be admired or even understood by the more passionate Russian. 'Send me Hegel,' wrote Dostoevsky to his brother from Siberia when he came out of prison, 'my whole life depends on it.' 'Unless I know why I am here and what I am,' cried Tolstoy through the lips of the hero of *Anna Karenina*, 'I cannot live.' It was Dostoevsky's old colleague on the *Vremya*, Apollon Grigoriev, who once remarked that the Russian never knew how to distinguish between life and thought, between the practical and the abstract. The problems of ethics and metaphysics are, for the true Russian of all periods, a vital part of life and therefore a vital element in any fiction which seriously professes to reflect life.

There is a further point to remember if we wish to understand the philosophical background of Dostoevsky's great novels and the extremes to which he drives his heroes in the pursuit of their ideas. The lack of a long-established national tradition and of the discipline of character which proceeds from it makes the Russian thoroughly experimental by nature. 'The Englishman,' wrote Herzen who lived long in England, 'thinks it indelicate to overstep certain limits, to attack certain questions.' The Russian stands at the opposite pole; he acknowledges, as Count Kayserling recently put it, no *cultural* values; and in this as in other respects Dostoevsky is the most representative of Russians. 'Everywhere and in everything,' he wrote, 'I go to the uttermost limit; all my life I have overstepped the mark.' The Russian will accept no principle and no convention until he has explored its very foundations; and if he finds that the first stone has not been well and truly laid he will recklessly pull down the whole edifice about his ears. The assertion of a principle is of infinitely more importance to the Russian mind than any practical results which may flow from it (a point generally overlooked by foreign critics of the present régime in Russia); and if we find in Dostoevsky's novels people who murder for a principle, live on bread and water for a principle or commit suicide for a principle, we should remember that such types are far less unfamiliar and fantastic to the Russian than to the English reader, and that many of Dostoevsky's apparently most extreme and improbable characters had their counterparts in the annals of the period in which he wrote. About the time of the first appearance of *Crime and Punishment* a student in Moscow murdered a money-lender for motives similar to those of Raskolnikov; the conspirators in *The Devils* had prototypes in real life; and if we read the fantastic stories of self-immolation from religious motives which mark certain epochs of Russian history we shall be less disposed to greet with incredulity the suicide of Kirillov.

Crime and Punishment is the story of a young student Raskolnikov who commits a murder on principle. From complex motives which he himself finds it difficult to analyse, he murders an old woman money-lender, together with her sister who unexpectedly comes on the scene while the act is being committed After the murder he feels unable to make use of the money and jewellery which he has taken, and he hides them. There is no evidence to connect him with the crime; but his nerves are unhinged and his strange behaviour brings on him the suspicions of the astute detective in charge of the case. Before his guilt is actually established he confesses, is sentenced to eight years in Siberia and is followed thither by the girl Sonya who has been living as a prostitute to support her family. He goes to Siberia repenting not of his crime but of his failure to 'hold out'; but after an illness in the prison, his 'conversion' is effected through the influence of Sonya. The theme of the book is the analysis of the motives of the murder and of its reactions on the murderer; and in this theme Dostoevsky embodies the whole problem of the relations of the *ego* to the surrounding world, of the individual to society, which is, in effect, the central problem of both ethics and metaphysics.

The form in which the problem presented itself to nineteenth-century Europe was the outcome of the romantic movement. Rousseau had broken up the fixed mould of ethical and social convention. The native goodness of man when untrammelled by social chains was the corner-stone of his philosophy. He asserted both the dignity and the rights of the individual. In the days when he was under strong romantic influence, Dostoevsky made Devushkin in *Poor Folk* ask 'whether he was a man or a boot-sole' and Golyadkin in *The Double* 'whether he was a man or a rag', anticipating almost verbally the question which was to torment Raskolnikov's fevered mind. But romantic individualism implied not only the vindication of the downtrodden, but the self-assertion of the proud. The Byronic hero hurling defiance at society and its conventions is as much a romantic figure as the poverty-ridden clerk in his garret. Raskolnikov has both these opposite strains of Romanticism in his blood; he is a Devushkin or a Golyadkin aspiring to be a Napoleon.

For the romantic movement had found in history a hero more mighty even than Byron. The names of the two great idols of continental Romanticism had been coupled by Alfred de Vigny: 'La moue de Byron et celle de Bonaparte ont fait grimacer bien des figures innocentes.' The influence of Napoleonic legend on romantic literature deserves a special monograph; and nowhere was the influence greater than in Russia where historical figures so readily assume superhuman proportions. When Raskolnikov raves of becoming a Napoleon ('I wanted to become a Napoleon,' he told Sonya, 'that is why I killed her') he is speaking the idiom not perhaps of the age in which he was created, but of the age in which his creator was young; and we shall not do him full justice unless we understand that his was one of the innumerable 'innocent faces' which grimaced in imitation of Byron and Bonaparte.

But if Raskolnikov owes something to romantic influences, he owes more to the experiences of his creator in the convict settlement at Omsk. It has been suggested in a previous chapter that one effect of these experiences was to shatter Dostoevsky's belief in the accepted canons of morality and lead him on the quest for another truth beyond the frontiers of good and evil as ordinarily conceived. The essence of Raskolnikov's crime lies in the determination to discover this new 'good', a good based on self-assertion instead of self-submission. So much seems certain; and we may perhaps go further and seek the genesis of the conception of Raskolnikov in the impression made on Dostoevsky by one particular criminal whom he calls Orlov. He met Orlov, who 'had cut the throats of old men and children in cold blood', in the prison hospital. 'Never in my life', he writes, 'have I met a stronger, more iron character. . . . It was complete victory over the flesh. . . . This man had unlimited self-control, he despised all torture and punishments, and feared nothing on earth.' Orlov treated the rest of the world with a lofty condescension, and looked on Dostoevsky (the latter felt) as 'a submissive, weak, pitiful and in every way inferior being'. It is clear that Orlov inspired Dostoevsky with a kind of awe as one who had achieved for himself spiritual equilibrium, 'a complete victory over the flesh', beyond the confines of good and evil; and it is this ideal which is sought by Raskolnikov and after him, more successfully, by Kirillov. Raskolnikov can never be an Orlov (as Dostoevsky himself could never be an Orlov), because he is weak; and the question which agitated Raskolnikov, which agitated Dostoevsky and which is taken up once more by Nietzsche, is the fundamental ethical question of *Crime and Punishment*: Does Raskolnikov fail merely because he is weak? or because of some spiritual essence in mankind which makes it impossible for him to find ultimate satisfaction in the position of the amoral superman?

The philosophy of the superman is the natural offspring of subjective idealism, which is the counterpart in metaphysics of Romanticism in art. The Russian mind, through lack of disposition or lack of training, never took kindly to metaphysical speculation. But it was quick to seek in the fashionable German philosophy of the day a solution of the ethical problem, a new sanction for morality in the place of the now discredited sanctions of religion. The search was arduous. By the time German philosophy had found its way into Russia in the 'thirties, Kant's 'categorical imperative' had been rejected by his own countrymen; and the 'father of modern philosophy' never had any influence in Russia. The later idealists of the extremer kind offered little solid ground on which to construct a durable edifice of morality. For if phenomena are to be ultimately deduced from the human consciousness, if all reality derives from the *ego*, how can there exist any external standard or sanction of conduct? Is not man's highest obligation an obligation to his own self? and is not his highest vocation the development and assertion of his own personality? The motive of Raskolnikov was to prove himself a superman, to assert his right to transgress moral conventions.

I wanted to kill without casuistry [he told Sonya], to kill for my own sake, for myself alone. I did not want in this matter to lie even to myself. I did not kill to help my mother—that's nonsense. I did not kill in order, having got money and power, to become a benefactor to humanity. Nonsense! I just killed; killed for my own sake, for myself alone. . . . Money was not the chief thing I needed when I killed her; it was not money I needed but something else. . . . I wanted to know, and to know quickly, whether I was a worm like everyone else, or a man. Shall I be able to transgress or shall I not? Shall I dare to stoop down and take, or not? Am I a trembling creature, or have I the *right*?

Raskolnikov was not, however, altogether consistent. Inconsistency is regarded by some as a demerit in philosophers; but Dostoevsky is an artist, not a philosopher. The great characters of Dostoevsky, like those of Shakespeare and like human beings, are frequently inconsistent; and commentators may debate over the motives of Raskolnikov's crime as they have debated in the past over those of Iago's hatred or Hamlet's procrastination. The passage just quoted should have been sufficient to prove Raskolnikov a convinced egoist; it is not hard to adduce others equally explicit to prove him a rationalistic altruist. A Newton or a Kepler, he argues, would have been justified in sacrificing one, a hundred, a thousand human lives 'in order that his discoveries might become known to the whole world'. In history, it is the 'benefactors and teachers of humanity' who have claimed and used the right to shed blood. And later he justifies his own crime to his sister by insisting that the victim was 'a vile and loathsome vermin, an old usurer obnoxious to all, a vampire living on the lives of the poor'. If Raskolnikov were a pure egoist, these arguments based on the benefit to humanity of the crime would be irrelevant. We may, if we please, dismiss them as the excuses of a mind bent on acting egoistically but anxious to cover its egoism with a veneer of altruism. But even this theory disposes of Raskolnikov's claim to be deemed a convinced and consistent egoist; for such a person, if he existed, would not feel the need to disguise himself in the sham colours of altruism.

The fact is that Dostoevsky has never sat down, as a good philosopher should, and thought out his Raskolnikov in one piece. There are in Raskolnikov—and it is one reason why he is a human being and not a lay figure—elements of two divergent standpoints. The romantic individualism popular in Dostoevsky's youth, but now, in the 'sixties, already obsolescent, was the basis of Raskolnikov's philosophy; but Dostoevsky also used him, in a manner indefensible in a philosopher but quite legitimate in an artist, as an exponent of the fashionable rationalistic ethics of Chernyshevsky which he had attacked two years before in *Memoirs from Underground*. Halting between these two opinions, Raskolnikov is never quite sure whether he has committed murder for his own sake or for the sake of humanity. But whether he has acted on the theory that, being a superman, he makes his own moral laws and is subject to no external code, or on the theory that, ethics being purely rational and utilitarian, the killing of 'a vile and loathsome vermin' is an act of virtue, the hollowness of the theory is exhibited in the result. The sequel reveals to us not the pangs of a stricken conscience (which a less subtle writer would have given us), but the tragic and fruitless struggle of a powerful intellect to maintain a conviction which is incompatible with the essential nature of man. The tragedy for Raskolnikov is the collapse of the principle on which he has acted.

It is unnecessary to review in detail a novel so famous and so familiar to every reader. The leading incidental characters in *Crime and Punishment*—the hero's mother, his sister Dunya and her suitor Luzhin, the dull and level-headed student-friend Razumikhin, the inimitable drunkard Marmeladov, the examining magistrate Porphyry Zosimov—are perhaps better drawn than those of any other novel of Dostoevsky. But there are two characters who, though they scarcely influence the action, form part of the philosophical framework of the book, and who require notice here: Svidrigailov and Sonya Marmeladova.

In the construction of *Crime and Punishment*, Svidrigailov is evidently an afterthought. He does not appear in the first outline of the plot which Dostoevsky sent to Katkov, or in any of the manuscript drafts of the novel which survive. When he is first casually named as the former employer and persecutor of Dunya, it is by no means clear that he is afterwards to be introduced to us in person; and it is probable that Dostoevsky at that moment had no such intention. Svidrigailov makes his first appearance exactly half-way through the novel. He never quite becomes acclimatized, never moves quite on the same plane as the other characters. He remains to the last a mysterious figure, a symbol rather than a man; and this gives to his symbolical role—the only role he plays—an enhanced significance.

The genesis of Svidrigailov, like the genesis of Raskolnikov himself, can be directly traced back to *Memoirs from the House of the Dead*. The criminal A——v, a 'noble' by birth, is there described as

a bundle of flesh with teeth and a belly and with an insatiable thirst for the coarsest, most bestial bodily lusts. .. He was an example of the lengths to which the mere bodily part of a human being will go when unrestrained by any standard, any law. How it disgusted me to watch his everlasting mocking smile! He was a monster, a moral Quasimodo. At the same time, he was clever and intelligent, good-looking in a certain way, well-bred, and had capabilities.

This description exactly applies to Svidrigailov. He is a more consistent, more successful and infinitely meaner Raskolnikov. Strip from Raskolnikov the sympathetic halo which surrounds him, his recklessness, his inconsistencies, his altruistic impulses; and he stands revealed as the complete hedonist preaching individual self-satisfaction as the ultimate good. The philosophy of the superman and the rationalistic ethics of the utilitarian end alike in pure hedonism. The fundamental similarity between the outlook of the two men is emphasized from the outset of their relations. At their first meeting, Svidrigailov tells Raskolnikov, to the latter's profound disgust, that they are birds of a feather. He presses Raskolnikov with merciless logic:

Why should I restrain myself? Why should I give up women if I once have a taste for them? It is, at any rate, an occupation.

Or, later, still more brutally:

If you believe that one should not listen through keyholes, but may brain old women with anything that comes handy—well, you had better clear out as quick as possible ... perhaps to America.

The clear-headed and acute wit of Svidrigailov plunges a search-light into the muddled obscurity of Raskolnikov's distracted mind.

Yet even in Svidrigailov, Dostoevsky does not attain complete unhuman consistency. From the outset Svidrigailov is free with his money (though we may suggest that Dostoevsky himself had so little regard for money that readiness to open the purse-strings scarcely counted with him as a virtue); and the culminating scene, in which he releases Dunya when she is in his power and offers her the opportunity of shooting him, is surely incompatible with the principle of unrestrained self-indulgence. His suicide remains obscure and ineffective. We are doubtless intended to infer the moral bankruptcy of hedonism; but the point is not well made. The truth is that it was necessary to remove Svidrigailov rather hurriedly from the stage in order to leave it free for the closing scenes of Raskolnikov's tragedy. The puppet had done his work; he had made our flesh creep and our gorge rise; and it was time to bundle him unceremoniously back into his box. For Svidrigailov, alone among the characters of *Crime and Punishment*, is a puppet; and this is perhaps the best answer to those who, following the malicious Strakhov, attempt to discover in him a portrait of his creator.

The figure of Sonya is simpler. The 'pure prostitute' was a favourite character in the French fiction of the period; and though those of us who love Sonya may shrink from recognizing her as a descendant of Victor Hugo's Fantini, it would be idle to deny the relationship. But the Russian genius has not much in common with the French, and least of all in its attitude to women; and Dostoevsky lifts Sonya clean out of the sentimental atmosphere of a French *camélia*. She too becomes a symbol; she represents the extreme of self-submission, as Raskolnikov and his nightmare double Svidrigailov represent the extreme of self-assertion. As their philosophy is based on self, hers is based on the negation of self—a fact with which Raskolnikov does not fail to taunt her: she has 'murdered and betrayed herself for naught'. Dostoevsky resists, or never feels, the temptation to make the path of self-submission either smooth or glorious; no halo surrounds Sonya save the halo of suffering. 'I bowed down not to you,' said Raskolnikov when he had kissed Sonya's feet, 'but to the whole suffering of mankind.' It is perhaps a conscious echo when, after his confession, Sonya bids him 'bow down and kiss the earth which he has defiled'. In Sonya, we trace the germ of the doctrine which afterwards became the central truth of his religious and moral belief, the doctrine of salvation through suffering. It is only the germ; for *Crime and Punishment*, though technically the most perfect, is also in a sense the most limited of Dostoevsky's major works. It pierces the hollowness of the attempt to base ethics either on egoism or on rational altruism; but it scarcely attempts to probe the deeper levels of moral feeling. *Crime and Punishment* will perhaps always remain the most popular of Dostoevsky's novels, just as *Macbeth* is in a sense the most popular of Shakespeare's tragedies. But as nearly every lover and student of Shakespeare will prize *Hamlet* or *King Lear* more highly than *Macbeth*, so the lover of Dostoevsky will turn for the highest inspiration to *The Idiot* or *The Brothers Karamazov*.

Yet inconclusive though it may be, *Crime and Punishment* occupies a cardinal place not only in Dostoevsky's work but in Russian literature. Raskolnikov is the Russian Faust. The epic drama of Goethe has a wider sweep and a looser texture than Dostoevsky's novel; for it grew over a period of more than thirty years, and expanded far beyond the limits of its original theme. But the fundamental problem of both is the same. The hero of both is a young student, intelligent and ambitious, whose intelligence breeds an ironical half-pity, half-contempt for his fellow-men, and whose ambition leads him beyond the bounds of accepted morality in search of power and, through power, of happiness. Faust tempted by the devil, Raskolnikov the victim of his own dialectic, stride across the forbidden line in search of satisfaction; and the dramas revolve round the tragic failure of their quest. They seek salvation in transgression, and fail to find it.

How then shall we be saved? Goethe approaches the positive side of the problem, after many digressions, at the end of his monumental *Second Part*; Dostoevsky in the rather cursory pages of his Epilogue. There is a superficial parallelism in the conclusions. Both Goethe and Dostoevsky invoke the Eternal Feminine. Faust is led through the choirs of heaven to the feet of 'A Penitent, once named Gretchen'. Raskolnikov falls at the feet of the purified prostitute Sonya; and Dostoevsky ends on the note of the Angels' song in Faust:

> Love leads but them that love
> Into Paradise.

But this is not the essence of the matter—less so even for Dostoevsky than for Goethe; for Sonya occupies a less vital place in Raskolnikov's tragedy than Gretchen in Faust's. For the real solution we must look, in both cases, behind these mythical figures. In Goethe's case it is not far to seek. On the eve of his death, Faust contemplates the dykes he has built, the land he has reclaimed, and sees the highest achievement in the draining of a foul marsh. In work continually progressing, never completed, he discovers at last the moment to which he would say, 'Tarry awhile, thou art so fair!'

> For this is wisdom's last decree:
> He, only he, earns life and liberty
> Who daily conquers them anew.

And when he dies the Angels take up the same strain:

> Who strives and labours on unceasingly
> Him can we redeem.

It may be doubted whether the doctrine of perennial labour as an end in itself, in which Goethe took refuge, can prove ultimately satisfying to the human mind; and it did not satisfy Dostoevsky. The contrast between the solution of Goethe and that of Dostoevsky has all the vividness of a clash of national temperament. For the Russian, salvation must come not through action, but through suffering, and through suffering voluntarily accepted; and it is in search of this solution that he sends Raskolnikov to Siberia.

Raskolnikov, though he had failed to 'hold out' and had given himself up to justice, went to Siberia unrepentant, still convinced of the rightness of his premises and regretting only his failure to live up to them. In this state, he remains for the first eight months of his captivity; morose, unpopular with his fellow-convicts, he receives in silence the gracious ministrations of Sonya. At the end of this time, he falls seriously ill. After his recovery, he returns from the hospital to find that Sonya has also been taken ill, and for the first time he misses her. When at the end of a few days she reappears, he throws himself at her feet:

Love brought to them resurrection; the heart of one contained infinite sources of life for the heart of the other. . . . Instead of dialectic, life had dawned, and in his consciousness something completely new was bound to evolve itself.

He remembered her Bible which lay under his pillow.

He did not open it even now; but a thought flashed through his mind: 'Can her convictions now fail to become my convictions? her feelings, her aspirations at any rate . . . ?'

Now all this, despite the sentimental colour, possesses a certain verisimilitude. Raskolnikov, his body enfeebled by sickness, his spirit broken by captivity, lowers his flag, confesses his error, yields himself up to Sonya and makes his peace with the conventional morality which he had outraged. It is not hard to find cases of conversion brought about by transportation and hard labour. Raskolnikov, on the eve of his captivity, had predicted that 'twenty years of unceasing persecution' would break his resistance as water wears down a stone; and Dostoevsky was perhaps thinking of the change in his own outlook which had been wrought by his sojourn in the prison. But are *we* to accept from Raskolnikov, the broken convict, the solution which Raskolnikov in the fullness of his powers scorned and spurned ? The answer of Dostoevsky is in the affirmative; but in order to find his answer convincing, we must first embrace his faith that the way to spiritual strength lies through physical weakness and physical suffering. This faith, which becomes the cornerstone of Dostoevsky's later novels, finds its first expression in Sonya.

Dostoevsky seems himself to have felt that his solution, as it stands in *Crime and Punishment*, was incomplete. He had demonstrated the conclusions to which the postulates of a philosophy of self-assertion lead; he had shown the bankruptcy of an intellectual faith in self struggling in vain against the saving weaknesses of human nature; and in his concluding sentences he leaves us on the threshold of the other world—the world not of the ethical problem, but of the ethical ideal—which he will one day reveal to us:

Here begins a new story—the story of the gradual renewal of a man, the story of his rebirth, of his gradual transition from one world to another, and of the revelation to him of a new, hitherto quite unknown reality. This might form the subject of a new story, but our present tale is ended.

CHAPTER XV

The Ethical Ideal—The Idiot

THE 'new story' which was to tell of the regeneration of Raskolnikov remained unwritten. It is doubtful whether it could have been written; for the Raskolnikov of the Epilogue of *Crime and Punishment* is already a sickly shadow of his former self and carries no manner of conviction. It is easier to beat a sword into a plough-share than to convert an intellectual into a saint. A hero of a different calibre was needed for the new masterpiece germinating in the novelist's brain. A new method of approach was required. Dostoevsky left Raskolnikov, the eternal student, wrestling with life in his dark garret by the light of the tiny candle of philosophy; and turned aside to create *The Idiot*.

Between the day when he dictated to his betrothed in Petersburg the last chapter of *Crime and Punishment* and the day when he wrote the first lines of *The Idiot* in Geneva, many events had occurred in Dostoevsky's life—his marriage, the flight from Petersburg, the sojourn at Dresden, the journey via Baden to Switzerland. The mood of the books is not merely different, but sharply contrasted; though it is hard to say how far the contrast should be attributed to the changed conditions of Dostoevsky's life and how far to the change of theme. In *Crime and Punishment* the atmosphere is one of torturing enquiry; in *The Idiot*, of triumphant conviction. The link of thought between them is plain; they are both books about ethics. But the approach is no longer speculative and external. It comes from within, and is the expression of Dostoevsky's ethical faith. Religion, which fills so large a place in the novelist's later works, is still ignored or relegated to a secondary place. In *The Idiot*, as in *Crime and Punishment*, Dostoevsky is primarily occupied with ethics.

There is perhaps hardly a great work of literature which so baffles description as *The Idiot*. The hero, a prince of an ancient Russian house, is a sufferer from epileptic fits which, from early youth, have impaired his health and his mental faculties. He returns to Russia half-cured in order to take up an inheritance. Two women fall in love with him, the young daughter of a general and the discarded mistress of a rich merchant. Half loving both, he prepares to marry the latter from motives of pity; but she, in order to save him from sacrificing himself, escapes at the last moment to another suitor, who, maddened by jealousy, murders her; and the prince and the murderer spend a night together in vigil by the putrefying corpse. The murderer goes to Siberia; the general's daughter marries a fraudulent adventurer by whom she is soon deserted; and the prince returns to Switzerland in a state of physical prostration and renewed mental derangement. There are one or two subplots, of which the principal culminates in the attempted suicide of a youth who is slowly dying of consumption; and there are two irrelevant but extremely graphic descriptions of the horrors of capital punishment.

This bare summary of the plot suggests bedlam. The impression of the book itself is quite otherwise. It is the most profoundly tragic, even the most painful, of Dostoevsky's works; but in spite of this, or perhaps because of it, it is incomparably the sanest and most serene. *The Idiot* is marked by a pervading serenity unknown to his other major novels. Critics who see in Dostoevsky above all a great thinker have little use for *The Idiot*; for the rare passages in it devoted to philosophical questionings are palpably the weakest in the book. But those who regard Dostoevsky the abstract thinker as altogether subordinate to Dostoevsky the artist and the creator of new worlds will find themselves returning more often and more lovingly to *The Idiot* than to any other of his masterpieces. The quality in Dostoevsky which gives him his permanent place among the great writers of all time is his faculty of creating for us a new world, of lifting us on to a new plane of existence, where our old standards, hopes, fears, ideals lose their meaning and are transfigured for us in a new light. And this quality is supremely revealed in *The Idiot*. Myshkin does not belong to our world; he does not even belong to the Russian world. He is a vision which, perhaps, never quite succeeds in becoming real. But he embodies the most perfect and the most satisfying expression in literature, visionary and fantastic though it may be, of the Russian ethical ideal. The theme of the novel is the story of the contact of this strange visionary world with the world which we know.

There is no novel of Dostoevsky whose scope and purpose have been so clearly defined for us by the author himself. In a letter to his niece Sonya, written when he had just completed the first part of *The Idiot*, he says:

The idea of the novel is my old favourite idea, but so difficult that I for long did not dare to attempt it; and if I have attempted it now, it is certainly because I found myself in a desperate situation. The principal conception of the novel is to depict the positively good man. There is nothing in the world more difficult, particularly nowadays. Of all writers (not merely our own, but European writers too), those who have attempted to depict the positively good have always missed the mark. For it is an infinite task. The good is an ideal, and both our ideal and that of civilized Europe is still far from having been worked out. In the whole world there is only one positively good man, Christ. . . . Of the good types in Christian literature, the most perfect is Don Quixote. But he is good only because at the same time he is ridiculous. The Pickwick of Dickens (an infinitely weaker conception than Don Quixote, but still immense) is also ridiculous and succeeds in virtue of this. A feeling of compassion is produced for the much ridiculed good man who does not know his own worth, and thus perhaps sympathy is evoked in the reader. This rousing of compassion is the secret of humour. Jean Valjean is also a powerful attempt; but he arouses sympathy by the immensity of his misfortune and the injustice of society to him. In my novel there is nothing of this kind, nothing whatever, and I am terribly afraid that it will be a complete failure.

The appreciation of Pickwick and the criticism of *Les Misérables* are unusually penetrating and just. Mr Pickwick is in his origin and essence a figure of fun; and the pathos of Jean Valjean resides not in himself, but in the artificial circumstances in which he is placed. Both Dickens and Victor Hugo had had a strong appeal for Dostoevsky at different periods of his life, Dickens during his sojourn in Siberia, and Hugo at the time of his first European journey. But their influence was now a thing of the past, and the hero of *The Idiot* owes nothing either to Pickwick or to Valjean. The influence, on the other hand, of the Christ of the gospels and of Don Quixote is patent for all to see. Even the physical description of Myshkin, 'of a little more than middle height, very blond, with thick hair, sunken cheeks and a thin, pointed, almost completely white beard', seems to be inspired by the Christ of the orthodox ikon. In the scene where he is introduced to the three daughters of General Epanchin, Myshkin relates how in Switzerland, when all the others despised him, he used to gather the children around him and 'teach them or rather simply be with them'. His treatment of the sinning Mary is palpably inspired by the stories of Mary Magdalene and of the woman taken in adultery; and the first sight he recalls on his journey abroad, the sight which aroused him from lethargy and gloom, was an ass—an animal of undoubted biblical associations. 'Since that day I have been terribly fond of asses . . . and my former sadness passed away completely.'

And besides the figure of Christ Himself, we find reflected in Dostoevsky's hero some of the characteristic forms which Christianity had assumed in Russia. Readers of Tolstoy's *Childhood* will recollect the figure of the Yurodivy, the strange pilgrim who wanders over the countryside from house to house receiving alms, whose physical deformities and mental derangement are the pledge of his holiness. The Yurodivy was still a familiar figure in Russian life when Dostoevsky wrote; and the cognate tradition of the Pure Fool —the simple man whose apparent folly confounds the wisdom of the mighty—a tradition which dates back to the earliest Russian folk-lore, has survived every vicissitude of Russian history, reappearing even in recent Soviet fiction. Myshkin, with his holiness and his ignorance, with his epilepsy and his periods of recognized insanity, may not unjustly be counted the greatest incarnation in Russian literature of the Yurodivy and of the Pure Fool. 'You turn out to be quite a Yurodivy,' said Rogozhin to him, 'and such as you God loves.'

The influence of Cervantes is secondary, but significant. Few of the heroes of European literature have been successfully transplanted on Russian soil. It was Pushkin himself, that cunning blender of European and Russian tradition, who remarked that 'a Brutus and a Pericles transported to Russia turn into mere swash-bucklers'. Turgenev's Faust and King Lear are unmistakably Russian figures and retain but a faint external resemblance to their alleged prototypes. The outstanding exception to this rule (in virtue perhaps of some subtle affinity between Russian and Spanish character and ideals, between one extremity of the European continent and the other) is Don Quixote. The Knight of the Sorrowful Countenance has always been a living figure in Russian literature; and his appeal to Dostoevsky is well attested. Not only does Dostoevsky devote a long passage in *The Journal of an Author* to 'the greatest and saddest book ever created by the genius of man'; but Aglaya, the heroine of *The Idiot*, quotes at length Pushkin's famous fragment *The Poor Knight* and solemnly applies it to Myshkin. If we seek a parallel in western literature for the main theme of *The Idiot*, the clash between the world of reality and the world of the ideal, we shall search in vain until we open the pages of Cervantes' romance. Don Quixote, in the quaint phraseology of Coleridge, is the 'personification of the reason and the moral sense, divested of the judgment and the understanding'. The same words might be applied to Myshkin; such judgment and understanding as he possesses are of another world than that in which he moves. But there is still a profound difference between the two artistic conceptions. Cervantes disguises—or, we should rather say, expresses—his tragedy in laughter. Dostoevsky restricts his comic muse to the introductory scene in the ante-room of the Epanchins, where the old family

L

servitor is scandalized by the guest who places himself on terms of familiar equality with a servant. Once he has plunged into the heart of his theme, the reader is kept on the rack of ever deepening tragedy. If we go to *Don Quixote* for a parallel to the theme of *The Idiot*, we can find the counterpart of its culminating effect of pain only in the last three acts of *King Lear*. And if it be asked how, out of all this torment, Dostoevsky wrings a triumphant faith in the ethical ideal of Christianity, the answer lies in the very essence of tragedy. For the property of tragic art is to transfigure and transmute, to lift us through the human plane of pity to a new plane of consciousness, where the death of Cordelia and the agony of Lear, the humiliation of Aglaya and the recurrent insanity of Myshkin, lose their human significance in a world of higher spiritual values.

It is worth while pausing to consider the nature of the ethical ideal which Dostoevsky embodies in the figure of Myshkin. It is distinctly enough a Russian, not a western, ideal. It does not correspond with Russian reality any more than western ideals correspond with western realities; indeed, owing to what Dostoevsky calls elsewhere the 'broadness' of the Russian character, there is probably an even greater divorce between ideal and practice in Russia than in the west. But the ideal has a relation to, and an influence on, reality which is as clearly defined in Russia as elsewhere.

In the first place, the ethical ideal presented to us in Myshkin is a passive rather than an active ideal. Nothing could be further from the western conception of a good man as one who performs good works. You can imagine Myshkin sharing his crust with a beggar, or working a miracle, or throwing away his life for an impracticable ideal; but you cannot imagine him building a public library or endowing a hospital. So far as good works are concerned, Raskolnikov, who gave his last pence to help the Marmeladovs, has more to his credit than Myshkin. The reader unacquainted with *The Idiot* might easily imagine from a mere sketch of the plot that Myshkin's role in it is purely negative; but no reader of the novel itself will be tempted to make that mistake. Myshkin is the dominant figure throughout. The servitor in the first serio-comic scene in the anteroom at General Epanchin's; the self-willed heroine, Aglaya; the wild man of blood and lust, Rogozhin; the proud and innocent harlot, Nastasya Philippovna; the self-conscious youth, Ippolit; the coarse-grained pugilist, Keller—all the characters in turn feel the force of his commanding personality, and see in him their natural mentor and confessor. Yet it is hard to discover in the whole course of the story an act of any importance performed by Myshkin, except in obedience to the will of one of the other characters. The supreme Christian virtue which finds its expression in Myshkin is described by the Russian word *Smirenie*, for which there is no exact English equivalent. It is usually translated 'humility', but includes the ideas of renunciation and spiritual peace. It is the opposite of the familiar Greek conception *Hybris*, which implies pride, presumption and spiritual revolt. *Smirenie* is an essentially passive virtue; it is achieved through humiliation and suffering; and the importance attached to it by Dostoevsky explains the suffering to which he subjects his favourite characters. The doctrine of salvation by suffering comes to occupy the central place in his later work.

The ideal of Myshkin is, then, one which expresses itself in suffering rather than in action, and subordinates action to feeling. The moral and psychological relation between man and man is all-important; the action which proceeds from it relatively indifferent. In the antinomy between feeling and action the west has constantly given the preference to the latter; and the western forms of Christianity have tended more and more to regard religion as enjoining or forbidding certain courses of action. Yet it would not be hard to show that Dostoevsky more accurately represents the primitive Christian tradition of the gospels. The two great commandments of Jesus, as contrasted with the Hebrew ten, enjoin not actions but states of feeling—to love God and to love one's neighbour. The beatitudes, the most characteristic utterances of the early Christian ethic, declare the blessedness of certain states of virtue ('the pure in heart', 'the merciful', 'they which do hunger and thirst after righteousness'), and of certain states not now generally regarded as intrinsically virtuous ('the poor in spirit', 'the meek', 'they that mourn'). In only one of the eight ('the peacemakers') does Jesus affirm the blessedness of any form of action; and even this is action of a rather negative kind. And it is surely significant that the supreme achievement of Jesus' career on earth is a Passion, undergone in obedience to the will of a Divine Father. In depicting in Myshkin the ethical supremacy of suffering and submission, Dostoevsky has given us the only tolerable representation in modern literature of the primitive Christian ideal.

The subordination of action to feeling obviously has a profound effect on the conception of sin. It relegates to the background the formalistic conceptions of sin found in the Hebrew and the Greek religions, and makes the sin inherent not in the action but in the state of feeling. It follows that sinful actions are more venial than sinful states of mind. The woman taken in adultery (at that time one of the cardinal sins) escapes with no more than a formal condemnation; the Pharisees and the rich, whose actions may be unimpeachable but whose mind and feelings are corrupted, are denounced in terms of unmeasured bitterness. It is in the same spirit that Dostoevsky pours out his wrath upon nihilists and atheists, but reserves his infinite tolerance for thieves, liars and drunkards. Like Jesus, Myshkin is a friend of publicans and sinners. He is more at home with the disreputable Lebedev and the drunken, dishonest Ivolgin than with General Epanchin; he has no social or moral fastidiousness to make him cleave instinctively to the spotless Aglaya rather than to the soiled Nastasya Philippovna; it is always the degree of need which determines the direction of his attention. Many commentators, principally German, have denounced the Russian ideal depicted in Myshkin as hostile and dangerous to western civilization; but these commentators generally fail to note that it is the Russian ideal which has retained, in something like its original form, the spirit of primitive Christianity which, rightly or wrongly, has been rejected or profoundly modified by western civilization. The moral outlook of Western Europe has become affected with notions proper to the police court and the criminal code; we are tolerant of feelings and opinions and intolerant of actions. We fail to understand why the debauchery of the prodigal son, driven by hunger to a tardy repentance, is more venial than the envy of the elder brother; why the one repentant sinner is exalted above the ninety-nine respectable citizens who have not sinned; and why Mary who sat at Jesus' feet in passive contemplation is preferred to Martha who made ready the supper. The Russian, insistent on feeling and indifferent to action, understands, and Myshkin is the very embodiment of this spirit; we, by precept if not by practice men of action, live in a world of different values.

The world of transmuted values into which we are borne in *The Idiot* is a world from which the ordinary stimuli of self-interest are excluded; and in presenting us with an ideal of pure self-sacrifice Dostoevsky continues his warfare, begun in *Crime and Punishment*, against the apostles of 'enlightened self-interest'. *The Idiot* thus provides the positive complement to the negative argument of *Crime and Punishment*, and is in a spiritual sense the sequel promised in the concluding pages of the earlier novel. It is not necessary to review in detail the practical applications of the ideal as we find them in *The Idiot*—the literally complete absence of thought for the morrow; the contemptuous attitude to money; the unqualified acceptance, not as a paradox but as a self-evident rule of conduct, of the principle that giving is more blessed than receiving. But no commentary on *The Idiot* can omit to consider its application to the relationships of sex; for *The Idiot* is, and in a way peculiar to itself, a unique love story.

There is no reason to suppose that Dostoevsky was ever directly or indirectly influenced by the attitude of the early church to the sex relationship. The Russian church does not share the veneration for virginity fostered in the Latin churches; in the popular cult, Mary is worshipped as mother-goddess rather than as virgin. Nor does Dostoevsky himself ever seem to have attached particular significance to virginity; his attitude to sex, though in some respects akin to that of primitive Christianity, was reached rather through the rationalistic channels of thought which had attracted him in his youth. It has already been noted that the rationalists vigorously disclaimed the theory of exclusive rights of possession in the sex relationship, and that Dostoevsky's early denunciation of jealousy was probably derived from them. But Dostoevsky, gifted with deeper insight or more turbulent passions than they, soon perceived the hollowness of their conception; sexual passion, as Dostoevsky knew it in real life, was self-assertive, exclusive and jealous, and seemed incapable of subsisting in any other form. Unable to reconcile himself to the abandonment, in this field, of the supreme ideal of self-sacrifice, Dostoevsky acquired, in theory (for we are not now considering his practice), an aversion or contempt for the sex relationship, based on its refusal to conform to a preconceived altruistic ideal. It is curious to trace in his novels the gradual development of his thought. In *Poor Folk* he had already given us a relationship based on pure altruism; but it was not a relationship of sex in the ordinary sense of the word, and the despair of Makar Devushkin at Varvara's marriage has nothing in it of sexual jealousy. In *White Nights*, we begin to approach the problem closer; the hero masters his nascent passion for the heroine in order to facilitate her happiness with another man. But it is not until Dostoevsky's return from Siberia that the issue is set squarely before us. Vanya, the hero of *The Insulted and Injured*, has a perfectly normal passion for the heroine, Natasha; but she in turn loves Alyosha, and the principle of self-sacrifice demands of Vanya that he shall further the success of her passion for his rival. The issue is further emphasized and complicated by the fact that Alyosha himself is too passive and too submissive to the will of another (his father) to be capable of ordinary sexual passion; and the novel ends in inevitable tragedy. In both Vanya and Alyosha, the sexual passion is represented as incompatible with the altruistic ideal. In the latter the ideal drives out sex; in the former sexual passion is forcibly restrained in the interests of the ideal. Between the rivals there is a contest not of sexual desire, but of competitive magnanimity; they fight each other with the weapons of disinterestedness. It may be observed by the cynic that the heroine probably suffers more in such a contest than in any primitive strife of rival lusts. But this observation, even if true, did not occur to Dostoevsky and, had it occurred, would doubtless have been dismissed by him as irrelevant; and the moral of an unsatisfactory and rather unpleasant novel is that sex relationships as ordinarily conceived are incompatible with our highest ideals. It has often been remarked that Dostoevsky nowhere attempts to portray a stable sex relationship; such a relationship remains for him, in theory, fundamentally egoistic (none the less so for being an *égoïsme à deux*), and a derogation from the ethical ideal of altruism and self-effacement.

Such was the background against which the story of *The Idiot* took shape in Dostoevsky's mind. The Jesus of the gospels is purely sexless; but the relation of the ethical ideal to sex had tormented Dostoevsky too much for him to ignore it. We are indeed warned at the outset of something abnormal in Myshkin. 'Perhaps you do not know,' he remarks to Rogozhin in the first chapter of the book, 'but owing to my inherited illness I have no knowledge of women.' But the intention is surely to represent him as sexually innocent rather than sexually impotent. To assume definite physical incapacity in Myshkin would be to weaken the point of the story. The growth in him of a normal human love for Aglaya is strangled only by the higher claims of the altruistic ideal, which forces him to sacrifice himself now to Aglaya, now to Nastasya Philippovna, according to their respective needs, and precludes him from making either the demands or the assumptions which human passion implies. And lest the reader should be tempted once more to see in Myshkin not the apotheosis, but the *reductio ad absurdum*, of the ethical ideal, we must insist that *The Idiot* is not a representation of the real world, and still less a sermon purporting to offer us counsels of perfection for our conduct, but the vision of an imaginary world of embodied ideals, a world where 'they neither marry nor are given in marriage, but are as the angels which are in heaven'. 'An ideal is an idea,' wrote Tolstoy years afterwards, 'when its accomplishment is possible only in *idea*, in thought, when it appears attainable only in infinity and when the possibility of approaching it is therefore infinite. If the ideal were attainable, or if we could even picture its attainment by mankind, it would cease to be an ideal.'

The tragic impression of *The Idiot* is so overwhelming that (the parallel of *King Lear* once more suggests itself) the minor characters are, as it were, driven by its sheer power from the middle of the stage, and fail to retain our full attention except when they come within the circle of fierce light which beats down on the head of the central figure. By comparison with Myshkin, all the rest, including even Aglaya and Nastasya Philippovna, shrink to something less than life-size. Yet many of them deserve closer study. Aglaya is incomparably the most attractive of Dostoevsky's heroines; she is the only innocent young girl in the whole range of his novels who seems entirely true to life. Enough has been said in an earlier chapter of the originals from which she and her parents are unquestionably drawn. Between mother and daughter there exists that subtle resemblance of character, not apparent at first sight, but revealing itself more and more clearly as you delve deeper, which is so common in real life and so rarely achieved in fiction. The fundamental characteristics of both are an unflinching uprightness which makes them intolerant of compromise and of middle courses, and a 'shamefacedness' which prevents them from giving free rein to their most generous impulses. They are among the most charming and altogether life-like of Dostoevsky's more objective creations.

The figure of Nastasya Philippovna also contains, as we have seen, elements from real life. Her sensitive pride resulting from a sort of inferiority complex may owe something to Polina Suslova. On the other hand we cannot ascribe to Suslova the capacity for self-sacrifice which is developed to so high a power in Nastasya; and the scene in which she falls in love with the man who, in her physical degradation, first recognised her moral nobility and innocence, was, as we know, inspired by Martha Brown. Yet when all is said, Nastasya is of dramatic rather than human proportions. The sentimental strain of the 'pure prostitute' is in her blood; and her creator's insistence on her past wrongs becomes laboured and tedious. Except, perhaps, in the final scene between the two women (unreal and melodramatic, and in places suggestive of Balzac) our human, and not merely our conventional, sympathies are definitely on the side of Aglaya. It is rarely that a novelist succeeds in making the innocent heroine more convincing and more attractive than the woman of fragile virtue who is her rival; but Dostoevsky has performed this unusual feat.

The suitor and eventual murderer of Nastasya, Rogozhin, is a human figure at his first introduction, but develops disappointingly into a puppet of the stage. He is the embodiment of unbridled and uncalculating passion, just as Svidrigailov was the embodiment of cold and cynical self-indulgence. He dogs Myshkin much as Svidrigailov dogged Raskolnikov; like Svidrigailov, he appears and disappears mysteriously at unexpected moments, makes signs and

drops dark hints, glides through closed doors, and strikes terror by
the look in his eyes. Rogozhin is a figure who, particularly in the
later scenes, reminds us of Dostoevsky's early essays in the manner
of Hoffmann. The final scene of his ghoulish vigil by the corpse of
the murdered Nastasya is one of extraordinary power. Some of the
details are apparently borrowed from the proceedings, as read by
Dostoevsky in the Russian press, of a contemporary murderer
who, like Rogozhin, covered the body of his victim with 'American
oil-cloth' and surrounded it with 'four bottles of disinfectant'. But
though these fantastic particulars may be reproduced from real life,
the atmosphere remains none the less reminiscent of the 'horrors'
fiction current in Dostoevsky's youth. Rogozhin performs his role
in the story of *The Idiot*; he makes our flesh creep, and even plays
on our emotions. But we scarcely consider him as a man.

The artistic function of most of the remaining characters is to
serve either as a foil to Myshkin or as an illustration of his power to
influence even the most unpromising material. The most significant
of them is Ippolit, a youth of sixteen (we must allow something for
the greater precocity of the Russian adolescent) who knows himself
to be slowly dying of consumption, and whose soul is divided
between bitter revolt against this motiveless and meaningless
sentence of pain and death and a normal youthful desire for bom-
bastic self-assertion. The character, if it were altogether convincing,
would probably be intolerably painful; but Ippolit never quite
grips us. In a sense he is too realistic; for boredom and irritation are
powerful rivals of compassion even in real life. In Ippolit Dostoevsky
presents to us in its starkest form the problem of pain, to which he
will return, more subtly and more maturely, in *The Brothers Karamazov*. But if we remember Ippolit with emotion, it is perhaps most
of all on account of his last dialogue with Myshkin:

Well then, just tell me yourself how, in your opinion, it would be best
of all for me to die ? So that it may happen most—most honourably, I
mean ? Tell me that.
    Pass by us and forgive us our happiness, said the Prince quietly.

It is one of the great answers in literature.

CHAPTER XVI

Ethics and Politics—The Devils

THE interest of Dostoevsky in 'socialists' and 'nihilists' (both words were then new and strange) dates from his visit to the Geneva Congress of the League of Peace and Freedom in September 1867. The episode of the young nihilists in *The Idiot*, in which this interest found its first expression, is a rather tedious excrescence which clashes a little with the prevailing tone of the novel. But it contains a curious passage which reveals the train of thought running from *Crime and Punishment* through *The Idiot* to *The Devils*. Myshkin is discussing the perverted psychology of murderers who (like Raskolnikov) 'refuse to consider themselves criminals and think they had the right, and even that they had performed a good action'; and one of his interlocutors remarks that the attitude of the young nihilists betrays 'a similar distortion of ideas and of moral principles.' The ethical theory which, individually, produced the crime of Raskolnikov, leads socially to revolution. The Raskolnikov of private life is the nihilist of politics. Such is the thesis which Dostoevsky seeks to establish. The ethical problem of *Crime and Punishment* becomes the ethico-political problem of *The Devils*.

The germ thus planted in Dostoevsky's mind while he was writing *The Idiot* was suddenly fertilized a year later by a striking event which came home to him in a peculiar way. During the year 1869 a student of Moscow University named Nechaev, a revolutionary fanatic who had consorted with Herzen, Ogarev and Bakunin in Switzerland, began to organize his fellow-students for the coming revolution. The summer was to be devoted to propaganda throughout Russia; and the revolution was to break out in the spring of the following year. As often happens in Russian enterprises, vagueness of purpose was offset by minute precision in details of organization. The movement was to be carried on by groups of five, each responsible through its chief to a higher group. Nechaev himself pretended to be one of a central committee, which seems to have been the product of his own imagination; and in the name of this fictitious committee he enforced rigorous discipline and claimed implicit obedience from all whom he enrolled as confederates.

In this summer of 1869 the Dostoevskys, who had just reached

Dresden from Italy, were joined by Anna's brother, who had been a student of the Agricultural Academy of Moscow. He described the life of the students and their revolutionary leanings, and painted in particularly sympathetic colours a comrade named Ivanov. There was nothing unusual in these stories; but a few months later, the milieu which young Snitkin had described was luridly revealed to the world by the lightning-flash of a spectacular crime. On November 21st Ivanov was murdered by Nechaev and three of his fellow-students in the garden behind the Academy and his body thrown into the pond. It turned out that the five of them had formed a group in the revolutionary organization; that Ivanov's ardour for the cause had subsequently cooled; and that his comrades, fearing treachery and denunciation, had killed him at the instigation, and under the leadership, of Nechaev. Nechaev himself escaped to Switzerland; his three accomplices, together with many other members of Nechaev's organization, were arrested and eventually brought to trial in Petersburg in July 1870.

The profound impression made on the Russian world by this tragedy was intensified in the case of Dostoevsky by the peculiar knowledge of the scene and the *dramatis personae* which he had derived from his brother-in-law. Having at the moment just completed *The Eternal Husband*, he was casting round for a plot for the new novel which he owed to Katkov; and he pounced eagerly upon the Nechaev affair. It seemed admirably adapted to illustrate the idea, which had lain dormant in his mind since he wrote *The Idiot*, of the essential relation between nihilism and crime. He had merely to transplant the action to a provincial town, change the names of the actors and create a few supplementary characters; and he had ready to his hand all the materials for a stirring topical tale of crime with an unexceptionable moral.

But there was another ingredient which Dostoevsky was anxious to add to his brew. The last vestiges of the radical in him had long ago disappeared. But looking back on his unregenerate radical youth he perceived, or thought he perceived, that the nihilist of the 'sixties was the logical offspring of the radical idealist of the 'forties; and he resolved to express this relationship by making the Nechaev of his novel (the real Nechaev was the son of a serf) the son of a typical radical of the previous generation, who would play one of the leading roles in the story. He selected for his purpose a sincere but rather ridiculous idealist named Granovsky, long since dead; and he begged Strakhov to send him a biography of this worthy to aid him in his task. In the person of Stepan Trofimovich Verchovensky he produces a fairly detailed caricature of Granovsky; of his vague and sentimental liberalism; of his pusillanimity and lack of decision when faced with practical issues; of his passion for teaching and preaching; and of his interest in medieval, and particularly in Spanish, history. We do not know why Dostoevsky hit on Granovsky, whom he had never seen, as his typical liberal of the past generation; but the result, from an artistic point of view, justified the choice. Stepan Trofimovich is one of the most brilliantly drawn figures in the whole range of Dostoevsky's creation, and the interest of *The Devils* flags only when he is not on the stage. He is the only character in the novel who is wholly ridiculous and almost wholly lovable.

Such were the materials on which Dostoevsky began to work in the early months of 1870. We cannot tell how much of the novel in its present form was actually written during this time; but the first, and some isolated chapters of the second, of its three parts belong in the main to this original stratum. In all this section the fiction is maintained of a narrator who, though not himself an important actor in the story, is well acquainted with the principal personages and only relates what he has seen or heard. In later sections, this fiction altogether disappears and the story is related frankly and directly by the omniscient author. The degree to which this fiction is maintained provides a rough-and-ready clue to the order of composition of different chapters of the novel.

In March 1870, Dostoevsky hoped to complete the novel 'in three months.' He wanted to be rid of it; for a new idea was tormenting him and was filling his notebook with jottings even as he was writing *The Devils*. Already in 1868, before he had finished *The Idiot*, he had conceived the idea of a great novel to be called *Atheism*, which was to depict the spiritual pilgrimage of 'a Russian of our class' (it is a letter to Maikov from which we quote) through Atheism, Catholicism and Dissent to a belief in 'the Russian God.' The idea remained dormant for twelve months and re-emerged in a new form. Dostoevsky had now conceived a cycle of five novels grouped under the general title *The Life of a Great Sinner*; and detailed notes of the plan, made between December 1869 and May 1870, are extant. The *Great Sinner* had in original intention nothing to do with *The Devils*. The latter, relatively unimportant in Dostoevsky's eyes, could be polished off in quick time to discharge his debt to Katkov; and he could then sit down seriously to write his masterpiece.

But things did not work out like that. The mind of Dostoevsky was not made to advance simultaneously on two parallel lines; the lines always converged at no very distant point. It was true that in 1866 he had managed to write *The Gambler* as it were between two chapters of *Crime and Punishment*. But *The Gambler* was a slight matter; and *Crime and Punishment* was then too nearly complete to be exposed to danger. *The Devils*, not yet half written, was no match for the *Great Sinner*; it was drawn violently into the orbit of the new constellation, and its original framework was shattered by the forcible intrusion of ideas from the new plan. 'In the summer,' wrote Dostoevsky to Strakhov shortly afterwards, 'there emerged a new personage with pretensions to be the real hero of the novel, so that the previous hero (a curious figure, but not really deserving the name of hero) fell into the background.' There was nothing for it but a complete re-modelling. The story of Nechaev was retained as the framework of the plot. The 'curious figure' of Stepan Trofimovich continued to be the hero of the first scenes, which were left as they had already been written; and the conclusion, in which he once more holds the centre of the stage, was executed in accordance with the original plan. But the rest was transformed. The qualities of the hero of the *Great Sinner* were grafted on to Stavrogin, the son of Stepan Trofimovich's patroness, a relatively unimportant person in the original *Devils*, who now displaced Stepan Trofimovich as its principal hero; and from the *Great Sinner* came also 'the lame girl', Stavrogin's unacknowledged wife, and Kirillov, the half-mad superman. The welding of all these elements into a final concerted plan was scarcely complete when, in the autumn of 1870, the first chapters were sent off to Katkov; and we can well believe the author when he tells Strakhov that 'nothing he had written had ever given him more work.' *The Devils* was not finished until after his return to Russia nearly a year later; its publication in the *Russky Vestnik* continued throughout 1871, and was only completed in the following year.

It has been necessary to dwell at length on these particulars, partly for the light they throw on the capricious working of Dostoevsky's inspiration, which was particularly fertile at this period, and partly because, in default of some understanding of their causes, the glaring defects of *The Devils* are a serious bar to the enjoyment of it. The most casual reader cannot fail to perceive the general faultiness of its construction and the uncertainty as to the person of the narrator. The careful reader will probably enquire why, more than half-way through the book, we are suddenly introduced to 'a certain rascal Captain Lebyadkin,' although the gentleman in question has already made two or three conspicuous appearances; why, in the same chapter (which despite its present position belongs to the earliest stratum of the novel), the activities of Peter Verchovensky are explained to us as if we had not already heard of them *ad nauseam*; and why, in one conversation, Stavrogin is consistently addressed as Prince, a title found in the manuscript of the plan of the *Great*

Sinner, but bestowed on him nowhere else in *The Devils*. These blemishes, relatively excusable in the serial version, remained unnoticed and uncorrected in subsequent editions; but they need not be a stumbling-block to the reader who possesses the clue to the conditions in which the novel was originally written.

The external inconsistencies between the two strata are perhaps artistically less harmful than the change in the tone. The original version was based on an historical event, the conspiracy of Nechaev; and the characters belonging to this stratum, except the purely tendencious figure of Verchovensky—Nechaev himself—are palpably drawn more or less closely from life. The minor conspirators, Liputin, Lyamshin, Shigalev and the rest, were types which Dostoevsky had known twenty years before in the circle of Petrashevsky. They are lightly touched, but not unsuccessful, caricatures. The figure of the repentant nihilist, Shatov, who plays in the novel the role of the murdered Ivanov, presents particular problems. Anna's brother had, we are told, described to Dostoevsky the personality of Nechaev's victim. But when we come to study Shatov we find in many of his traits the unmistakable image of his creator. He is the one character in the novel whom Dostoevsky makes entirely sympathetic. 'He was normally gloomy and uncommunicative, but occasionally, when his convictions were attacked, he became nervously irritated and was very unrestrained in speech.' We remember Dostoevsky in the circle of Belinsky or later in Madame Krukovskaya's drawing-room. Stepan Trofimovich calls him 'le meilleur et le plus irascible homme du monde.' He is at first an enthusiastic socialist and, like Dostoevsky, takes charge of the printing-press of the confederates. He becomes converted, adopts Slavophil tenets, and makes 'the people' the corner-stone of his belief in God; he is even taunted by Stavrogin with 'degrading divinity into an attribute of nationality'—a charge which might, not altogether unjustly, be levelled at Dostoevsky himself. So many resemblances cannot be accidental. There is no reasonable doubt that Shatov is a self-portrait or, it would be fairer to say, a self-idealization of the author. Dostoevsky had dramatized himself as the victim of the crime of which he had heard so much.

The Devils, unlike any other novel of Dostoevsky, is rich in elements of caricature. The most famous of his victims, and the only one who was in a position to hit back, was Turgenev. It is a bitter piece of work. In the person of Karmazinov, Dostoevsky ridiculed the personal appearance and the mannerisms of his rival, parodied the affectations of his literary style, and raked up once more a hoary but malicious legend that Turgenev, in his youth, under the stress of a storm at sea, had appealed to the sailors with tears in his eyes to save him first on the ground that he was the only son of his mother. These insults seem to have left Turgenev relatively indifferent. Strangely enough, the item in the caricature to which he took the bitterest exception was that part which seems to us most legitimate and least offensive. The half-Europeanised Russian liberal, of whom Turgenev was the type, seemed to Dostoevsky to occupy much the same position *vis-à-vis* the nihilists as did the idealists of a previous generation; and Karmazinov, like Stepan Trofimovich, is depicted as a sympathizer, out of vanity rather than from conviction, with the nihilists. The very name Karmazinov suggested the Russian form of the French word *cramoisi*; it is as if an English novelist had labelled a friend of the Reds 'Mr. Pink.' The charge went home; and it became an unforgotten and unforgiven incident in the famous literary quarrel between the two novelists of which some account has been given in an earlier chapter.

Besides the two major caricatures of Granovsky and Turgenev, there are in *The Devils* a host of minor parodies, probably more than have been detected even by the industry of modern critics. The speech of the mad professor at the 'literary *matinée*' at which Karmazinov gave his reading is closely imitated from a speech actually delivered a few years previously by a professor of Petersburg University, who paid for his attack on the government by exile to the provinces. The poems circulated by the nihilists in *The Devils* are close parodies of poems published abroad by Dostoevsky's Geneva acquaintance, Ogarev.[1] And there are, apart from these parodies, broader strokes of satire such as this at the expense of the sentimental jury, a frequent butt of the Russian writers of the time:

If you have been caught stealing, run off home quickly and murder your mother; then you will at once be acquitted of everything.

Or this at the expense of an American magnate:

He left the whole of his vast fortune for building factories and teaching the applied sciences, his skeleton to the students of the local academy, and his skin for a drum on which should be played day and night the American national anthem.

The writing of *The Devils* revealed in Dostoevsky an unfamiliar and unexpected vein of satire. The caustic witticism is an effect which we seldom find in any of his other novels. Had he finished *The Devils* in accordance with his original design, it would have been one of the

[1] See note on p. 179.

lightest and easiest to read, though probably not one of the greatest of his novels.

But when we cross the uncertain and shifting line which, in our present version of *The Devils*, separates the first stratum from the second, we leave the atmosphere of satire and caricature for one of theory and imagination. Peter Verchovensky, though he plays the historical role of Nechaev, belongs in spirit to the second stratum. He is no longer even a caricature; he is the walking embodiment of a theory. He is drawn with as little wit as understanding, and remains totally unconvincing. In order to demonstrate the fundamental identity of moral evil and political nihilism—and this is the task which Dostoevsky has at heart—it is scarcely sufficient to put up a lay figure who exclaims in a moment of expansion, 'I am a rascal and not a socialist,' and about whom we are never allowed to make up our minds whether he is a fanatic who practises crime for righteousness' sake, or a monster whose criminal instincts are masked in an assumed guise of revolutionary fanaticism. And that is all Dostoevsky has to offer in support of his thesis. The tortured questionings of *Crime and Punishment* are replaced by crude dogmatic assertion. It is no wonder that, in a country where literary productions have always been judged by their supposed political tendencies, the younger generation raged against the author of *The Devils*, the more so as he had once seemed to be one of themselves. Their indignation was no surprise to Dostoevsky; he had anticipated, and obtained, a sort of *succès de scandale*.

Even Verchovensky remains, at any rate in original conception, a character of the real world. But when we leave the original characters of *The Devils*, and turn to Stavrogin and Kirillov, those uninvited and not altogether welcome intruders from the plan of the *Great Sinner*, we have passed over into the world of pure imagination. It is true that a distinguished Soviet critic has expended considerable ingenuity in the search of an historical original for Stavrogin, whom in 1924 he identified with Speshnev, one of the members of Petrashevsky's circle, and in 1926 with the anarchist Bakunin. But the former identification is extremely problematical, the latter purely fantastic; and it may be suggested that the fact that Stavrogin can be identified by the same critic almost simultaneously with two completely different historical personages is an impressive argument against the plausibility of either hypothesis. It is difficult to understand how any sensitive reader can fail to be aware of the difference in tone which separates Stavrogin and Kirillov from the other *dramatis personae* of *The Devils*. The rest are characters, more or less convincingly portrayed, from the real world; Stavrogin and Kirillov are pure fictions of the imagination, and their inspiration is literary and philosophical rather than historical. Their relation to the political theme of *The Devils* is fortuitous and artificial; they look backward to Raskolnikov and forward to Ivan Karamazov.

Stavrogin represents a more advanced stage in the development of Raskolnikov; he is a Raskolnikov who has lost his ardent faith in the exaltation of self as the highest canon of morality, but continues, disillusioned, bored and half-hearted, to follow its dictates, mocking at the same time his lost faith and himself. His literary ancestors, like those of Raskolnikov, must be sought among the romantic writers of western Europe; he is a typical victim of romantic *ennui*.

Sa barbe n'était pas encore poussée que ces amusements l'avaient lassé déjà. . . . Il aimait à battre ses chiens, bientôt il battit ses prostituées. . . . À mesure que l'animal se développait dans son cerveau appesanti, le dieu s'éteignait dans tout son être. L'intelligence inactive sentait des forces sans but, le cœur se rongeait dans un ennui sans terme, dans une souffrance sans nom. Trenmor n'avait rien à aimer. Autour de lui tout était vil et corrompu; il ne savait pas où il eût pu trouver des cœurs nobles, il n'y croyait pas.

The quotation has nothing to do with Stavrogin; it was penned a quarter of a century before he was created. But it analyses his character more accurately and more pungently than any passage in *The Devils* itself or in any of the numerous critiques which have been written on it. It is George Sand's description of the most romantic, and at one time the most famous, of her novels. *Lélia*. It would be too much to assert that Dostoevsky had Trenmor in his mind when he created Stavrogin, though he was an admirer of George Sand and had certainly read *Lélia* in his youth; but the type was a commonplace at the time. In Musset's *Confession d'un Enfant du Siècle*, Desgenais sends his mistress with a bouquet to offer herself to his friend Octave; it is an exploit which Dostoevsky would have been proud to attribute to Stavrogin if he had thought of it. The disillusioned hero, who titillates his jaded palate by seeking experiences ever more and more bizarre and piquant, is not peculiar to one author or one novel or one country. The precise genealogy of Stavrogin cannot be established, and there are elements in him peculiarly Russian and even peculiar to Dostoevsky; but we know well enough the stock from which he springs.

The figure of Kirillov is first roughly sketched in the plan of the *Great Sinner*: 'in the vagaries of his imagination he has infinite dreams, extending to the overthrow of God and the putting of himself in his place.' He is forced into the plot of *The Devils* by a rather repulsive melodramatic device. He has resolved, on philo-

ill himself; but being a sympathizer
promised to make his suicide coin-
committed by them, in order that,
onfessing himself its author, he may
of detection. The occasion on which
e is the murder of his friend Shatov.
y that nothing will induce him to
but ends by playing his part and
ter Verchovensky. We may assume,
this time no longer responsible for
, and indeed his whole connection
rally unintelligible. It is a mere
f many weaknesses of *The Devils*.
reader resides not in this miserable
rgument which leads to his resolve
ian, 'the last enemy that shall be
erman, the last enemy to be over-
can overthrow that, he is complete
es supreme; he is the man-god, the
Christianity. But the only way in
overcome the fear of death is to
ne can he achieve godhead; and
g sacrament of the religion of the
expressed by the old and saintly
Makar Dolgoruky in *A Raw Youth*: 'A man who bows down to
nothing can never bear the burden of himself.' The suicide of
Kirillov is, in Dostoevsky's eyes, the logical issue of the ethical
theory of Raskolnikov; and Kirillov, the fanatic of logic, the rebel
not only against morality, but against God, is the prototype of
Ivan Karamazov.

In Kirillov, Dostoevsky transposes the problem of the superman,
which has occupied him so much, into the religious key. It is at this
comparatively late stage of his career, in passages which have crept
into *The Devils* in virtue of an afterthought, that Dostoevsky first
embarks on the seas of religious thought. In *Crime and Punishment*
and *The Idiot*, he is content to take orthodox religion for granted.
The incipient superman, Raskolnikov, believes 'literally' in God
and in 'the resurrection of Lazarus'; the exponent of the ethical
ideal, Myshkin, except in his one strange diatribe against the
iniquities of Roman Catholicism, expresses no sort of religious
belief. But from *The Devils* onward, religion not unmixed with
politics occupies a large place in Dostoevsky's thought and work;
and some of the religious ideas adumbrated in *The Devils* will

M

reappear in his later and specifically religious novel *The Brothers Karamazov*.

The Devils has been, since the Bolshevik revolution, a happy hunting-ground for those in search of quotations to demonstrate Dostoevsky's profound prophetic insight into revolutionary mentality. Already after the revolution of 1905, Merezhkovsky had called him 'the prophet of the Russian revolution'; and there are many passages in *The Devils* which may justify the title in the eyes of those Russians who are opponents of the present régime.

My starting-point [says Shigalev] is unlimited freedom, my conclusion unlimited despotism.

A generation or two of debauchery [says Peter Verchovensky] is now indispensable—unparalleled vulgar debauch, when man turns into a filthy, cowardly, cruel, selfish reptile, that's what we need; and a little drop of nice fresh blood just to accustom people. ... Well, then the turmoil will begin. It will be such a tossing as the world has never seen. The face of Russia will be darkened, and the land will mourn for her old gods.

Not knowing how to look after their own affairs [says Stavrogin] they are all terribly fond of accusing other people of being spies.

These quotations are not devoid of wit and of insight into the potentialities of the Russian character; but they prove little except a certain lack of originality in modern political invective. Beside these quotations we must place one of the most moving (and, from the political point of view, most absurd) passages in the book—the scene at the deathbed of Stepan Trofimovich. The evangelical bible-seller, whom he has encountered on his last journey, reads to him the story of the unclean devils who entered into the swine. The eyes of the dying man are opened; and he perceives, as in a vision, that Russia was the man afflicted of devils; that he himself, and his son Peter, and the other radicals and nihilists, are the swine into whom the devils have entered and who are rushing headlong down a steep place into the sea; and that when they have passed ignominiously away, Russia will sit healed and glorified 'at the feet of Jesus.' Such is the significance of the title of the novel, and such Dostoevsky's diagnosis of the mission and fate of the Russian revolution.

The success of *The Devils* encouraged Dostoevsky in the political bent which his mind had taken; and for the next six or seven years his interests lay principally in the political sphere. Then once more he turned back to religion, and wrote the last great work in which he endeavoured to express the most fundamental ideas from his plan of *The Life of a Great Sinner*. There are long passages in *The Brothers Karamazov* which in depth and maturity surpass, perhaps, anything Dostoevsky had yet written; but the book is a mighty *tour de force* by one whose zenith is already passed, and lacks the eager, stumbling spontaneity of its predecessors. After his return to Russia in 1871, Dostoevsky was not again revisited by the fertile fever of inspiration of that wonderful quinquennium which had produced *Crime and Punishment*, *The Idiot* and *The Devils*, and, by way of recreation, *The Gambler* and *The Eternal Husband*.

NOTE TO CHAPTER XVI

The fate of one of the parodies in *The Devils* is sufficiently amusing to merit a note.

In 1869 Ogarev published in Geneva, with a dedication to Nechaev, a short doggerel poem called *The Student*, singing the praises of a student who devoted his life to the revolutionary movement. It was of course prohibited in Russia. But Dostoevsky must have seen it in Dresden; for in *The Devils* he introduces among his samples of nihilist literature a poem entitled *A Noble Character*, 'evidently printed abroad,' which is in fact a close parody of Ogarev's *The Student*.

In 1874 agents of the Third Section (Secret Police) of the Imperial Chancery discovered copies of *A Noble Character* being circulated in Russia as a serious revolutionary propaganda pamphlet; and having ascertained that it was reprinted from the *Russky Vestnik* of three years before, the Third Section addressed to the Ministry of the Interior a querulous letter enquiring why so inflammatory a document had been allowed to pass the censorship. The Ministry of the Interior replied in due course explaining that the poem had originally appeared in an 'indubitably well-intentioned' novel written 'with the wholly laudable and useful object of exposing the revolutionaries.' It is improbable that Dostoevsky ever knew to what base uses his parody had been turned; for this official correspondence was first published in the Soviet journal *Krasny Archiv* (Vol. III, 1923).

CHAPTER XVII

Return to Russia

THE ten years of life which remained to Dostoevsky after the return to Petersburg in the summer of 1871 are, for the biographer and for the reader, something of an anticlimax. Already in the last years abroad a certain ordered monotony had descended on his life. The multiple uncertainties of his earlier career had been reduced to one—the prolonged financial crisis which made a hand-to-mouth existence seem like second nature to him. Now after the return to Russia this one remaining uncertainty ceased, under Anna's practical management of his affairs, to play its former dominant and menacing role. The growing security of his financial position, the tranquillity of his domestic happiness, the passage of years, combined to calm his tempestuous emotions; and the biographer of the last decade finds little to chronicle save his now relatively methodical activities, his uneventful journeys, the ailments of his children, and petty quarrels about money with jealous relatives. The tumults and excitements of the heroic age had given place to the sedate period of bourgeois respectability.

Anna's first son was born, just a week after their arrival in Petersburg, in the furnished lodgings in which they had hastily established themselves; and it was not till September that the problem of a permanent home seriously presented itself. Save for the payments from Katkov for *The Devils* they were penniless as ever; and beyond the contents of their travelling-trunks they had not a possession in the world. The furniture of Dostoevsky's former flat had, we may assume, been appropriated by Emilia Fyodorovna or, more probably, seized by the landlord to meet the unpaid rent. His library had been left in the care of Paul Isaev who, having no other use for the books, had sold them one by one to defray the needs of existence. The furniture which Anna had pledged more than four years ago to enable them to escape from Petersburg, had been lost through failure to keep up the interest payments. Even the crockery and household utensils which she had left with various relatives had been dispersed, lost or broken. It was a heart-rending beginning for the returned exiles. Most of all did Anna regret some cups with painted shepherdesses which had belonged to her father, and a drinking-glass with a wonderful painted fly on the lip which the unsuspecting guest, as he took up the glass to drink, invariably tried to flick away. It was some consolation when a large basket came to light in an attic of the old flat; it was crammed with Dostoevsky's old notes, manuscripts and correspondence, which Anna spent many happy hours sorting and labelling.

A new flat was taken, and furniture purchased on the instalment system. Both these transactions were carried out in Anna's name; so that when the creditors, who learnt of Dostoevsky's return some months after the event, fastened once more on their victim, they found no tangible assets in his possession and no weapon to use against him save the old two-edged threat of the debtors' prison. Instead, moreover, of a man who put his hands to his head in despair and made fantastic promises which he had not the faintest prospect of fulfilling, they found themselves confronted by a determined woman who argued and fought and bargained, and whose promises carried with them the conviction that, once made, they would somehow be executed to the letter. On the plea of saving her husband from anxieties which endangered his health, Anna soon took the control of these affairs from his unresisting hands; and the financial pre-occupations which had tormented him almost unceasingly for thirty years receded more and more into the background of his consciousness.

The beneficent control exercised by Anna over the debit side of Dostoevsky's budget was soon extended to his sources of income. The writing of the last chapters of *The Devils* had proceeded slowly and with many delays. It was not till December 1872 that the final instalment appeared in the *Russky Vestnik*. Its frankly melodramatic episodes, its caricatures of persons still living or recently dead, its topical significance which excited the rage of the radicals and the enthusiasm of the conservatives, combined to make *The Devils* a sensational popular success. The trial of Nechaev, who had just been handed over by the Swiss authorities, brought vividly back to men's minds the dramatic circumstances of his crime; and an edition of *The Devils* in book form, if issued at once, promised to be a lucrative undertaking. Warned by the unproductive results of her husband's previous bargains with publishers, Anna determined to publish the book herself. It was the day of small business; and the story of Anna's operations gives a vivid impression of the primitive organization of trade in the Petersburg of the 'seventies. The paper was purchased, and an order given to a printer to print 3,500 copies. As soon as the order was completed and the first consignment of the books delivered at the Dostoevsky's flat, an advertisement was inserted in the principal morning newspaper of the publication of *The Devils* by the author in book form at the price of 3 roubles 50 kopeks. At 9 o'clock messengers from the leading bookshops already began to arrive at the flat to obtain copies of the book for sale. Relying on the public demand, Anna insisted on cash payments, refused to deal on a 'sale or return' basis, and haggled with each and all over the discount, which varied from 20 to 30 per cent. according to the number of copies taken by the purchaser. Dostoevsky, who worked at night and never rose before midday, slept peacefully through the excitements of this busy morning. When he finally appeared, 115 copies had been sold; but the incredulous author-publisher refused to believe the good tidings until the bundle of rouble notes was flourished before his eyes by his triumphant wife. In the evening another dealer came and purchased 300 copies outright for provincial circulation. It was January 22, 1873, 'a notable day in our lives,' as Anna remarks with conscious pride. For nearly forty years she continued to publish her husband's works.

By this time, Dostoevsky's literary abilities had sought another outlet. Like many other great creative artists, he secretly despised pure art and coveted the mantle of the prophet. The prohibition of the *Vremya* and the failure of the *Epocha* had left him with the sense of an unfulfilled mission. His beliefs were not always consistent and seldom perfectly lucid; but he had a passionate unwavering faith in their immense importance for himself and for humanity. Already in the autumn of 1867 he had written from Geneva that he wished, on his return to Russia, to publish a weekly journal 'the object and form of which are now completely clear in my mind.' Now at the end of 1872, when *The Devils* was at last off his hands, the opportunity occurred to realize his ambition. Among the new acquaintances made since his return from abroad was Prince Meschersky, an unprincipled and undistinguished publicist, who had recently founded a weekly paper, the *Grazhdanin*. According to Anna's *Memoirs*, he approached Dostoevsky with an invitation to become editor of the *Grazhdanin*; according to Meshchersky's own more circumstantial account, the first suggestion emanated from Dostoevsky. But whichever version is the correct one, the proposal was made and enthusiastically accepted. The salary was fixed at 250 roubles a month, exclusive of pay at the normal rate for contributions; and for the first time since he left the Engineering Department in 1844, Dostoevsky had a fixed employment and a regular salary. It was this aspect of the matter which appealed to Anna; and Dostoevsky found his satisfaction in the opportunity of addressing the world in a series of monthly articles under the title *The Journal of an Author*.

The summers following their return to Russia were spent by the Dostoevskys at Staraya Russa, a little health-resort on the shores of Lake Ilmen. There was no railway. In summer, the village was reached by a steamer from Novgorod; in winter, you drove across the ice in sleighs. The summer of 1873 saw Dostoevsky detained in Petersburg by his editorial duties. He could only visit Staraya Russa at rare intervals and for a few days at a time; and this, like other short periods of separation from his family during the last decade of his life, produced a flood of letters which reveal him in the role of a passionate husband and almost comically anxious parent.

Anna, my joy [he writes on July 20th], I am impatiently awaiting a letter from you. . . . You are my only joy, and without you it is terribly hard for me here alone. You can never understand my loneliness here. I am now in complete loneliness, and nothing but unpleasantnesses into the bargain. Write to me in detail about the children, what Lily and Fedya are doing. Write to me in detail about their sayings and their pranks.

A few days later there is another letter:

In the night of Saturday to Sunday, among other nightmares, I saw Fedya climb up on the window-sill and fall from the fourth storey. As he fell headlong, turning over and over, I covered my eyes with my hands and shrieked in despair: 'Farewell, Fedya!' and at once woke up. Write to me as soon as you can about Fedya, and whether something did not happen to him on the night of Saturday to Sunday. I believe in second sight, all the more because it is a fact, and I shall not be at ease until I get your letter.

Hypochondriacal as in the days of his youth, he worries her to distraction not only over the children, but over himself. In the same letter he draws this alarming picture of his health:

Apart from all this [his gloom and depression], I am seriously afraid of falling ill. Yesterday evening I had attacks of fever, my back ached and my legs felt heavy. Today however I am a great deal better, only I sleep badly, nightmares, bad dreams, and my digestion is out of order. Write to me at once every time you get a letter from me.

A week or two later he writes that he 'has never been in such a bad way, not even after his worst fits,' and he fears a stroke which will certainly finish him off. Then, after two letters in this strain, he suddenly becomes conscience-stricken and terrified lest Anna should take him seriously and hurry back to Petersburg to the detriment of the children's health; he sends a hurried telegram assuring her that all is well, and begging her not to return. Separated from Anna, he always relapsed into the same state of pathetic, childish fears, worries and helplessness.

The editorial duties which compelled him to toil alone in Petersburg through the heat of the summer, soon began to feel intolerably irksome. Dostoevsky had long become incapable, if indeed he had ever been capable, of a life of disciplined regularity. He could neither write nor edit to order. There was no divergence in political convictions to fear; for Meshchersky was as good a conservative as Dostoevsky himself, and attested the ardour of his Slavophil creed by dressing his office messenger, to the public amusement, in Russian blouse and top-boots. But Dostoevsky was totally unfitted to deal with the delicate situations which arise between editor and proprietor when the latter participates actively in the management of the journal. When the Slavophil poet Tyutchev died, Dostoevsky planned an appropriate obituary article; but he had to put it aside in order to make room for one from the pen of Meshchersky himself, which, we are assured, required innumerable corrections of grammar before it was fit to appear. Dostoevsky possessed none of the suppleness and the patience necessary for the discharge of the functions he had undertaken. Meshchersky seems to have been an easygoing chief, and the irritability was all on the side of the subordinate, but relations between them became more and more difficult. Dostoevsky's irritability was a by-word in the office of the printer who produced the paper, and who frequently had to complain of the difficulty of serving two masters. At the end of the year, Dostoevsky asked to be relieved of his post. His last personal contribution to the *Grazhdanin* appeared in January 1874, and two months later he formally laid down his functions as editor.

The mood had changed once more. He had for the moment had enough of politics and criticism, and his thoughts turned back to the relatively tranquil waters of fiction. The matter was clinched by an unexpected visit from Nekrasov. Relations between Dostoevsky and Nekrasov had been intermittent and uncertain. The short-lived friendship of 1845–6 had ended in a violent quarrel, in which Dostoevsky reproached Nekrasov with his share, real or supposed, in the 'literary pimple' lampoon. In the early 'sixties they were once more on friendly terms, and negotiations were at one time on foot for Nekrasov to contribute some poems to the *Vremya*; but they broke down, and the political quarrel between the *Vremya* and *Sovremennik* again embittered relations between the two writers. Now in the 'seventies, the *Sovremennik* having ceased to exist,

Nekrasov was editing the other great radical journal, the *Otechest-vennye Zapiski*, which had published most of Dostoevsky's early stories; and in April 1874 he called on Dostoevsky (they had not met for more than ten years) to ask him to give his next novel to the old journal.

The scene is described in Anna's *Memoirs* in a revealing passage which is symptomatic of much in their characters and their relation-ship to each other:

I knew that since our return from abroad Fyodor had not met Nekrasov, so that his visit must have some particular significance. My curiosity was so great that I could not help myself, and took my stand behind the door which led from the study to the dining-room. To my great joy I heard Nekrasov invite my husband to become a contributor and write a novel for the *Otechestvennye Zapiski* of the following year; he offered a price of 250 roubles a folio, whereas Fyodor had hitherto received 150 roubles.

Nekrasov seeing our very modest surroundings probably thought that Fyodor would be extraordinarily pleased by such an increase in his rate of pay and would at once consent; but Fyodor, after thanking him for the proposal, replied:

'I cannot give you a definite answer for two reasons. In the first place I must write to the *Russky Vestnik* and ask whether they require my novel. If they have enough material for next year, then I am free and can promise you my novel. I am an old contributor of the *Russky Vestnik*. Katkov has always been sympathetic and attentive to my requests, and it would be ungentlemanly of me to leave them without giving them the offer of my work. This can be cleared up in two or three weeks. I ought to warn you, Nikolai Alekseevich, that I always receive an advance on my work, an advance of two or three thousand.'

Nekrasov quite agreed to that.

'The second question,' continued Fyodor, 'is what my wife thinks of your proposal. She is now at home and I will ask her at once!'

My husband came to me.

Then a curious scene occurred. When Fyodor came up to me, I hurriedly said to him:

'Well, why ask? Agree, Fedya, agree at once.'

'Agree to what?' my husband asked in amazement.

'Why, good heavens! To Nekrasov's proposal.'

'But how do you know about his proposal?'

'I listened to the whole conversation, I was behind the door!'

'So you were eavesdropping? Oh, Anna! Aren't you ashamed?' cried Fyodor sadly.

'Not in the least. You have no secrets from me, and would have told me all the same. Well then, what does it matter if I did eavesdrop? It wasn't other people's business, but our own.'

Fyodor could only raise his hands at such logic.

Fyodor returned to the study and said:

'I have spoken to my wife, and she is very glad for my novel to appear in the *Otechestvennye Zapiski*.'

Nekrasov continued to be a little hurt that in such a matter it had been necessary for Fyodor to consult his wife and said: 'Well, I should never have imagined you "under the thumb" of your wife.'

A hasty journey to Moscow revealed the fact that Katkov, having just secured *Anna Karenina* (for a price, as Dostoevsky afterwards learned with indignation, of 500 roubles a folio), was not particularly anxious for another big novel, and could offer no payment in advance; and Nekrasov's proposal was accepted.

In the cold and damp of the Petersburg climate, Dostoevsky had developed a chronic catarrh of the lung; and in 1874 he went for six weeks in the summer to Bad Ems in western Germany to undergo one of the fashionable cures. The visit was repeated in the two following years and again in 1879. The voluminous letters which he wrote to his wife during these summer absences are surely the most monotonous ever penned by a great author. His mind revolves in an unending circle of unchanging preoccupations. The themes never vary: his symptoms and the progress of his cure; the number of bottles of Kränchen or Kesselbrunnen he has drunk (for as the years went on Dostoevsky became a more and more decided valetudinarian); the stupidity of the German and the affectations of the travelling Russian; his loneliness and boredom; his passionate devotion to Anna, expressed sometimes in terms so personal that she saw fit to obliterate certain passages before bequeathing the letters to posterity; his constant anxieties for the children, and his delighted interest in anecdotes of their sayings and doings. The gaming-table had lost its old fascination; the *Wanderlust* of his earlier years had vanished; and when Anna suggested that he might go on to Paris to buy her some dresses, and sent him money for the purpose, he rather angrily refused. His annual journeys to Ems had become a wearisome routine, and he longed for nothing but to escape from the artificial society of the German watering-place to the domestic felicity of his home. Only once, he went on from Ems to lay a last wreath and drop a last tear on the grave of his never-forgotten Sonya in the little cemetery at Geneva.

When at the end of July 1874 he returned home with some rough notes for the new novel in his pocket, his wife greeted him with an unexpected proposal. They had no money, for Nekrasov was not so generous with advance payments as Katkov had formerly been; and peace and quiet were necessary for the writing of the novel. Why should they not winter at Staraya Russa, where houses could be rented for 15 roubles a month? Dostoevsky was dumb-founded and began to think of objections—in particular the fear, which never quite left him, that Anna would be bored with his exclusive company. But it was Anna, of course, who had her way; and they settled down to their winter of tranquillity and isolation, he to write *A Raw Youth*, and she to discharge the tasks of mother, housekeeper and copyist in which she found the well-ordered ideal of her existence.

The reasons adduced by Anna for this winter retirement were those of economy and health; and we may discern another motive of which she was perhaps scarcely conscious, but which nevertheless is extremely characteristic. The simple possessiveness of her nature had not diminished since the day when she had carried off Dostoevsky from the insidious clutches of his Petersburg relatives; it had rather been enhanced, perhaps a little coarsened, by success. She wanted her husband—the hero with all his laurels, the child with all his weaknesses—for herself alone. She had lived with him for more than four years abroad in splendid solitude; and she had come to grudge every activity and every relationship of which she was not the sole arbiter. In Petersburg he belonged too much to his relatives and friends; and when he visited them she, always a hater of society and devoted to the family hearth, sat half-annoyed and half-contemptuous at home. The relatives had indeed, since the return from abroad, not given serious trouble; her hold over husband was now far too secure to be endangered from this or any other quarter. But she was not one of those who know how to make victory tolerable for the vanquished. She was heartily and unanimously detested by all her husband's relatives, and his meetings with them discreetly took place, not indeed without her knowledge, but in her absence. In such circumstances these meetings inevitably seemed like temporary desertions to the other camp, and never ceased to fill her with a certain uneasiness and resentment. Emilia Fyodorovna, whom he occasionally visited for the sake of his dead brother's memory, was no longer a claimant on his bounty; for her sons were now well established. Paul Isaev, on the other hand, continued to exploit the charity of his soft-hearted stepfather. Not long before the latter's return from abroad, he had increased his lightly borne responsibilities by marriage. His wife pleased Dostoevsky, and even the more fastidious Anna; but her lot was unenviable. The civil service, the time-honoured refuge for idle sons of the Russian educated classes was not open to Paul; for he had failed at school to reach even the minimum standard required for this not too exacting career. Through the intermediary of Maikov and other friends of Dostoevsky he obtained employment from time to time, generally in banks; but he held none of these posts for long. He had not, if we may believe one of his stepfather's letters written in a moment of exasperation, learnt his multiplication tables until the age of twenty; and it is scarcely to be supposed that he had any aptitude for finance. But this seems to have mattered little; for insubordination or insolence generally led to his resignation or dismissal before there had been time to detect his incompetence. For the rest, he lived on what he could beg from his stepfather or, on occasion, from other relatives. A child was born, and then another; when the third came, the position was desperate, and it was taken to the Foundling Hospital. Still pity was the dominant feeling in Dostoevsky's attitude; he would neither judge nor condemn; and when Paul complained of an insulting letter received from Anna Grigorievna, he hastily wrote to explain that he had not seen the letter and that his wife's sentiments must not be confused with his own. What passed between husband and wife on the subject of Paul Isaev must be left to the imagination; for there are no records. There was not much softness in Anna's composition; but it is difficult to blame her for the restraint which she strove to place on her husband's promiscuous generosity. His letters to Paul are fewer and curter as time goes on; in one, he writes that he will never again ask any of his friends to help his stepson to a post; in another, he calls him brusquely to account for money entrusted to him. The improvement in Dostoevsky's material circumstances implied a tightening of his wife's control; and Paul Isaev, in these years of Anna's undisputed reign, fades gradually from the narrowing circle of his preoccupations.

The older generation of the Dostoevsky family remain dim figures. Of Andrei, the next brother to Fyodor, we hear little save that he was a tolerably successful engineer. The youngest brother, Nicholas, was frankly a parasite, living on Fyodor's bounty at the rate of 50 roubles a month, supplemented by occasional gifts when funds were plentiful, and when Anna was not there to interfere. Varvara and Vera lived in Moscow. The youngest sister, Alexandra, was in Petersburg, and Dostoevsky saw her sometimes; but her husband refused to recognize him in the street, and she could scarcely be induced to mention Anna's name. It is clear that in most of these relationships the conventional tie alone remained; and the family would have drifted altogether apart, peacefully and painlessly, but for a development which provided them with two powerful specifics against mutual indifference—a common cause and a bone of contention.

The affair which agitated the whole Dostoevsky clan for ten years and was not fully liquidated until after Fyodor's death was the estate of Aunt Kumanin. This old lady, the sister of Fyodor's

mother, has already made a few dim but imposing appearances on
the horizon of his biography. The wealth of her husband made her
a unique figure in the Dostoevsky family. When their father died,
the youngest children had been taken into the Kumanin household;
and one of Fyodor's earliest surviving letters, addressed to Uncle
and Aunt Kumanin, bears witness, by its more than deferential
tone, to the respect which they inspired. The respect was fully
justified by results. Uncle Kumanin died in 1863 and left Fyodor
3,000 roubles at one of the many critical moments in his career; and
in the following year Michael and Fyodor each successively obtained
10,000 roubles from Aunt Kumanin for the purpose of carrying on
the doomed *Epocha*.

It required no profound knowledge of human nature to realize
that the death of the wealthy and childless widow was an event
anticipated with interest by her next of kin; and when he wrote
The Gambler in 1866, Dostoevsky included in it a quite recognizable
caricature of Aunt Kumanin. The eccentric old 'grandmother'
arrives with her sedan-chair at Roulettenberg, where the hungry
heirs are awaiting a telegram from Moscow to announce her death,
and proceeds, under their very eyes, to gamble away their expected
inheritance at the roulette table. Aunt Kumanin was now in her
dotage, and there was probably no danger that the portrait would be
recognized by its original. But the sequel came near to bearing out
Dostoevsky's premonition. In August 1869 at Dresden, he learned
from a letter of Apollon Maikov that the old lady had died, and had
left 40,000 roubles of her fortune to a monastery; and on the advice
of Maikov, he wrote impassioned letters to relatives and lawyers
enquiring whether the will could not be contested on the ground
that the testatrix had been, for the past four years, 'not right in her
mind.' The source of Maikov's information is unknown; but it
turned out to be a complete mare's nest. Aunt Kumanin, whatever
may have been the state of her mental faculties, lingered on till the
spring of 1871 and died only a few months before Dostoevsky's
return to Russia.

The principal property left by her consisted of an estate in the
province of Ryazan. The will was so complicated that it took three
or four years of wrangling between lawyers to determine that the
property must be divided, in three equal parts, between the
Dostoevskys and two other families of nephews. In 1873, the year
of his editorship of the *Grazhdanin*, we find Fyodor constantly
occupied with lawyers over this question. When the legal issue was
settled, the estate was put up to auction. But no buyers were forthcoming; and it remained, in accordance with the usual practice, to

assemble the heirs and effect a division of the land. It was not until 1879 that the opportunity occurred of bringing all the interested parties simultaneously to this remote spot fifty miles from the railway. Fyodor was at Ems taking his cure. But Anna, who had long held his Power of Attorney, found his absence no obstacle; and lest he should consider it necessary to interrupt his cure or to trouble her with unnecessary advice, she vouchsafed him no information about the impending division until she was actually on her way to Ryazan. She might reasonably have more faith in her own than in her husband's capacity as a negotiator; and in reply to his reproaches, she was able to point to '200 dessiatines of forest and 100 dessiatines of arable land' secured by her skilful bargaining. But even this unhappily did not settle the matter. The property was real estate and descended only to the males, namely to the three surviving Dostoevsky brothers and to the sons of the dead brother Michael. It was all the more unfair in that Michael and Fyodor had already received 10,000 roubles each; and, contrary to the original intention, these benefactions do not seem to have been debited to their shares under the will. There was no doubt of the legal position, but the sisters had a moral grievance and loudly demanded compensation. In the old days Fyodor, as his sisters well knew, would have been incapable of turning a deaf ear to a moral claim far weaker than theirs; but now the hard-headed Anna was at his side to remind him of the rights and needs of his own children. Against Anna, he could do nothing; but the reproaches and appeals of his sisters continued, if we may believe his daughter's biography, to embitter the last weeks of his life.

We have anticipated in order to be done, once for all, with this last financial complication of Dostoevsky's career. We return to the winter of 1874–5 when, sitting quietly in Staraya Russa, he began to write *A Raw Youth*. The dispute over the inheritance of Aunt Kumanin is reflected in more than one passage of the novel. The trouble between the different groups of heirs evidently inspired the lawsuit over an estate between the hero's father Versilov and the two Princes Sokolsky. In this affair there was a conflict between legal and moral right. The law is on the side of Versilov; but a private letter of the testator is clear evidence of an intention to benefit the two Princes. It is tempting to speculate whether this position may not reflect, consciously or unconsciously, Dostoevsky's secret opinion of the respective merits of the moral claim of his sisters and the legal rights of himself and his brothers in the Kumanin inheritance. Nor is this all. One of the pivots on which the confused plot of *A Raw Youth* turns is a letter written by the heroine to a

N

lawyer in which she discusses the possibility of appointing a curator to control her father's affairs on the plea that he was no longer *compos mentis*. The letter falls into unknown hands; and the writer is terrified lest it should come to the knowledge of her father and deprive her of her place in his affections and in his will. We can hardly doubt that, in creating this episode, Dostoevsky had in mind his own letters of 1869 to Maikov, in which he had proposed to contest Aunt Kumanin's will, and his subsequent anxieties lest some interested party should make use of them to ruin his credit with the old lady. It is clear that the troubles of the Kumanin inheritance played a larger part in Dostoevsky's life and thought during his later years than the rather scanty references in his extant correspondence might lead us to infer.

The writing of the novel proceeded with a regularity hitherto unprecedented in Dostoevsky's literary career; and publication of instalments in the *Otechestvennye Zapiski* continued throughout 1875. In June he went once more to Ems for his cure; in August Anna gave birth to another child; and in September, fortified by the receipts from the new novel, they went back to live in Petersburg. *A Raw Youth* falls by general consent below the four other great novels of its author's maturity; but it contains much material which will repay examination.

CHAPTER XVIII

Dostoevsky as Psychologist—A Raw Youth

A Raw Youth was the only one of Dostoevsky's major works to be published in a journal whose political views were diametrically opposed to his own. In Russia, literature and politics are never far apart. His last novel had been frankly political; and several of his letters written at the end of 1874 bear witness to his embarrassment lest anything in his new novel should be rejected by Nekrasov on political grounds. The point is important; for these fears limited both choice and treatment of his subject. In most of his great books Dostoevsky is primarily occupied with the problems of life and philosophy: in *Crime and Punishment* with the meaning of ethics; in *The Idiot* with the ethical ideal; in *The Devils* with the relations between ethics, politics and religion; and in *The Brothers Karamazov* with the foundations of religion. His views being what they were, Dostoevsky could not, in the columns of a radical journal, have expressed himself freely on any of these subjects. *A Raw Youth* discusses none of them, or discusses them superficially and incidentally; in essence, it is concerned only with the psychological reactions of human beings on one another.

Now if, as there is good reason to maintain, Dostoevsky is a mediocre philosopher and a supreme psychologist, it might be inferred that *A Raw Youth* would repay study more, not less, than his other great novels, and that critics are wrong in having relegated it by common consent to the lowest place. Nevertheless, though moving in a field where its author is a supreme master, *A Raw Youth* must be pronounced a failure. The considerations of expediency which confined his pen to neutral themes placed a fatal curb on the sweep of his genius. The new novel raises no vital problem, or raises problems only to drop them again unprobed; the characters are, so to speak, working *in vacuo*; their aims are petty and obscure; they are animated by no dominant idea; and the principals seem to revolve in vicious circles of purposeless self-dissection. 'It is all like dream and delirium,' exclaims the hero at one moment; and at another he describes his condition of mind as 'an undecypherable chaos of feelings and emotions,' The reader may be left to apply these apposite definitions to the book as a whole;

or he may even prefer the sweeping judgment expressed by the hostile Turgenev in one of his private letters:

I took a glance into that chaos. God! what sour stuff—the stench of the sick-room, unprofitable gibberish, psychological excavation.

The explanation of the artistic failure of *A Raw Youth* is not far to seek. A genius so rich and so discursive as Dostoevsky's requires the discipline of a compelling idea to give form to his artistic creation. *Crime and Punishment* and *The Idiot* (the latter with some digressions) display this fundamental unity of idea. In *The Gambler* the sheer momentum of physical necessity (he wrote it in a month to save himself from Stellovsky) supplied the discipline; and the story, though lacking in idea, is technically excellent. In *The Eternal Husband*, also written at unusual speed, the central idea, slight as it is, is sufficient to maintain the unity of a short novel. *The Devils* suffers from dichotomy; it gravitates round two central points instead of one; but the force of gravity is there. In *A Raw Youth* these compelling forces are completely lacking; and the result is a novel more formless than any Dostoevsky ever wrote.

The book as it stands derives from at least three sources. In *The Journal of an Author* for 1876 Dostoevsky wrote:

When eighteen months ago Nekrasov invited me to write a novel for the *Otechestvennye Zapiski*, I was on the point of beginning my *Fathers and Sons*; but I restrained myself and thank God for it. I was not yet ready. So for the moment I wrote *A Raw Youth* as the first trial of my idea. . . . I took a soul still sinless, but already stained by a fearful possibility of moral corruption, by early hatred of his insignificance and his illegitimacy, and by that 'broadness' with which a soul as yet pure admits into itself thoughts of vice, already cherishes them in its heart and plays with them in dreams—dreams still modest, but already daring and stormy. All this left exclusively dependent on its own strength, its own reason and, of course, on God. Such are the outcasts of society, 'casual' members of 'casual' families.

Such was the theme of *A Raw Youth* as it originally took shape in Dostoevsky's mind—an illegitimate son in his relations to society and to his father; and his theme constitutes the sole fragile claim to unity which the completed novel possesses.

But other ingredients went to complete the brew. The note-books for *The Life of a Great Sinner* had, as we have seen, already been tapped for *The Devils*; and still larger draughts were made from this source for *A Raw Youth*. The hero's 'idea' of 'becoming a Rothschild' by self-privation and the ceaseless accumulation of money comes straight from the note-books. In *The Life of a Great Sinner* it would probably have had some significance and some relation to the whole; in *A Raw Youth*, it is thrust into the foreground of the first few chapters, and then fades pointlessly into oblivion. The character of Lambert is taken from the note-books, where he appears as a Frenchman and a type of 'the national lack of principle.' In *A Raw Youth* he fulfils a necessary, if melodramatic, part in the plot as a not unskilful blackmailer, but has no particular moral significance. These extraneous elements scarcely make for unity. *The Great Sinner* and the illegitimate son have coalesced; but there remains something imperfect and artificial in the blend.

The third element of *A Raw Youth* is the character of the father, Versilov, who is second in importance only to the hero. He is, unfortunately for the success of the novel, another composite figure, made up of the odds and ends of ideas which had fermented in Dostoevsky's mind for thirty years. We find in Versilov unmistakable echoes of *The Double*, of Prince Valkovsky in *The Insulted and Injured*, or Velchaninov in *The Eternal Husband*, of the note-books for *The Life of a Great Sinner*, and, through them, of Stavrogin in *The Devils*; and on top of all this welter, the same syncretic and unco-ordinated figure became the mouthpiece for political theories about Russia and Europe which were germinating in the background of Dostoevsky's mind as he wrote, and which found full expression in *The Journal of an Author* in the two following years.

The result of this confusion of elements is an incoherence which increases as the novel proceeds. The outlines of the two principals grow more and more blurred, their motives and their feelings more and more complicated; there are powerful and poignant scenes between them, particularly in the first book; but the mutual relations of two unknown, or insufficiently known, quantities fail to attract the reader's consistent attention and interest. It is permissible that father and son should be impenetrable to one another; it is artistically fatal that they should be so often impenetrable to the reader. And all this is held together by a plot which, for crudity and confusion, rivals the later plots of those other undisciplined masters of fiction, Balzac and Dickens. The mainspring of the action is the letter, already referred to in the previous chapter, which puts it in the power first of the son, and then of the father, to blackmail the woman with whom they are both in love (but so vaguely and indeterminately that there is no real anticipation here of the Karamazov *motif* of rivalry between father and son). And lest this well-worn device of melodrama should not seem feeble enough, there is another secret letter which gives the son a momentary opportunity for blackmailing the father. The second letter soon drops out of the plot altogether, and is forgotten; but by this time the mind has begun to wander, and the reader, looking back, asks himself in bewilderment whether there were, after all, two secret letters or one. No novel of Dostoevsky's contains so long a list of *dramatis personae*, or so few characters who leave any definite impression on the mind of the reader after the book is closed; and of no novel of any author is it so impossible, even after four or five readings, to give a concise and coherent account.

The interest of the novel resides therefore not in the plot, but in its character as a psychological study. When the Russian novelists were first translated in the latter part of last century, the French critic Lemaître summarily dismissed their works as 'Kalmuck exaggerations of French romantic ideas.' The verdict has in it a small element of truth; the psychology which Dostoevsky presents to us, and which western Europe has reborrowed from him, is directly descended from the psychology of the French romantics. The hero of *A Raw Youth* possesses all the perpetual mobility and paralysing self-dissection of a Rousseau or a Benjamin Constant. But he belongs to a later generation than these pioneers. He is more sophisticated, and has reduced his psychological complications to the manageable formula of the 'double', which Dostoevsky had already adopted in his pre-Siberian story of that name. The magical machinery which had pleased him in those early days had long been forgotten; but the idea of the duality of human nature had taken an ever firmer root in his mind. Most good romantics found the richness of their nature enhanced by postulating its division between two variously defined but always antipathetic elements. It was a natural revolt against rationalism and, by making human nature more complicated, made it seem once more more interesting and more spiritual. In the form in which the idea eventually reached Dostoevsky, there are clear traces of Hegel, whose influence on nearly ever branch of thought during the middle years of last century has never been fully assessed. The Hegelian postulate of thesis and antithesis, to be resolved ultimately in a higher synthesis, was applied to psychology; and in the view of Dostoevsky and others, the presence of the 'lower' as well as the 'higher' element was necessary in order to produce the synthesis by which alone humanity could achieve true unity and partake of the divine perfection.

The point in which Dostoevsky may lay claim to originality, and in which he anticipated more recent psychological theories, is the identification of this 'lower' element (which he calls the 'double') with the unconscious or the subconscious man. He first explored the subconscious hell which seethes in the depths of each man's soul, and whose waters have since been charted with so much ingenuity by the psychoanalysts. It is the 'double', the uncharted element in his nature of which he is himself scarcely aware, which makes Stavrogin pull the harmless Gaganov's nose, bite the governor's ear, marry Lebyadkin's idiot sister and (in the chapter which Katkov refused to publish) rape the little girl. 'The truth is, I don't know how the desire suddenly came over me to do it ... mere folly,' is Stavrogin's own explanation of the first of these actions; and he is sincerely incapable of explaining any of them. The hero of *A Raw Youth* analyses this state of mind with more subtlety but with the same result:

I remember that I could at certain moments remain fully conscious of the folly of a decision, and yet at the very same moment proceed with full consciousness to carry it out.

But the clearest case of all is Versilov who, under the influence of the 'double' within him, writes an outrageously insulting letter to the woman whom he loves and respects, conspires with the unmitigated blackguard Lambert to blackmail her, and threatens her life with a revolver. The subconscious element is once more emphazised by the narrator:

Did he want to kill her at that moment? My opinion is that he himself did not know; but he probably would have killed her if we had not struck aside his hand.

In the concluding chapter of *A Raw Youth* Dostoevsky, in the person of the hero, gives us for the first and last time something like a full analysis of the 'double' and its operation:

Gradually, I have come to a certain explanation: in my opinion, at these moments, on that last day and on the day before, Versilov was simply incapable of having any fixed purpose and even, I think, did not reason at all, but was under the influence of a sort of whirlwind of feelings. Of course, I do not at all admit real insanity—the more so, as he is not now in the least insane. But the 'double' I do admit certainly. What then precisely is the 'double'? The 'double,' at any rate according to a medical work by an expert which I afterwards read for the purpose, is nothing else but the first stage in some serious mental derangement which may lead to a pretty bad conclusion. Indeed, Versilov himself, in the scene at Mama's, explained to us with the most extreme frankness the then 'bifurcation' of his feelings and his will.

The medical aspect of the phenomenon engages Dostoevsky's attention only in passing. It was not his intention to suggest that the 'double' is pathological, except in so far as there is a pathological element in all human nature. The 'double' remains an essential element in every fully developed character. It is part of life itself.

I am as full of life as a yard dog [says Versilov in one place]. I am capable of experiencing in complete comfort two contradictory feelings at one and the same time—independently, of course, of my own will.

And when after the stormy scenes of the novel, the 'double' finally vanishes from Versilov's life and he returns peacefully to the hero's mother, with whom he has lived intermittently all these years, he is 'only one half of the former Versilov'—a broken and exhausted man. Remove the antithesis, and you can never arrive at the perfect synthesis. Do away with the sense of sin, and you cannot have salvation.

The idea is carried still further. It is not only the individual human being who carries his 'double' within himself; every human emotion carries in it the germ of its opposite. All love contains its element of hate, suffering its element of pleasure, and humiliation the element of pride. This duality of the emotions seems first to appear in *Memoirs from Underground*, the story written in the year after the crisis of Dostoevsky's liaison with Suslova, and is prominent in *The Gambler*, the novel which specifically reflects that liaison. It has been suggested in an earlier chapter that this conception was the most direct and important influence which Suslova exercised on Dostoevsky's artistic development. The same duality reappears in Raskolnikov's attitude to the detective Zosimov, his repulsion for whom proves to have a fatal power of attraction. Next we trace it, in a half-mocking form, in *The Eternal Husband*—every hate contains its element of love; for the husband both hates and loves his rival, and both hates and loves the child who is 'not his own.' In *The Devils* the inner antithesis of pride and self-humiliation forms the keynote of the mysterious character of Stavrogin. The composite emotion of love-hate forms, in *A Raw Youth*, the basis of the feelings of the son for his father and of the father for the heroine; and, most brilliantly and convincingly of all, it inspires, in *The Brothers Karamazov*, the relations of Katerina to Dmitri Karamazov.

These manifestations of duality are, as we should expect, particularly prominent in Dostoevsky's treatment of sexual love. It is in a sense correct to say that sex plays an important part in his psychological theories. But this should not be taken to imply that Dostoevsky deliberately seeks, like some modern theorists, to interpret the phenomena of psychology in terms of sex; it is rather that sex is for him a normal undifferentiated manifestation of human psychology.

The love-hate emotion is not fundamentally different in the the relationship from what it is in any other. But the analysis of sexual passion which emerges from Dostoevsky's novels involves a further refinement of the theory of duality. Sexual love contains in its active form a desire to inflict, and in its passive form a desire to undergo, pain; the former expresses itself in the male desire for domination, the latter in the female desire for submission, though the roles of the sexes may in practice be reversed, as they seem to have been in Dostoevsky's liaison with Suslova. Sexual love in Dostoevsky is invariably associated with suffering rather than with happiness—a fact which suggests that Maria Dmitrievna and Suslova played a more important part in the formation of his ideas on sex than did his second wife; and the man who, in his letters, protests in terms of passionate sincerity the unclouded happiness of his second marriage, fails to depict anywhere in his novels a tolerable or stable sex relationship. There is a time when Raskolnikov thinks he hates Sonya. 'If I loved Dmitri,' exclaims Katerina in *The Brothers Karamazov*, 'perhaps I should not now pity him, but hate him.' In the world of Dostoevsky's fiction, sexual love has more in common with hate than with pity; and it is because pity is the predominant element in Myshkin's nature that he is incapable of it.

Now in stressing the association of sexual love with suffering Dostoevsky is not unique, and perhaps not even original. Novalis, the German romantic, had drawn attention to the intimate link between the sexual passions and the infliction of pain, and between both and religion, thereby anticipating much that has been written by psychologists of a later date. Alfred de Musset's *Enfant du Siècle* is a man who cannot conceive love except in terms of suffering, undergone by himself or inflicted on his mistress. In the year after the completion of *A Raw Youth*, Dostoevsky published in *The Journal of an Author* a short story entitled *A Gentle Spirit*, which has so many points of contact with the last chapters of the *Confession d'un Enfant du Siècle* that it is difficult not to suspect the direct or indirect influence of the latter. Théophile Gautier, in his preface to the poems of Baudelaire, is even more explicit:

La volupté unique et suprême de l'amour gît dans la certitude de faire le mal, et l'homme et la femme savent de naissance que dans le mal se trouve toute volupté.

And Baudelaire sought his chief source of inspiration in the aesthetic value of pain.

In western Europe, these revelations of human perversity were regarded as mere romantic aberrations or outpourings of spleen, and were not, at any rate before the close of the nineteenth century, taken very seriously as psychology, or perhaps even as literature. In Russia, in the work of Dostoevsky, they came to play for the first time a profound and essential part in normal human psychology. Nor was his interest in the sadistic impulses of human nature solely or primarily connected with sex. The mysterious human love of cruelty in all its aspects had for him an ever-increasing fascination. Side by side with the occasional studies (principally in *Memoirs from Underground* and *A Gentle Spirit*) of the man tormenting the woman who is at his mercy, there is a long series of episodes, beginning even with the pre-Siberian stories, of cruelty suffered by children at the hands of their parents or natural protectors. An episode of the same nature, written for *A Raw Youth* and still preserved in manuscript, was omitted from the published version, either on Dostoevsky's own initiative or at the instance of Nekrasov; but three or four cases from actual life are discussed in the pages of *The Journal of an Author*. Perverted parental love expressing itself in cruelty provided Dostoevsky with another mysterious and engrossing example of the duality of human emotion.

The theories of psychology with which Dostoevsky confronts us would lose much of their interest if we did not believe them to be of universal, or at least of general, application; and the frequent parallels from western writers quoted in this chapter should suffice to dispose of the idea that Dostoevsky confines himself to the analysis of morbid phenomena peculiar to himself and, perhaps, to his countrymen. But it is not out of place for the biographer to enquire how far these theories reflect the characteristic features both of the author's own personality and of the Russian mind.

The theory of the 'double' does not, so far as we can trace its origins, seem to have been born of personal experience. It was rather, in its genesis, a literary conception of western origin; and it was used by Dostoevsky, not only for literary purposes, but to introduce some semblance of order into his diagnosis of his own character. Consistency is not a common human virtue, if indeed it be a virtue at all; but few human characters can have been so incoherent and so ill co-ordinated as his. A multiplicity of conflicting impulses tore his soul asunder; and since he could not reduce it to unity, it was convenient, and to some extent reassuring, to imagine it as a duality. The earliest manifestations of this rather self-conscious dualism are connected with the nervous disorders of his early manhood in Petersburg, when 'his nerves were beyond his control', and he was capable of insulting those whom he loved best. 'My heart is full of words, but I cannot utter them,' says Versilov in the language of one of Dostoevsky's early letters to his brother; 'it seems as if I were *split in two*.' Then came the period after the return from Siberia, when the official biography speaks of the 'bifurcation' of his character, which enabled him to judge with one part of his nature the feelings and actions of the other part—the period when the sins of the flesh and a lively moral judgment were capable of existing side by side in apparent harmony. The 'double' became a convenient symbol, not merely of the opposition of higher and lower impulses, but of the opposition between high ideal and low action which is a commoner and less abstruse phenomenon than Dostoevsky seems sometimes to suggest. Then, later still, in the evening of his days when the storms of life had been quelled, the 'double' could be used to point a moral as well as to adorn tales. It appears in a letter written to a lady admirer in the last year of his life as the voice of moral duty or conscience:

It is a powerful consciousness—a need of rendering an account to oneself; it is the existence, in the very nature of this need, of a moral duty to yourself and to mankind. That is what dualism means. If your mind were less developed, you would be less subject to conscience and would feel none of this dualism; on the contrary self-satisfaction would be born. Yet, all the same, this dualism is a great torment.

There is in this later Dostoevsky, relatively well disciplined and coherent, a shade of smugness which had been altogether absent from the years of ferment when the 'double' had been an active phenomenon in his life.

The 'double', then, in its relation to Dostoevsky's own nature, is a literary theme invoked first to diagnose a disease, and then to point a moral. It has no peculiar root in his own psychological experience. We reach a somewhat similar result when we approach the question how far Dostoevsky's theories of the duality of man and of human feelings are applicable to humanity as a whole and how far they are peculiar to his countrymen. It is a question we can scarcely escape; for he himself in many places thrusts it upon us. In common with most Russian writers (for the Russian is by nature and tradition self-conscious), he continually insists on the difference between the Russian and the European character, and on the 'broadness' of the Russian nature which harbours this strange duality. 'The way of life is broad,' exclaims Golyadkin as he reflects on the haunting presence of his double.' 'Human nature is broad,' muses Dmitri Karamazov, more than thirty years later; 'I would have narrowed it,' and Dostoevsky includes in the speech of the District

Prosecutor who arraigns Dmitri an indictment of the 'broadness'
of the Russian soul:

We are immoderate, we are an astonishing blend of good and evil; we
are lovers of enlightenment and of Schiller, and at the same time we riot
in taverns and pull out the beards of our drunken boon-companions. . . .
We are broad natures, Karamazov natures—this is my point—capable
of accommodating every possible contradiction and of contemplating
simultaneously the two infinites, the infinite above us, the infinite of
lofty ideals, and the infinite below, the infinite of the lowest and most
repulsive degradation. . . . We are broad, broad like mother Russia
herself; we find room for everything, we reconcile ourselves to everything.

Many years earlier Dostoevsky had placed a similar indictment of
the Russian character in the mouth of Svidrigailov in *Crime and
Punishment*. Svidrigailov suggests an explanation of the phenomenon
—the lack of any 'sacrosanct traditions' in the educated classes. In
The Journal of an Author Dostoevsky adopts the explanation in his
own person, and ascribes the 'broadness' of the Russian to 'two
hundred years of the absence of any independence of character and
two hundred years of insults against his own Russian nature.'
Unconfined by any recognized tradition, the Russian sways from
side to side of the 'broad path' of life, a helpless victim of the fundamental duality of his nature and his feelings.

The question which haunts Dostoevsky throughout *A Raw
Youth* is whether this characteristic 'broadness' should be counted
among the defects or among the assets of the Russian soul.

I have always marvelled [writes his hero] at this capacity of man—
and, it seems, of the Russian man *par excellence*—to nurture in his soul
the loftiest ideal side by side with the meanest baseness, and both in
perfect sincerity. Is this a peculiar broadness of the Russian, which will
carry him far, or is it simply viciousness ? There's the question.

It is symptomatic of the moralizing tendency of Dostoevsky's
later years that the duality which he has so mercilessly exposed
eventually becomes for him the symbol and source of Russia's
unique achievement. For as duality is necessary to the complete
man, so does the Russian, in virtue of his duality, offer to the world
a unique example of complete humanity and universal comprehension. The western ideal, based largely on tradition, has about it
something mechanical and material. For the Russian, virtue is not
a matter of tradition, it is a perpetual individual achievement; and
there is a corresponding contempt for mere conventional honesty.
'The Russian can be saint, but he cannot be an honest man,' wrote

the critic and philosopher Leontiev. The Russian who, by reason of the duality of his nature, had the experience of sin in his inmost soul, may fall behind the European in the mechanical practice of virtue; but he alone can know the meaning of true holiness.

The questionable psychological doctrine of the 'double' had, it will be seen, led Dostoevsky to some equally questionable and extremely curious deductions in the spheres of religion and nationality. These deductions fall outside the scope of *A Raw Youth*, or are but faintly adumbrated there. They had perhaps not yet taken final shape in Dostoevsky's mind; and he would, in any case, have found it hard to express them in the pages of Nekrasov's journal. But these questions of nationality and religion were to absorb Dostoevsky during the five years of life which remained to him after the completion of *A Raw Youth*. In *The Devils*—and in part even earlier—he had established an intimate relation between nationality and religion; and the two became, as time went on, more and more inextricably mingled in his thoughts, each being portrayed in turn as an aspect of the other. It is however possible to make a broad distinction. *The Journal of an Author*, which extended over the years 1876 and 1877, is devoted primarily to national questions, and *The Brothers Karamazov*, written in the three following years, primarily to religion. There can, half a century later, be no conflict of opinion on the relative value of the two studies. The problems of Russian nationality, at any rate in the narrow form in which they were conceived by Dostoevsky, are obsolete, the problems of religion perennial; and—what is more important—Dostoevsky was a mediocre publicist and a supreme novelist. Nevertheless, his nationalistic writings proved in the highest degree acceptable to the taste of his day; and it was *The Journal of an Author* which firmly established his position among his contemporaries as the prophet and interpreter of Russian civilization.

CHAPTER XIX

Dostoevsky as Publicist—The Journal of an Author

In August 1875, whilst Fyodor was still writing *A Raw Youth*, Anna gave birth to her last child, a son, whom they named Alyosha. He was the only one of their children to inherit the father's disease, and died at the age of three in an epileptic fit. Not long after his birth, the Dostoevskys moved back from Staraya Russa to Petersburg.

The decision not to spend a second winter in Staraya Russa was dictated by a new project. The finances of the family were now reasonably secure and allowed Dostoevsky to realize a long-cherished, but financially speculative, ambition. His *Journal of an Author*, which had appeared in the pages of the *Grazhdanin*, had enjoyed a fair measure of popularity; and Dostoevsky now decided to resume the writing of articles, social and political, under the same title, and to issue them in the form of an independent journal. The business manager of the enterprise was, or course, Anna. She negotiated with printers, drew up and published advertisements of the new venture, received subscriptions and saw to the despatch of the journal to subscribers. The flat served as an office, and the staff consisted of an errand-boy. It was not perhaps the least arduous of Anna's duties to ensure that her husband should punctually discharge the single task allotted to him—the writing of the articles; but in this, too, she achieved remarkable success. Throughout 1876 and 1877 *The Journal of an Author* appeared with exemplary regularity. Its circulation approached four thousand in the first year, and touched six thousand in the second. The expenses being virtually confined to the printer's bill, the margin of profit was substantial.

Like his earlier journalistic work in the *Vremya* and the *Epocha*, *The Journal of an Author* belongs to Dostoevsky's ephemeral writings and has little interest for a later generation. It consists of a loosely-knit series of essays on matters of topical interest, sometimes literary, but more often political, varied with an occasional short story or sketch. Its central and constantly recurring theme is the idealization of 'the people.' It is a rather special form of cult. There is not, in Dostoevsky, any attempt to minimize the vicious propensities inherent in the Russian, as in most other peoples; the cult takes little account of actions. It is the cult of that ideal which, if we may believe Dostoevsky, has its home in the heart of every member of the Russian people (it is only the intelligentsia who have lost it), and which finds its highest expression in them. Dostoevsky nowhere states the grounds of his belief, which is the product partly of his Siberian experience, partly of his subsequent inoculation with Slavophil doctrine. The peculiar blessedness of the Russian people has ceased with him to be a question of fact or argument; it is an article of faith which you must take or leave as it stands.

It must be emphasized from the outset—for it is vital to the understanding not only of Dostoevsky, but of the Russian temperament— that this cult does not imply either any practical knowledge of the people or any interest in the amelioration of the conditions in which they live. The conception of Christianity which found its most perfect expression in *The Idiot* had, as we have seen, nothing to do with humanitarianism or good deeds. *Memoirs from the House of the Dead* exhibited a complete and disconcerting indifference to prison reform; and the prolific disquisitions in *The Journal of an Author* on the subject of the people are equally innocent of any humanitarian or reforming spirit. His early novels like *Poor Folk* and *The Insulted and Injured* suggest by their very titles sympathy with the down-trodden and oppressed; but the sympathy is sentimental, not practical, and is part of a literary tradition. Dostoevsky himself had known poverty; but it was the poverty of the impecunious bourgeois, such as he depicted in Raskolnikov, not the poverty of the labouring masses in country or in town. He was not insincere, but only muddle-headed; and when, on nearly every page of *The Journal of an Author*, he elevates the people above the bourgeoisie, he is idealizing a class of which he knew nothing at the expense of a class which he knew through and through and to which he himself belonged. 'In our whole literature,' wrote the critic Rozanov, 'there never was a writer whose ideals were so completely severed from current realities.' It is a perfectly just criticism, and is a necessary antidote to much that has been written by undiscriminating enthusiasts in praise of Dostoevsky's political acumen.

It was this lack of any contact with the people which facilitated the confusion of Dostoevsky's thought. We have seen how, in the 'sixties, the single word *Narod*, with its twin meanings of 'the people' and 'the nation', had presided over his painless and unperceived conversion from the ideals of democracy to those of nationalism. There are whole chapters of *The Journal of an Author* in which, with wearisome iteration, the true wisdom of the people is contrasted with the false wisdom of the intellectuals, and the latter are reproached for having separated themselves from the people; and the unwary reader, particularly if he has been brought up in the traditions of western democracy, might well imagine that Dostoevsky was a fervent, though perhaps rather sentimental, radical and reformer. It was the old mistake which Herzen had made when he saw him in London in 1862; and even now, in works of criticism, reference is sometimes made to Dostoevsky as a champion of the 'insulted and injured'. In truth, he cared for none of these things. His interest lay in moral, and not at all in political or social issues. The object of his cult was an abstraction; and he was one of the popularizers, if not one of the creators, of the myth of 'the holy Russian people' which has been so startlingly exploded in recent years.

In short, Dostoevsky exemplifies in his own person the rift—the lack of mutual comprehension—between the Russian intelligentsia and the Russian people. It is a real practical problem of Russian history; and Dostoevsky was not the first to write of it, though nobody has written of it with greater emphasis than he. Historically, it began with the creation of a half-Europeanized intelligentsia by Peter the Great; and this is the reason of the hostility with which all writers of the Slavophil school regard Peter's memory. It grew continuously down to the middle of the nineteenth century; and Dostoevsky hardly exaggerates when he refers to two Russias, the Russia of the intelligentsia and the Russia of the people. His statement of the problem is admirable; but he failed altogether in his diagnosis of the causes and in his prescription of the remedy. He reduces the issue to the question of religion; he believes that the intelligentsia, by abandoning its religion for democracy and utilitarianism and economic materialism, had consummated its own divorce from the people. The remedy is for the intelligentsia to return, by one and the same process, to religion and to the people; and we thus reach the identification of religion and the people which had already been hinted at in *The Devils* and which finds its full development in *The Journal of an Author*.

Curiously enough, another and far acuter observer, a writer of very different opinions, Paul Milyukov, also discusses this divorce between intelligentsia and people in terms of religion. But whereas Dostoevsky puts the blame on the intelligentsia which, in going away from the church, has gone away from the people, Milyukov, writing nearly thirty years later, had the insight to perceive that the people, like the intelligentsia, were fundamentally indifferent to the official religion. It is to the failure of the church in Russia to provide, as it had done in Western Europe, a common tradition and culture for intelligentsia and people alike that Milyukov traces the rift between them; and this analysis, though far from being a complete explanation, is valid as far as it goes. The disease was real enough; but Dostoevsky's diagnosis was false and his remedy meaningless. And although, partly as the result of his influence, a considerable section of the Russian intelligentsia returned, in the thirty years following his death, to religion, the movement did nothing to bridge the rift or stay the approaching dénouement. The rift grew until, in a moment of crisis, the people turned on the intelligentsia as on an enemy utterly alien to itself in tradition and outlook, and swept it from the face of Russia. Of Dostoevsky's two Russias, one swallowed up the other.

The cult of the people occupies the central place in the *Journal*; but it is jostled closely by another theme almost equally dear to Dostoevsky's heart, the eternal contrast between Russia and the west—or, as Dostoevsky (in common with most Russian writers) generally phrases it, Russia and Europe. The theme had occurred to Dostoevsky on the occasion of his first journey to Europe in 1862, not indeed as the result of observation—for remarkably few of Dostoevsky's ideas ever came from external impressions—but as the result of a theory. He discovered that western civilization was built on the basis of the individual, on the self-assertion of the *ego*. It was not an original discovery. The first of all Slav political theorists, Krizhanin, had written at the end of the seventeenth century that 'the Europeans consider enjoyment the highest aim of man . . . and pervert the gospel of Christ into a gospel of enjoyment'. In Dostoevsky's day, it was not, at any rate in theory, altogether untrue; for this was the heyday of J. S. Mill and the utilitarians and of the economic doctrine of *laissez-faire*. The more questionable side of this popular doctrine was that Russian civilization was innocent of the principle of egoism and was based on the conception of universal brotherhood. Yet this belief, which was the stock-in-trade of the Slavophil enthusiasts under whose influence Dostoevsky fell, forms the burden of all his subsequent dissertations on Russia and Europe and, in the last ten years of his life, of his ethical and religious teaching. The ultimate formula of Dostoevsky's ethical-religious-national creed was as follows: on the one side—egoism = Catholicism = antichrist = Europe; on the other—brotherhood = Orthodoxy = Christ = Russia.

The most important influence in the consolidation of this strange, but fervently held belief was the once famous political treatise of a publicist named Danilevsky. Danilevsky had been an ardent Fourier-ist in his youth and knew Dostoevsky in Petrashevsky's 'circle'. He

o

was arrested with the others, but after three months' imprisonment was liberated by the Commission of Enquiry. The evolution of his opinions had been not unlike that of Dostoevsky's own; and in 1869, during the period of Dostoevsky's residence abroad, he published in the *Zarya*, at the very time when *The Eternal Husband* was appearing in the same journal, a long series of articles entitled *Russia and Europe*. There Dostoevsky certainly read them. They made an immense impression on Russian thought, and particularly on the Slavophils; and they formed the foundation of nearly everything which Dostoevsky afterwards wrote on the subject. It may therefore be appropriate to summarize the powerful, though often perverse, arguments of Danilevsky's work, which has entered so deeply into subsequent political theory that it cannot even now be treated as entirely obsolete.

Anticipating some of the ideas enunciated fifty years later by Spengler, Danilevsky declared that the Germano-Latin civilization, following the same cycles as the ancient civilizations of Greece and Rome, had achieved its ideal culmination in the sixteenth and seventeenth centuries, and its material culmination in the nineteenth century. It was now a body in which the soul had long been extinct, and nothing remained in front of it but the disagreeable process of decomposition. Western civilization was now purely material, and built on brute-force; in Russian civilization alone did moral forces still predominate. The contrast of civilizations is bound up with a contrast of characters. In opposition to the self-seeking individualistic European, the character of the Slav, 'a stranger to violence, full of softness, obedience and respect, has the fullest correspondence with the Christian ideal'. In the European, individual qualities are predominant, in the Slav social qualities; and this fact explains the phenomenon, noted by Dostoevsky as well as by Danilevsky, that whereas the Frenchman or the Englishman who loses his nationality may still remain an estimable individual, the denationalized or Europeanized Russian becomes 'a worthless rag'. The European deprived of his national or social status falls back on his individuality, the Russian so deprived degenerates into nothingness.

It is perhaps scarcely worth while to subject this doctrine to serious criticism. It might be reasonably pointed out that the lack of individualism, which Danilevsky found in the Russian, derived mainly from the absence of a long-standing national tradition. The Russian of the nineteenth century assimilated easily because he had not developed a strongly marked national character of his own—a state of things which rather confirmed the view taken by the westerners of the undeveloped nature of the Russian national character (though it did not necessarily justify their desire to develop that character on European lines). But this lack of national individuality, already idealized by Danilevsky, was elevated by Dostoevsky into the supreme and characteristic virtue of the Russian people. The Russian was hailed by him as the 'all-man' (there is no translation of the Russian compound which, in some chapters of *The Journal of an Author*, appears on every page), who is alone capable of understanding, assimilating and teaching the purely national and therefore narrow European; and the poet Pushkin, who showed remarkable skill in introducing into Russian literature the forms and traditions of more than one literature of western Europe, became the typical representative of the Russian genius. The Russian must not allow himself to be Europeanized; but he is, and must remain, the super-European and the teacher of Europe. The notion may appear to the western mind somewhat fantastic; but it still persists, where much else has been radically altered, as a powerful element in the Russian national psychology.

But neither Danilevsky nor his pupil Dostoevsky was content with these abstract musings on the Russian character or on the role of the Russian people in European civilization. They plunged boldly into the morass of international politics and, by attempting to find for their theories practical applications compatible with the patriotic aspirations of the Imperial Russian Government of their day, involved themselves in a maze of confusion and self-contradiction. The first point in *Russia and Europe* in which we can detect Danilevsky in flagrant inconsistency is the chapter in which he endeavours to define his attitude to Peter the Great, the stumbling-block of all writers who are ambitious to construct theories of Russian history. For while Danilevsky is bound by his hypothesis to condemn Peter's social and political reforms at home, he is content to give unstinting praise to his martial achievements abroad. Peter the reformer remains, for the sake of the Russian people and its ideal of brotherhood, the villain. Peter the conqueror becomes, in the teeth of all theories of brotherhood, a national hero; and Danilevsky, like Dostoevsky after him, returns again and again, with the persistence of an uneasy conscience, to a passionate denial that Russia is an imperialistic country.

The embarrassed attempt of Danilevsky to reconcile his conception of the Russian as the disinterested elder brother of Europe with the not altogether altruistic foreign policy of the Imperial Government is taken up with renewed fervour by Dostoevsky. It leads him into many strange places. It is however fair, before we quote some of his more outrageous lapses from good sense and good

taste, to recall the circumstances in which *The Journal of an Author*
for 1876 and 1877 was written and published. These were the years
when Russia first took her stand as the champion and liberator of
the enslaved Slav races of the Balkan peninsula, when she seemed on
the eve of driving the Turk from Europe and establishing herself at
Constantinople. In 1875 there had been revolts against Turkish
rule in Herzegovina and Montenegro, followed in the next year by
risings in Bulgaria. Patriotic Russian feeling was thoroughly roused
on the side of the oppressed brother Slav and brother Christian;
and in April 1877 public opinion compelled Alexander II to declare
war against the Turk. The first campaign of the Russo-Turkish
War was favourable to the Russian arms. But early in 1878 the inter-
vention of the other Powers, and particularly of Great Britain,
stopped the Russian advance almost under the walls of Constantinople, and eventually compelled Alexander to relinquish a substantial part of his gains and of his ambitions.

The Journal of an Author for these years was therefore written in
an atmosphere of pan-Slav excitement and jingoistic emotions,
raised to fever-heat by a successful war. Patriotic feelings were
exacerbated by the undisguised opposition of most of the other
Powers to Russian designs; and diatribes against Great Britain and
France filled the press. It is against this background that we should
read the following passages of *The Journal of an Author* for April
1877, the month of the declaration of war:

We need the war for ourselves; we are arising not only for the sake of
our brother Slavs harassed by the Turks, but for our own salvation.
War will clear the air which we breathe and in which we stifle, sitting
as we do in helpless rottenness and spiritual suffocation.

The second passage has a still more familiar ring:

If society is unhealthy and infected, even so good a thing as prolonged
peace, instead of being beneficial to society, becomes harmful. Never has
a generation passed in European history, since we can remember it,
without a war. And there is a reason: war, evidently, is necessary for
some purpose, is health-giving and eases humanity.

The last passage ends with a threat to England:

Perhaps not we, but our children, will see the end of England.

And elsewhere France is dismissed even more cavalierly:

The fate of Poland awaits France, and she will cease to exist politically.

Dostoevsky had no hesitation in proclaiming a European war:

As soon as the war begins, it will turn into a pan-European war. The eastern question and the eastern war will, by force of fate, be merged into the pan-European war. ... The most essential and important part of this last fateful struggle will consist in the fact that it will solve the thousand-year-old question of Roman Catholicism and that, in the place of the latter, will arise a revived Eastern Christianity. ... I am convinced that the war will end in favour of the eastern allies, that Russia has nothing to fear if the eastern war is merged into a pan-European war, and that it will even be better if that is the solution. Of course, it will be a terrible thing, the spilling of so much precious human blood! But there is comfort, at any rate, in the reflection that this shedding of blood will save Europe. ...

It is unnecessary to continue the quotation. These ravings read now almost as pathetically as the vision, which Dostoevsky conjures up in another chapter, of Russia coming to the aid of Europe to deliver her from the menace of communism. It may seem to later ages painful and almost incredible that so great an artist should have diverted his pen to the service of jingo journalism. But Dostoevsky had always insisted on the moralizing aspect of art; and whether he wrote in the form of fiction or of essays, he began more and more to regard himself, not primarily as an artist, but as a teacher and a prophet. It would have shocked him to be told that *The Journal of an Author* would count for nothing with posterity beside *The Idiot* and *The Brothers Karamazov*; and his own view was that of many of his contemporaries. Strakhov in the official biography names *The Journal of an Author* with *Poor Folk*, *Memoirs from the House of the Dead* and *Crime and Punishment* as the four summits of different periods of Dostoevsky's artistic achievement; and this judgment not unfairly represents the stages of growth of his contemporary fame. He had returned to Russia in 1871 with his name made, principally by *Crime and Punishment* and *The Devils*, as a great novelist. *A Raw Youth* had not sensibly enhanced or diminished his reputation. But *The Journal of an Author* at once gave him new rank as an idol of Russian national opinion. It hit the mood of the moment by providing a religious and philosophical foundation for the prevailing patriotic enthusiasm. It is easy for us to see that the magnificent edifice was built on sand; but in the intoxication of the Russo-Turkish War, and for many years afterwards, it looked remarkably like solid rock.

The Journal of an Author not only made Dostoevsky a public figure, but it brought him a new circle of friends. In 1873, when editing the *Grazhdanin*, he made the acquaintance of Pobedonostsev, who had been the tutor of the future Tsar Alexander III, and who was afterwards to become Procurator of the Holy Synod, and the most energetic champion of reaction during the ensuing reigns. In the last years of Dostoevsky's life there were frequent meetings between the novelist and the statesman, who found a common ground of thought and action in the defence of orthodoxy. Through the influence of Pobedonostsev, the heir to the throne was pleased to accept copies of *The Devils* and of *The Journal of an Author*; and it was probably at Pobedonostsev's instigation that the tutor of the Tsar's younger sons called on Dostoevsky and begged him to visit his charges. The great writer seemed well qualified to play the role of Aristotle to these young Alexanders, and to inculcate in their minds a salutary sense of 'the part which they might take in the present-day constitution of society and the benefits they might confer on it'. He also met the nephew of the Tsar, the Grand Duke Konstantin Konstantinovich, who distinguished himself from his fellow Romanovs by a taste for literature and had pretensions to be regarded as a minor poet.

In the more intimate sphere of personal friendships there had also been changes. Relations with Strakhov had, since Dostoevsky's return from abroad, lost the cordiality of earlier years. There was no longer active co-operation, and Strakhov had become a satellite of Tolstoy, whose imperious temperament demanded exclusive worship. Even with Maikov, Dostoevsky seems to have had moments of friction; Yanovsky did not live in Petersburg; and Wrangel had passed altogether out of his life. The two most constant of his newer friends were Orest Miller, who afterwards collaborated with Strakhov in writing the official biography, and a young professor of philosophy, Vladimir Soloviev.

Soloviev is generally placed by critics at the head of the not particularly distinguished roll of Russian philosophers. He was only twenty-three when he first met Dostoevsky in 1873. Their friendship ripened, and was at its height four or five years later. Soloviev afterwards wrote commentaries on the religious and philosophical implications of Dostoevsky's work; and his ideas coincided to a considerable extent with those of Dostoevsky. It would be unprofitable to attempt an analysis of this intercourse between the trained philosopher fresh from the schools and the aging novelist prolific in ideas but inexact in thought, or to assess the share of influence which each exercised on the other. The exchange provided mutual inspiration to both; and Dostoevsky seems to have derived from these conversations the definitely religious, even ecclesiastical, train of thought which scarcely appears in his earlier works but emerges into prominence in *The Brothers*

Karamazov. The importance of Soloviev for the biographer of Dostoevsky is the part, intangible but certainly important, which he played in the conception of the novelist's final masterpiece. Some contemporaries thought that the figure of Alyosha in the novel had been drawn from Soloviev.

In the summer of 1877, in consequence of the war, Dostoevsky abandoned the journey to Ems which had been his regular summer routine for the past few years, and accompanied his family to the country estate of Anna's brother somewhere in the province of Kursk. In the course of the summer, he made a pilgrimage to Darovoe, the farm which had once belonged to his parents, where he had spent the short serene summers of his boyhood, and where his father had been murdered. It had been inherited by his sister Vera who used it, like her parents, as a summer retreat for her family. It was just forty years since he had last seen it; and he wandered step by step over the once familiar ground, reconstructing long-forgotten scenes and reflecting on the adventurous life that lay between. It was only now, after forty years of uneasy wandering east and west, that he had begun to know again the domestic tranquillity of those summer days of his boyhood.

It was perhaps here in the peace of Darovoe that Dostoevsky traced in his mind the first outlines of *The Brothers Karamazov* and, brooding on the scene where his father had met his death, decided to make a murdered father the theme of his coming novel. The hypothesis remains largely conjectural; for the one solid fact which supports it is that Dostoevsky gave the name of a wood on the farm, Chermashnya, to a village which plays some part in the action of *The Brothers Karamazov*. It was in any case about this time that Dostoevsky's restless mind turned back again to fiction; for he announced in the autumn that *The Journal of an Author* would 'for reasons of health' not be continued beyond the end of the year.

We are on firmer ground when we return to the role of Soloviev. He and Dostoevsky saw one another frequently during the winter; and in the spring of 1878 the young professor delivered a course of lectures on philosophy which Dostoevsky attended. The summer was once more spent by Dostoevsky in Russia; and in June the two friends visited together the famous monastery of Optina Pustyn, in the heart of the country in the province of Tula. It was the monastery to which Tolstoy made a pilgrimage a few years later, on foot and dressed as a peasant. They remained there two days, and had several conversations with Father Ambrosius, who became the original of Father Zosima, and some of whose speeches found their way almost verbatim into the novel. The monastery dominates the whole of the first half of *The Brothers Karamazov*; and the importance of this pilgrimage with Soloviev at the moment when it was beginning to take shape in Dostoevsky's mind can hardly be exaggerated.

Both going and coming, Dostoevsky halted in Moscow to negotiate with Katkov for the publication of the new novel in the *Russky Vestnik*. The price offered by Katkov was 300 roubles a folio, which compared favourably with the 150 roubles paid by him for *The Devils* and the 250 roubles paid by Nekrasov for *A Raw Youth*. Both Turgenev and Tolstoy in their day had received higher rates. But they were sufficiently well off to be able to bargain, and could afford to dispense with payments in advance, while Dostoevsky, whether by necessity or by habit, continued even now to demand and receive substantial advances. He returned from Moscow with the bargain struck and set eagerly to work. *The Brothers Karamazov* ran in the *Russky Vestnik* throughout 1879 and the greater part of 1880, and was published in book form towards the end of 1880, a few months before Dostoevsky's death. It is his final message to the world; and though it contains a few scenes where the inspiration seems to flag and interest slackens, it is by common consent almost the greatest, if not the greatest, of all his novels.

'If,' wrote Soloviev soon after Dostoevsky's death, 'we wish to express in a single word the social ideal at which Dostoevsky arrived, that word will be not "the people" but "the church". . . . The church as the positive social ideal was to be the central conception of the new novel or new series of novels, of which only the first, *The Brothers Karamazov*, was written.' The religion of the Russian people had been transmuted, under Soloviev's influence, into the religion of the Russian church.

CHAPTER XX

Dostoevsky as Prophet—The Brothers Karamazov

IT is perhaps a partial explanation of the religious fervour of Dostoevsky's later years that religion played no perceptible part in the first forty years of his life. The formal religious observances of his childhood passed easily and imperceptibly into the frank agnosticism of his Petersburg years. In the groups of Belinsky and of Petrashevsky he found himself among men who rejected the Orthodox church and all forms of religious dogma. But most of these men professed profound respect for the Christian ethic, in which they found support for their revolutionary creed; and Christ always remained for Dostoevsky the supreme personification of the ethical ideal. The effect of his four years in prison, during which his principal reading was the Bible, was to create in him a certain spiritual *malaise* and a vague longing for the support of some religious belief. Such at least appears to be the sense of a letter written by him immediately after his release to Madame Fonvisina, one of the women who befriended him on his journey at Tobolsk and later during his sojourn in the prison:

Many people have told me that you are very religious. But it is not because you are religious, but because I have felt and experienced it myself, that I tell you that at such times one thirsts 'like the parched grass' for faith, and finds it, because in unhappiness truth dawns. I can say of myself that I am a child of the age, a child of unbelief and scepticism; I have been until now and shall be, I know, to the grave. How many sufferings this thirst for faith has cost, and is costing me; it is all the stronger in my soul, the more arguments I have against it. Yet God sometimes bestows on me moments at which I am completely calm; at these moments I love, and feel myself loved by others, and in such moments I enfold in my heart a symbol of faith, which makes everything bright and holy for me. This symbol is very simple: it consists in believing that there is nothing more beautiful, more profound, more lovable, more reasonable, more courageous and more perfect than Christ, yes, and I tell myself with jealous love, that there could be nothing. More than that, if anyone proved to me that Christ was not in the truth, and it really was a fact that the truth was not in Christ, I would rather be with Christ than with the truth.

This exalted and hyperbolic utterance has been used and abused both by commentators who desire to prove that Dostoevsky was a believer from his earliest years and by those who are convinced that he remained a sceptic to the end. In assessing its value as evidence we must certainly remember that it was addressed to a woman whom he knew to be 'very religious', and to whom he owed a debt of deep gratitude and affection; and he would inevitably tend to exaggerate rather than to minimize the strength of these vague religious impulses. Neither the letters to his brother nor the published *Memoirs from the House of the Dead* make any mention of this 'thirst for faith'; and Wrangel specifically records that Dostoevsky at Semipalatinsk was rarely seen in a church and displayed a particular aversion to priests. He returned to Petersburg at the end of 1859 with the same religious convictions with which he had left it ten years before: acceptance of the ethical ideal of Christianity and rejection of its dogmatic content. It was the position reached by Renan in the famous *Life of Jesus*, published at the beginning of the 'sixties; but the course of the development which lay before Dostoevsky was the converse of that through which the French thinker had just passed.

The unperceived transformation of Dostoevsky's political views in the years after his return from Siberia has been traced in a previous chapter. In Russia, politics and religion are never far apart; and the movement of Dostoevsky towards political orthodoxy implied, at any rate, a strong urge in the direction of orthodoxy of religion. Russia is not the home of middle courses; and it was scarcely possible in the Russia of the 'sixties to find a middle position between radical materialism and conservative orthodoxy. The deserter from one camp sooner or later inevitably took refuge in the other. In this way, by the time he wrote *Crime and Punishment*, Dostoevsky had drifted into a position of acquiescence—it is still too soon to speak of active faith—in the dogmas of Christianity and of the Orthodox church. *The Idiot* belongs to the same stage of development; religious dogma plays no part in the ethical idea which Myshkin represents.

It was during the last years of his stay abroad, when homesickness weighed heavily on him, that references to 'the Russian God' and 'the Russian Christ' begin to come easily to Dostoevsky's pen; and in March 1870, just before the well-ordered plan of *The Devils* was shattered by the irruption from *The Life of a Great Sinner*, he told Maikov that the theme of the latter work was to be the great question 'with which I have tormented myself, consciously or unconsciously, all my life—the existence of God'. The growth of his belief is traced in significant words which he puts into the mouth of Shatov in *The Devils*:

'I believe in Russia, I believe in Orthodoxy. . . . I believe in the body of Christ. . . . I believe that Christ will come again in Russia.' 'And in God? in God?' 'I . . . I shall believe in God.'

Like Shatov, Dostoevsky believed in Christ, in Russia, in the Orthodox church; and through them he came at last to believe in God. When he returned to Russia in the summer of 1871, the conversion (if such it can be called) was complete. He was then nearing the end of his fiftieth year.

The myth of 'holy Russia' has been responsible for much misunderstanding of the state of religious belief among Russian intellectuals. Throughout the greater part of the nineteenth century, the intelligent and educated members of the governing classes in Russia, the aristocracy and the conservative intelligentsia, were agnostic by inclination and orthodox by rational conviction. The traditional culture of the upper classes went back to the French rationalists of the eighteenth century. Their intellectual capacities and training predisposed them to unbelief. But reason showed them that the state of civilization in which they lived was held together by faith, and that faith was, pragmatically speaking, a necessity. Their attitude is summed up once for all in Pascal's famous epigram: 'Mon cœur est matérialiste, mais ma raison s'y oppose.'

It is not therefore in any way singular that the foundation of the faith which Dostoevsky held in his later years was pragmatic and empirical. He followed the tradition of his age and class. He believed in, and recommended others to believe in, the doctrine of the Orthodox church because—to put the matter crudely—it worked, and because without it morality became impossible and life on earth intolerable. His was a reasoned, not an intuitive faith.

If a conviction of immortality [he wrote in *The Journal of an Author*] is indispensable for human existence, this conviction is presumably the normal condition of mankind; and if this is so, then the immortality of the human soul is an indubitable fact.

But despite this unashamed pragmatism, which has led some commentators to doubt the reality of his faith, there was in Dostoevsky's religion a certain mystical element which has misled others into treating him as a mystic. His somewhat incongruous vein of mysticism seems beyond doubt to have been connected with his epileptic seizures. It is an established fact that epilepsy, in common with certain narcotic drugs and perhaps certain forms of recurrent insanity, produces in its victim, at the moment prior to the attack, a sense of spiritual exaltation and triumph, a feeling of power to transcend the limits of the material world. The first recorded observation by Dostoevsky of this phenomenon belongs to the year 1865; and in a famous chapter of *The Idiot*, written three years later, Myshkin falls in an epileptic fit in the midst of a beatific vision of the beauty of the world. By this time Dostoevsky, who shared the popular belief that physical infirmity confers an unusual measure of spiritual insight, had come to attribute a definitely religious significance to these moments of epileptic exaltation; and this conviction gave to his religious faith a certain mystical quality, though he never at any time claimed for himself that sense of personal communion with God which is the foundation of mysticism.

Such was the essence of the religion to which Dostoevsky attained in the last years of his life and which, under the influence of Soloviev, came to be associated more and more closely with the teaching of the Orthodox church. In *The Brothers Karamazov* he set out to proclaim his faith to the world. Like all his later novels, it has a complex origin, and its roots may be traced back to the plan of *The Life of a Great Sinner*. So far as we can judge from the obscure hints in Dostoevsky's letters and note-books, the hero of the *Great Sinner* was to be a man of sin and passion; he was to be an unbeliever and an atheist; and he was to pass some years in a monastery from which he was to re-emerge into the world a changed man. But the plan was now ten years old and had been generously tapped both for *The Devils* and for *A Raw Youth*; and in *The Brothers Karamazov* he fundamentally modified the original idea by substituting three persons for one. In the novel as it stands Dmitri Karamazov is the man of sinful passions; Ivan is the intellectual sceptic; and it is Alyosha, the youngest brother, who has been brought up in the monastery and returns to the world to bring the light of the Christian ideal into everyday life. Alyosha must, in virtue of his role, be styled the hero of the novel; and since, as we saw in *The Idiot*, unbelief and hardness of heart are more antipathetic to the Christian ideal than active sin, Ivan not Dmitri is the villain. In fact, Dmitri constantly threatens to oust Alyosha from the role of hero. For the finished novel comprises two main themes, of which the second encroaches more and more on the first: the debate between Ivan, representing the principle of evil, and Alyosha, the type of the Christian ideal; and the redemption of Dmitri through sin and suffering.

The Brothers Karamazov is an epic of nearly 400,000 words; and an attempt to define its content may well seem almost as inadequate as to describe the *Iliad* as a poem about the wrath of Achilles. The key of the plot, an afterthought to the original conception of the novel, is the murder of the father of the three brothers, a revolting but impressive monster of lust and debauchery. He and Dmitri have been rivals for the same woman, a prostitute reminiscent in many of her qualities of Nastasya Philippovna in *The Idiot*. Words and blows have been exchanged, and threats uttered in the hearing of all; and when the old man is found murdered suspicion naturally falls on Dmitri. The murderer is in fact Smerdyakov, the old man's illegitimate son. Smerdyakov plays the same role in relation to Ivan as Svidrigailov to Raskolnikov in *Crime and Punishment*; he is the cruder, more logical exponent of the same opinions. He apes Ivan's ways of thought and puts his principles into practice. It was Smerdyakov's hand which killed old Karamazov, but in principle Ivan was the murderer. It was Ivan's unbelief which, communicated to Smerdyakov and carried by him to its logical issue, inspired the crime; and after Smerdyakov has hanged himself and Dmitri has been condemned to Siberia for the murder he had not committed, Ivan is driven to insanity by consciousness of his own essential guilt.

In the end, it is perhaps Dmitri, at once the most human and the most purely Russian figure created by Dostoevsky, who contributes most to the overwhelming impression of this tremendous tragedy. But the most vital thing in the book, in the intention of its author, is the long intermittent debate, spoken and unspoken, between Ivan and Alyosha. It begins in one of the early chapters where they return opposite and equally emphatic answers to their father's half-mocking question, 'Is there a God?' Then in a long and effective scene, Ivan states the reasons for his 'revolt' against God, the famous 'Legend of the Grand Inquisitor' forming part of his indictment. This book is entitled *Pro and Contra*. The answer is given in the next book, *The Russian Monk*, not by Alyosha, but by Father Zosima, the abbot of the monastery, who is on his deathbed. At Zosima's bidding, Alyosha, hitherto an inmate of the monastery, goes forth into the world; and throughout the rest of the action he is in constant colloquy with one or the other of his brothers. He is clearly intended by Dostoevsky to play the role of Myshkin in *The Idiot*, influencing morally the course of events without seeking himself to partake in them. But Alyosha has not the supreme quality of Myshkin. Even a Dostoevsky could not succeed twice in the most difficult task ever undertaken by a novelist. There is artistic compensation for this relative failure. The demands made on the nerves and emotions of the reader by the scenes of which Dmitri is the central figure, and scarcely less by the scenes between Ivan and Smerdyakov, are so tremendous that an intermediate relaxation of tension is imperative; and this relaxation is provided to some extent by the scenes in the monastery and by

others in which Alyosha plays the principal role. It was perhaps
artistically inevitable that Alyosha should, beside his titanic brothers,
appear a somewhat pale and puny figure. But the didactic purpose of
the book naturally suffers; and Ivan's denunciation of God remains
more powerful and more cogent than the defence which is put into
the mouths of Zosima and Alyosha.

It is perhaps a dim consciousness of this fact which has led an
influential school of Russian critics, who have had German and even
English disciples, to maintain that Dostoevsky remained to the end
of his life a sceptic, and that Ivan, rather than Alyosha or Dmitri,
is the true mirror of his creator. In the eyes of these critics, Dostoevsky's acceptance of Orthodox Christianity was never more than
formal; his real religion was a sort of anarchical mysticism beyond
the confines of Christian moral teaching and Christian doctrine.
There is some obscurity about the criticism of this school. It is
never quite clear whether they suppose the opinions which they
attribute to Dostoevsky to have been consciously held by him; or
whether they claim a profounder understanding than he himself
possessed of the true nature of his religion. The former hypothesis
will not easily be credited by those who have read either what
Dostoevsky wrote for publication or his private correspondence;
for a consistent course of conscious hypocrisy was altogether alien
to his character, and he constantly proclaims himself a Christian of
the Orthodox faith. The second hypothesis is both presumptuous
and dangerous. We have admitted that Dostoevsky's faith was the
product of reason rather than of intuition; and we are not inclined
to claim for it any great measure of spirituality. But we see no reason
to discredit the reality of his professed belief such as it was; and to
do so on the strength of Ivan Karamazov's argument might commit
us to deducing from *Paradise Lost* the conclusion that Milton's
innermost sympathies were on the side of Satan, not of the angels.

The problems of *The Brothers Karamazov* are the problems which
confront every Christian apologist—the problem of suffering and
the problem of sin. The problem of suffering had first been approached by Dostoevsky in *The Idiot* in the person of Ippolyt, the
youth of sixteen who is dying of consumption. The world of nature
seems to Ippolyt like 'some huge inexorable monster', to which
even Christ Himself had at last to submit; and he brushes aside the
facile explanation of the necessity of individual suffering for the
welfare of the world as a whole.

Good, then [he says]. I am prepared to admit that otherwise, that is
to say, without the perpetual devouring of one by another, it was im-

possible to establish the world. I will even admit that I understand nothing of the manner in which it is constructed. But what I know for certain is this: if I have once been given the consciousness that 'I am', what has it to do with me that the world is faultily constructed and that it cannot exist otherwise? Who after that will condemn me, and on what ground?

The indictment, which is a passing episode in *The Idiot*, is repeated even more forcibly twelve years later in *The Brothers Karamazov*. Ivan culls from the Russian press of the day heart-rending stories of cruelty to innocent children, and exclaims boldly that no considerations of 'eternal harmony' can justify these sufferings:

This harmony has been assessed too dearly; the price for entry is altogether too high for our pockets. I prefer to hand back my entrance-ticket; and as an honest man I am bound to return it as soon as possible. So that is what I am doing. It is not that I reject God, Alyosha; I merely most respectfully hand Him back the ticket.

The indictment is not answered, and could not be answered, on the rational plane. Indeed, it is clear that Ivan's objections are in great part those of his creator, and that Dostoevsky recognizes their validity as far as it goes. They can only be answered by transferring the issue to another and super-rational plane. In *Memoirs from Underground*, Dostoevsky had already insisted that man is fundamentally non-rational; and in *Crime and Punishment* he had disposed of the attempt to find a rational basis for ethics. The fruitless struggles of Ivan Karamazov to find a rational solution of the problem of suffering are mere 'Euclidean nonsense', the product of Ivan's 'poor earthly Euclidean mind',[1] The basis of life is something quite different. 'I live,' confesses Ivan, 'because I want to live, even in despite of logic.' We must love life, is Alyosha's reply, because it is only by loving life that we can attain any understanding of its meaning.

The belief in the blessedness of suffering belongs—to trace back its origins no further—to primitive Christianity; and the beatitude 'Blessed are they that mourn', forgotten or discredited by contemporary western Christianity, has always held an honoured place in Russian thought.

The strongest, most fundamental need of the Russian people [wrote Dostoevsky in *The Journal of an Author*] is the need of suffering, continual suffering, everywhere and in everything. The Russian people have, it would seem, been infected with this thirst from time immemorial.

[1] See note on pp. 231-2.

The strain of martyrdom runs through their whole history, springing not only from external misfortunes and miseries, but out of the very heart of the people.

A special form of the cult of suffering was the popular belief in the spiritual value of physical infirmity, a belief which was still strong in western Europe in the middle ages and survived to much later times in Russia. One of the letters written by Gogol when, towards the end of his life, he underwent conversion and fervently embraced Orthodoxy, is entitled *The Significance of Sickness*. He thanks Providence for having deprived him of health, which would have encouraged him to commit a thousand follies, and sent disease which ensures that everything that comes from his pen will henceforth possess deeper significance. We have noted the spiritual importance which Dostoevsky came to attach to his epilepsy; and we may recall the strange theory put into the mouth of Svidrigailov to explain why ghosts appear only to sick men:

There is no reason, of course, for a man in good health to see ghosts, because a healthy man is the most earthly kind of man and, probably, can live only an earthly life, for the sake of completeness and good order. Well, but let him fall ill, let the normal earthly order of the organism be upset, and the possibility of another world begins at once to declare itself; and the more ill he is, the more points of contact he has with the other world.

This doctrine, inherited from primitive and medieval Christianity, of the spiritualizing role of suffering was crossed, in Dostoevsky's youth, with a thoroughly incongruous strain of romantic enthusiasm. The thirst for experience, and especially painful experience, was proclaimed by half the romantic writers in England, France and Germany (most of all, in Germany) as an antidote to a humdrum bourgeois existence. Novalis hails suffering as the prerogative which distinguishes man from the brute; it is 'the token of his high estate'. This romantic cult of suffering, different in origin from the religious cult, yet identical in many of its expressions, is too well known to require detailed illustration. But a typical romantic passage from *Faust* will suffice to show how many of Dostoevsky's most characteristic and, according to modern judgment, most morbid ideas had been anticipated half a century earlier by the most representative of German poets:

No talk of pleasure! I vow myself to frenzy, to torturing enjoyment, to enamoured hate, to exhilarating spite. My breast, purged of the thirst for knowledge, shall henceforth reject no torments; the fate of all humanity I will embrace in my inmost self, seize in spirit the highest and the lowest, heap on my breast its weal and its woe; and thus, broadening myself to humanity's self, in the end, like humanity, be shattered in pieces.

Baudelaire refined still further on this romantic thirst for pain by making it the medium for aesthetic enjoyment, and showed the way to a host of 'decadent' poets, in whose work superficial parallels to Dostoevsky's may be found.

This cult of suffering, half religious, half romantic, became deeply engrained in Dostoevsky's mind. The infection (as he himself calls it in the passage previously quoted) is so profound and persistent that we suspect personal causes and look back to Suslova as its source. It was in his liaison with her that Dostoevsky had first experienced in his own person those romantic antitheses which recur again and again in his later works—love-hate, pride-humiliation, pleasure-pain. From this episode, Dostoevsky seems to have acquired the marked bent towards masochism which expresses itself in so many of his characters. Marmeladov drinks 'because he wants to suffer doubly'. Stavrogin seeks pleasure in his own humiliation. Liza Khokhlakova, a minor figure in *The Brothers Karamazov*, seeks relief after an hysterical scene with Alyosha, with whom she is in love, by crushing her finger in the door to make the blood flow—illustrating by anticipation the discovery of modern psychologists that self-inflicted pain is a common symptom of imperfect sexual satisfaction.

Such are the elements—religious, romantic and masochistic—which went to make up the doctrine of suffering as it ultimately took shape in Dostoevsky's mind. Even before his religious beliefs had assumed their final form he had worked out to his own satisfaction the intimate link between suffering and sin. He never fell into the vulgar error of those theologians, both western and oriental, who posited sin as the cause of suffering; but he believed firmly that suffering was the necessary psychological condition of the forgiveness of sin. The forgiveness which seemed important to Dostoevsky was not forgiveness by others, but the forgiveness of the sinner by himself; it was a process of his own conscience. And this forgiveness would only be won by voluntary submission to, and deliberate seeking of, suffering. He explains in a letter to Katkov that Raskolnikov is compelled to denounce himself to the police: 'the criminal decides to take the suffering on himself in order to redeem his crime'. Tikhon, in the suppressed chapter of *The Devils*, tells Stavrogin that he can '*forgive himself*, and win forgiveness for himself in this world, through suffering'. And Dmitri Karamazov, as we shall see, again and again hailed with joy the suffering which was to redeem him from the torturing consciousness of sin.

P

The answer of Dostoevsky to the problem of suffering becomes therefore part of his answer to the problem of sin; and we return to the point in the discussion at which Ivan, leaving the question of suffering behind, opens his attack on the dispensation which leaves humanity free to sin and to disbelieve. The attack is contained in 'The Legend of the Grand Inquisitor' which he recites to Alyosha. Christ returns to earth in sixteenth-century Seville at the moment when the Inquisition was at the height of its power and its activities. He is recognized and arrested. Confined in the dungeons of the Inquisition, He listens in silence to the Grand Inquisitor's denunciation. The error of Christ, declares the latter, was that He insisted on leaving humanity free. He had proudly and selfishly desired the worship of free men, and He had refused, by some overwhelming and incontrovertible miracle, to *compel* their obedience and their faith. The Catholic Church had corrected the work of Christ; by establishing itself on the firm basis of miracle, mystery and authority it had taken away freedom and given mankind happiness instead:

And men rejoiced that they were once more led like sheep, and that the terrible gift of freedom, which had brought them so much suffering, had been at last removed from their hearts.

Professing the name of Christ, but reversing the false principles on which He had acted, the church had taken charge of the consciences of its flock :

And they will have no secrets from us. We shall allow or forbid them to live with their wives or mistresses, to have or not to have children— according to the measure of their obedience—and they will submit themselves to us cheerfully and gladly. The most torturing secrets of their conscience—all, all will they bring to us, and we shall give them the answer; and they will accept our decision with joy because it will free them from their anxiety, from the present terrible torments of personal free decision.

'The Legend of the Grand Inquisitor' enables Dostoevsky to air his hatred, the time-honoured Russian hatred, of the Roman Catholic church by putting the condemnation of Christ into the mouth of one of its principal agents. In more than one passage of his earlier works he had compared Catholicism with Socialism: both strive to make a man happy by relieving him of his personal responsibility. Socialism deprives man of his individuality in return for 'warmth and a morsel of bread'; the church aims at the enslavement of men's consciences as the price of a rationalized machine-made happiness bestowed by an external power. Such in essence was the programme of the Grand Inquisitor. His argument is, within its own limits, as irrefutable as Ivan's argument against suffering; but the limits within which it operates and is valid imply, as Dostoevsky says elsewhere, 'the degradation of mankind to the level of cattle'. The defence of free will, not as a metaphysical but as a moral proposition, is one of the corner-stones of Dostoevsky's thought.

The evolution of his attitude to sin provides as curious a study as the analysis of his attitude to suffering. His conclusions were, as usual, reached not by observation, but by introspection and by theory. The doctrine of the essential goodness of human nature had been launched on modern Europe by Rousseau. In Russia, more than elsewhere, it retained the political affinities which Rousseau had given to it, and was proclaimed as an article of faith by the philosophical radicals. It found its most perfect expression in Chernyshevsky's novel *What is to be done?* In Dostoevsky's earlier works, his attitude to sin was purely conventional, even melodramatic. But when, in *Memoirs from Underground*, he set out to answer Chernyshevsky, he stoutly defended the conviction that man was not by nature good any more than he was by nature rational, and that there was in human nature a thirst for sin just as there was a thirst for suffering. The problem of sin as conceived by Dostoevsky was not the problem of Paul: The evil I will not, that I do. It was the problem of the will to do evil, the *nostalgie pour la boue*, which is presented in Svidrigailov and Stavrogin and, most graphically of all, in the sexually abnormal Liza Khokhlakova, who imagines herself watching a child being tortured to death while she sits and eats pineapple *compote*.

In *A Raw Youth* Dostoevsky had made his first attempt to discover the ultimate significance of this will to evil, this conscious or subconscious hell in every man's nature, and thereby to solve the problem of sin. He had there adumbrated the doctrine that the sense of sin, an awareness of the lower instincts of one's own nature, was the key to salvation, and that it was through the antithesis of good and evil within him that man arrived at the divine synthesis. In *The Brothers Karamazov*, he works out this doctrine in the person of Dmitri, who seeks salvation through sin and through suffering accepted in order to expiate it. In an epigram which was perhaps not intended to be taken too seriously, D. H. Lawrence defined the doctrine of Dostoevsky as 'sinning your way to Jesus'. There are passages in Dostoevsky which, interpreted in the light of a puritan tradition, might seem at first sight to lead to that conclusion. But a deeper understanding of his thought, and of Russian religious thought in general, reveals a totally different picture. The sense of sin which leads to salvation is not, for Dostoevsky, the sense of

personal sin which has played so large a part in Protestant theology.
It is a theory of what may best be described as communism in sin,
which first appears in one of the last chapters of *The Devils* and
occupies an important place in all Dostoevsky's later work. 'Each
and all have sinned before all men,' says Stepan Trofimovich in the
moment of vision which precedes his death. 'All have sinned before
all men in all things,' quotes Zosima in *The Brothers Karamazov*
from his dying brother. 'Each of us,' he tells Alyosha, 'bears the
guilt of all and of everything on earth, not merely the general world-
guilt, but each one individually for all and each on this earth.' It is
perhaps the only theory which can make tolerable the theological
doctrine of the Atonement. In ordinary western theology, the Atonement is presented in a form which is both incomprehensible and
repugnant to the sensitive mind; but for Dostoevsky, suffering for
the sins of others becomes the prerogative of every Christian.

There is no doubt that this sense of individual participation in
the general guilt, which may seem to some western minds an unreal
pretence, is profoundly ingrained in the Russian character, and may
presumably be connected with the deep-rooted communistic instincts
of the Russian. It probably accounts for the infinite tolerance which
has often been regarded as the most characteristic Russian quality.
Instead of censuring your fellow-man you recognize your share in
his guilt. When the jury-system was instituted in Russia in the
'sixties in imitation of western models, it was found extremely
difficult to secure convictions. Even in the clearest cases of crime,
jurors seemed to suffer from an irresistible impulse to acquit; and
in a passage of *The Journal of an Author* Dostoevsky tries to picture
their state of mind:

We sit in the jurors' box and perhaps we think: 'Are we ourselves better
than the defendant? Here we are, rich and secure; but if we were to find
ourselves in the same position as he, perhaps we should do even worse
than he—so we will acquit.' Perhaps even it is good that we should feel
thus; it is sincere mercifulness. It is perhaps the pledge for some sort of
higher Christianity which the world has not yet known.

And there is a curious passage elsewhere in the *Journal* where he
comments enthusiastically, but rather undiscerningly, on the scene
of Anna's death in Tolstoy's *Anna Karenina*:

All forgave and acquitted one another. . . . It turned out that no one was
guilty. They all unconditionally accused themselves and thereby acquitted
themselves.

It is not difficult to read danger into such a conclusion. Logically

speaking, the theory of Dostoevsky that all are to blame for the sins
of all may, it is clear, come to much the same thing as the theory of
Chekhov that nobody is to blame for the sins of anybody, least of all
for his own. But it is hard to imagine any reader of the last chapters
of *The Brothers Karamazov* receiving any such impression. From the
moment of Dmitri's arrest on the charge of murdering his father,
the genius of Dostoevsky takes entire charge both of our reason and
of our emotions; we are incapable of resisting or of questioning, of
thinking or of feeling otherwise than as he wishes us to feel. Throughout the long and nerve-racking scene of the magistrate's cross-
examination (the most powerful scene in the book, or anywhere in
Russian literature), and once more through the ordeal of the trial,
Dmitri becomes for us not merely the one figure in the novel, but
the one being in the world; and we can look at the world through no
other eyes than his. We attain, as we attained in *The Idiot*, to a
spiritual sense of transmuted values. Dmitri Karamazov, like Myshkin, has ceased to belong to the world in which he moves. He begins
to speak a language which his tormentors cannot understand. He
bears witness against himself; he declines to pursue, is not even
interested in, facts which speak for his innocence. He recklessly
disregards his interests, because he no longer sees those interests
with the eyes of other men. He never swerves from his conviction
that his sufferings are just. He suffers, if not for the death of his
father, then for his other sins; or if not for his own sins, then for the
sins of others. And since he accepts his suffering as a just expiation
for sin, it becomes his path to salvation.

Dmitri Karamazov is not merely the greatest character in Dostoevsky's last novel, and the one in whom his doctrines of sin and suffering are most profoundly expressed; he is one of the great tragic
figures of literature. There are moments when he belongs to the
sphere of pure poetry. In this respect he is unique among Dostoevsky's characters. Myshkin's effects are obtained, and enhanced, by
his altogether matter-of-fact manner; and except in the one speech
before his epileptic fit, which is deliberately high-falutin' rather than
poetical, he speaks the most ordinary prose idiom. But Dmitri
Karamazov continually speaks the language of poetry; his every
utterance conforms to the Miltonic definition 'simple, sensuous and
passionate'. 'Beauty', he exclaims once, 'is not only a terrible, it is a
mysterious thing. There God and the devil strive for mastery, and
the battleground is the heart of men.' He is fond of quotations both
from the Bible and from the Russian poets. Unlike most of Dostoevsky's characters and unlike Dostoevsky himself, he is intensely
sensitive to nature, and continually sees in it the mirror of his own

emotions. 'Stop; look at the night,' he says to Alyosha, 'see what a murky night, clouds, what a wind has got up!' It is the moment when jealousy of his father is surging up to its tempestuous climax. More often he is the poet of life and the sun. 'I love golden-haired Phoebus and his blazing light,' he exclaims with a play on words, 'light' and 'world' being identical in Russian. And before the trial he looks in the face the impending sentence of imprisonment in the Siberian mines:

Then shall we, men beneath the ground, sing from the bowels of the earth our tragic hymn to God, in Whom is gladness! All hail to God and His gladness! I love Him. . . .

I think there is so much of strength in me that I shall overcome all things, all sufferings, even in order that I may say, and say with every breath: I am! In the midst of a thousand torments—I am! I writhe in tortures—but I am! I sit in the prison, but I live; I see the sun, or if I cannot see the sun, I know that it *is*. And to know that the sun *is*—that is the whole of life.

In this force of poetic imagination, he is the counterpart of Othello, the most poetical of all tragic heroes. The parallel might be carried further. Indeed, in the whole range of literature there is perhaps no other figure with whom Dmitri Karamazov can be so well matched. 'Othello's mind,' wrote Bradley, in his *Shakespearean Tragedy*, 'for all its poetry, is very simple. His nature tends outwards. He is quite free from introspection, and is not given to reflection. Emotion excites his imagination, but it confuses and dulls his intellect. On this side, he is the very opposite to Hamlet with whom, however, he shares a great openness and trustfulness of nature.' Except perhaps for a strain of introspection which is inseparable from the modern man, and especially from the Russian, these lines could be repeated word for word of Dmitri. Both he and Othello were maddened by jealousy, though the situations were different and the particular difficulties which proved fatal to the one might have been readily surmounted by the other. The more diffuse and undisciplined vehemence of Dmitri's passion betokens a different national tradition. But the fundamental similarity of character remains; and there is no tragedy in the literature of the world to compare with these two for sheer tensity of emotion.

The sentence is passed; and we take our leave of Dmitri in the prison where he awaits transportation to Siberia. The drama is over. The last scene of all is the funeral of one of a band of schoolboys who are introduced half-way through the novel to provide a minor sub-plot. Alyosha makes a speech at the grave; but we are perhaps not wrong in supposing that he—or at any rate Dostoevsky —is thinking rather of the tragedy of Dmitri than of the dead boy.

'Karamazov,' cried Kolya, 'is it really true, as religion tells us, that we shall all rise from the dead and come to life again, and once more see one another, and Ilya and everyone?'

'Certainly we shall rise again, certainly we shall see one another and gladly and joyfully tell over to one another everything that has been. . . . Well, come now. Let us go hand in hand.'

'And for ever so! all our life hand in hand! Hurrah for Karamazov!' cried Kolya once more with enthusiasm; and once more all the boys took up the cry.

It is a formal, conventional ending, like the concluding platitudes of a Greek chorus, or the speeches of a Fortinbras or a Lodovico, which provide the necessary narcotic for our lacerated emotions when the tragedy is played out. Perhaps Dostoevsky contemplated a sequel; but we do not miss it. He had completed the story of Dmitri Karamazov's redemption through sin and suffering; and he had completed his work. When he laid down his pen at the words we have just quoted, Dostoevsky had only three months longer to live.

NOTE TO CHAPTER XX

The now fifty-year-old reference to 'Euclidean nonsense' may interest those who believe that Euclidean geometry was first seriously assailed by Einstein. The real pioneer seems to have been a professor of Kazan university named Lobachevsky, whose treatise on non-Euclidean geometry was published in 1833. Nobody but a specialist could presume to judge whether this apparent anticipation of later discoveries was a work of mathematical genius or merely a brilliant guess. But the overthrow of Euclidean geometry was so well known in Russia by 1880 that Dostoevsky, who was neither a mathematician nor a professional philosopher, and was writing not for mathematicians and philosophers but for the novel-reading public, could refer casually to 'Euclidean nonsense' as something which was being superseded by modern science.

In his commentary on *The Brothers Karamazov* (Legenda o Velikom Inkvisitore) published in 1894, the critic Rozanov writes:

'The relative and hypothetical character of human thought is the subtlest and deepest truth which for thousands of years has remained hidden from man and now at last has been discovered. The clearest and most striking evidence of this relativity is the admission in quite recent times of a doubt whether real space is confined to that which alone is known as such by man and alone can be thought of or imagined by him. The growth of so-called non-Euclidean geometry, which is now being worked out by the best mathematicians of Europe, and in which parallel lines meet and the sum of the angles of a triangle is somewhat less than two right angles, is an incontestable fact for all to see; and it leaves no doubt that the reality of existence is not identical with what can be conceived by the reason. Into the category of that which cannot be thought and nevertheless exists comes the existence of God, the unprovableness of which constitutes no objection to its reality.'

Modern writers have thought themselves daring and original for saying the same thing more than thirty years later.

CHAPTER XXI

Apotheosis

THE fame which had come to Dostoevsky in his last years brought with it new labours and responsibilities. He was frequently invited to give readings from his works in aid of various charities; and despite his nervous temperament there is abundant and unanimous testimony to his qualities as a reader, one auditor comparing his voice to 'a flow of molten lava'. The seclusion of his home was constantly invaded by admirers, for the most part students and women; some came with requests, others to seek advice, others merely to gaze on the object of their worship and to express to him their gratitude for all he meant to them. The number of his unknown correspondents increased continually. A Jew who had robbed a bank to provide medical treatment for his consumptive *fiancée* detected a hidden analogy between himself and Raskolnikov, and wrote long letters to Dostoevsky from prison beginning with an explanation of the motives of his crime and ending with a dissertation on the Jewish question. A young girl begged for advice whether she should continue her medical studies or marry a young man who was paying her attentions, but whom she thought 'poor-spirited'. Another wrote to lament her failure to pass her examination in geography. A mother consulted him on the moral upbringing of her children. A group of students of the Moscow University wrote to ask his opinion on the rights and wrongs of a street brawl in which they had been implicated. A lady whom he had met at Ems (the only one of these letter-writers whom he had ever seen) requested him to fetch a story of hers from the office of a journal which had rejected it, and to find a publisher for it.

Dostoevsky was visibly flattered by the volume of his correspondence, and savoured the universal recognition which he was at last enjoying. He took infinite pains with his replies which, though nearly all begin with complaints of over-work and sometimes of illness, are long, detailed and altogether human. No great man can ever have taken more trouble than Dostoevsky to satisfy the needs and curiosities of his unknown admirers. It was, after all, easier to be amiable to distant and unseen correspondents than to people with whom one was brought into constant personal contact; for, as he had insisted through the mouth of Ivan Karamazov, it is precisely one's neighbours, the people near to one, whom it is most difficult of all to love. It was always his friends who suffered most from his irritable and suspicious temperament; and these last years were no exception. 'He would come in like a black cloud,' records Soloviev, 'sometimes even forget to greet me, and seek every pretext to quarrel and to wound; he would see in everything an insult to himself, a desire to provoke and irritate him.' His wife too was sometimes the victim of these moods. 'At such moments,' wrote another acquaintance, 'an outsider would have thought him rude and despotic even to those nearest to him.' But Anna never failed to display the tolerance of perfect understanding; and neither she nor anyone else could have the faintest doubt of the completeness of her sway over him. In his heart, beneath these momentary exhibitions of self-conscious truculence, Dostoevsky was still possessed by the old desire, which goes back as far as his relations with Suslova, to prostrate himself absolutely before the woman he loved.

My darling joy [he wrote to her from Ems] what makes you think that you are 'the golden mean'? You are the rarest of women, and, what is more, you are better than any of them. You don't guess your own abilities. You not only run the whole house and my business affairs, but you carry all of us on your back, capricious and tiresome as we are, from myself to Alyosha. [This was written during the short lifetime of the youngest child.] . . . If you were made a queen and given a whole kingdom, I vow you would govern it better than anyone—you have so much intelligence, common sense, good heart and managing capacity.

The public recognition of his greatness never sapped for a minute his intense inward belief in Anna's superiority, or affected in any way the simplicity of his mind and of his domestic life. 'Marriage,' he had written to Strakhov, ten years earlier, 'makes three-quarters of human happiness, the rest of life a bare quarter.' The public triumphs of his last years, however magnificent, scarcely seemed to touch the kernel of his existence. In his callow youth his head had been turned by premature applause; but judging from his later life, few great men have been so little spoiled by fame or remained to the last so completely natural.

In the judgment of posterity, *The Brothers Karamazov* remains Dostoevsky's last achievement. But in the eyes of his contemporaries it was eclipsed by another event of the last year of his life, the Pushkin festival. The occasion was the unveiling of a statue of Pushkin which had been erected in Moscow. It had, like every other literary event in Russia, a strong political flavour. The erection of the